UNITED STATES
SPECIAL OPERATIONS FORCES

UNITED STATES
SPECIAL OPERATIONS FORCES

David Tucker
Christopher J. Lamb

COLUMBIA UNIVERSITY PRESS
NEW YORK

Columbia University Press
Publishers Since 1893
New York   Chichester, West Sussex
Copyright © 2007 Columbia University Press

Library of Congress Cataloging-in-Publication Data
Tucker, David, 1951–
United States Special Operations Forces /
David Tucker ; Christopher J. Lamb.
p.   cm.
Includes bibliographical references.
ISBN-13: 978-0-231-13190-2 (cloth : alk. paper)
ISBN-13: 978-0-231-50689-2 (electronic)
1. Special forces (Military science)—United States.
2. United States—Armed Forces—Commando troops.
I. Lamb, Christopher J., 1958– II. Title.

UA34.S64T83 2007
356'.160973—dc22
                    2006039198

Columbia University Press books are printed on
permanent and durable acid-free paper.
This book is printed on paper with recycled content.
Printed in the United States of America
c 10 9 8 7 6 5 4

*This book is dedicated to U.S. Special Operations Forces
and their families, to acknowledge and honor their sacrifices
on behalf of our collective security*

CONTENTS

TABLES

PREFACE

THIS BOOK IS THE RESULT of a collaboration of more than fifteen years, beginning in Abidjan, Ivory Coast, where we worked together in the U.S. Embassy, later in the office of the Assistant Secretary of Defense (Special Operations/Low-Intensity Conflict), and more recently in our respective academic institutions, the Naval Postgraduate School's Department of Defense Analysis, and National Defense University's Institute for National Strategic Studies. When it came to writing, one or the other of us took the lead with different chapters. Tucker is the primary author of the introduction and chapters 1, 2, 3, and 7; Lamb of chapters 4, 5, and 6, as well as the conclusion. Each read and commented extensively on the other's work. Tucker acted as a general editor.

This book is dedicated to U.S. Special Operations Forces (SOF) and their families, to acknowledge and honor their sacrifices on behalf of our collective security. Our hope is that the book will help readers better understand SOF, and that it will make a contribution to debate about the best way to organize and employ these forces for maximum strategic advantage against the nation's enemies. Without implying any shared responsibility for our statements or conclusions, we would like to thank individuals who assisted our research and writing by sharing personal experiences and reading and commenting on parts of the book: numerous students in the Department of Defense Analysis, some of whose work we cite in the notes; two colleagues in the Department, Peter Gustaitis and Hy Rothstein, for many discussions over the years; another, John Arquilla, for a number of helpful comments on the manuscript; for careful reading and critique of the Somalia chapter in particular, Jim Locher and Bob Oakley; and for editing assistance, Mike Casey and Matthew Shabat of the Institute for

National Strategic Studies. Ellen Tucker provided editorial comments and assistance and helped with the index. Because of this, the book is better than it otherwise would have been. The Smith Richardson Foundation provided financial support to Tucker and waited patiently for that funding to result in something. Steve Flanagan and Jim Shear, respectively the Director and Research Director for the Institute for National Strategic Studies, supported the research effort from its inception, for which we are grateful. Finally, the opinions expressed in this book are solely those of the authors and do not necessarily represent the views of the Department of Defense, the Naval Postgraduate School, or the Institute for National Strategic Studies.

                                                              D.T., C.J.L.

INTRODUCTION

In october and november 2001, small numbers of U.S. forces helicoptered into Afghanistan, hooked up with elements of the Northern Alliance, an assortment of Afghanis opposed to the Taliban, and, with their assistance and the support of Navy and Air Force aircraft, destroyed the Taliban regime in a remarkably short period of time. The U.S. Forces who did this were Army Special Forces (SF), an element of the U.S. military's Special Operations Forces (SOF). Trained to work with indigenous forces and personnel like the Northern Alliance, SF guided bombs with lasers and global positioning technology, while sometimes riding on horseback, combining the most modern technology with the most ancient technique of central Asian warfare. Using an American idiom, President Bush celebrated SF's success by describing their action in Afghanistan as "the first cavalry charge of the 21st century."[1]

SF's stunning accomplishment in Afghanistan brought them a prominence they had not enjoyed in the forty years since John F. Kennedy had anointed them the defenders of the liberal democratic faith against the threat of communism in what was then called the developing world. Yet, while it was important, SF's success in Afghanistan is not the only reason for SOF's current prominence. Another is the increased responsibilities that senior officials are giving SF and other elements of SOF in the war on terrorism. These responsibilities include asking the Special Operations Command (SOCOM), the military organization responsible for SOF, to take responsibility for worldwide counterterrorism operations. Still another reason for the current interest in SOF is the growing sense over the last fifteen years or so that warfare is changing, that smaller, more mobile, yet quite lethal forces, that is, SOF-like forces, hold the key to future success in war.

Given SOF's recent prominence and perhaps future significance, it is important to understand these forces. Assessments of our prospects in the war on terrorism as well as of prospective changes in warfare would be incomplete if not based on a thorough understanding of SOF—their capabilities and their limitations. For example, a senior official in the Defense Department is rumored to have said, as a summary of how the U.S. military should transform itself to meet its future requirements, that the Army should become like the Marine Corps, the Marines like SOF, and SOF like the CIA. It may be both useful and possible for the Army to become more like the Marines, but to suggest that the Marines could become more like SOF or SOF more like the CIA reveals ignorance of rather than insight into these organizations. The purpose of this book is to show why this is so with regard to SOF. We do so by explaining SOF core characteristics and how they influence the way SOF should be organized, trained, and employed for current and future security challenges.

To accomplish that end, we begin with a series of interviews of SOF personnel. Virtually every issue we subsequently discuss emerges in these interviews. They also provide a sound introduction to the character of SOF. Following these interviews, we discuss in chapter 2 the processes of selection and training that prepare SOF for the various tasks they perform. In considering selection and training, we learn a good deal about SOF, the kind of people they hope to attract, and the kind of military professionals they hope to produce. Following the chapter on selection and training, we present in chapter 3 a history of U.S. SOF. This history provides perspective on SOF and the array of issues and controversies surrounding them. It shows also that SOF's complex, often problematic relationship with other military forces and political leaders is not simply a contemporary phenomenon. The issues, controversies, and complexity are long-standing; awareness of them is essential background for understanding SOF. Chapter 4 takes an in-depth look at one particular episode from SOF's history, its involvement in the effort to capture Mohammed Farah Aideed, a Somali faction leader. This episode is perhaps the single most revealing case that one could study to understand how some SOF operate and the difficulty of providing proper command and control of these forces. In chapter 5, we begin the task of analyzing SOF as the previous chapters have revealed them. The chapter looks at roles and missions, at the ways in which SOF are used to accomplish our national objectives. Chapter 6 examines SOF and the future of warfare and how SOF and their traditional roles and missions might change. Chapter 7 presents a proposal for restructuring SOF and relevant decisionmaking processes in the U.S. government in order that SOF's capabilities be used to greatest effect. The conclusion summarizes our argument.

A brief description of SOF and their various missions will aid in understanding the chapters that follow, especially the first. The Department of Defense currently defines SOF as forces that are "specifically organized, trained, and equipped to conduct and support special operations." It defines special operations in turn as "operations conducted in hostile, denied, or politically sensitive environments to achieve military, diplomatic, informational, and/or economic objectives employing military capabilities for which there is no broad conventional force requirement." The official definition notes as well that special operations occur in peace and war, independently or in conjunction with conventional or foreign forces or civilian agencies, are often secret, often entail significant political and operational risk, and use special techniques and equipment.[2]

More specifically, each of the services has a component that it designates as SOF. SF, Army Special Forces, are known colloquially as "Green Berets," for their distinctive head gear. The most important organizational unit in SF is what is known as the Special Forces Operational Detachment Alpha or the "A Team," a twelve-man unit of officers (a Captain and a warrant officer) and senior enlisted personnel. Warrant officers are technical experts, combat leaders, and managers. They are commissioned officers but specialists, and so not on a career path that leads to becoming a general officer, unlike the Captains who head the team. The Captains, although the highest ranking soldiers on the teams, are usually the least experienced. Warrant officers are typically seasoned soldiers, as are the other members of the team. This creates interesting team dynamics.[3] The team contains specialists in weapons, engineering, medicine, communications and intelligence. It is so constructed that it can be divided into two smaller teams, each under the command of one of the Team's officers. Six "A-teams" make a company; three companies, a battalion; three battalions, a Group. Each Group and its subordinate elements focus on a particular region. Fifth Group, for example, focuses on the Middle East and Central Asia. Other Army SOF include Civil Affairs personnel, who specialize in working with civilian populations and foreign governments;

Psychological Operations forces, who specialize in the dissemination of information in support of SOF and other military units; the 160th Special Operations Aviation Regiment, which provides helicopter support to SOF; and the 75th Ranger Regiment, elite light infantry who specialize in raids and airfield seizures.

The Navy's SOF are the SEALs (short for Sea, Air, Land), whose progenitors were underwater demolition teams but who now, as their name suggests, operate in a variety of environments. They carried out a significant portion of the special operations in the Afghanistan campaign, for example. In June 2005, three SEALs on a reconnaissance mission in Afghanistan's mountains came under attack and were killed in action. Eight others SEALS died trying to rescue them when their helicopter was shot down. The eleven deaths were the greatest loss of life in a single mission in the history of the SEALs. As this episode indicates, like SF, SEALs operate in small teams. Unlike SF, however, SEALs focus on small-unit combat operations, rather than working with indigenous personnel. Also part of the SEALs' force structure are the special boat teams that carry the SEALs to their targets.

Air Force SOF are the pilots, navigators, and crew who fly Air Force special operations aircraft and combat controllers and pararescuemen. The combat controllers accompany SOF on their missions and coordinate air support. The pararescuemen, as their name implies, specialize in rescuing downed airmen and SOF. Among the least well-known SOF, combat controllers and pararescuemen are also among its most highly trained.

Historically, although they have designated certain elements that receive special training as "special operations capable," the Marines have resisted establishing separate "special" forces. Recently, given the demands of the war on terrorism and pressure from civilian leaders in the Pentagon, the Marines have developed a unit that will work within the Special Operations Command. Because this unit is new, we say little about it directly, although we do discuss the relationship between the Marines and SOF. We also say little about special mission units, a euphemism for SOF that specialize in combating terrorism and other secret and often especially demanding missions. These SOF highly value their operational security. What we say about them respects their security but is sufficient to make the points that need to be made.

SOCOM, the Special Operations Command, is the overall military structure in charge of SOF. SOCOM is a unique organization because it combines the usual duties of a command (operational authority over military forces) with the responsibilities of a service (recruiting, training, and equipping military personnel). In the past, SOCOM has seldom exercised operational authority over SOF. That has been more typically done by Special Operations Commands (SOCs) that work for each of the regional Combatant Commanders, the four-star generals with responsibility for U.S. military operations in the Middle East, Europe, Latin America, Asia, and now North America. Each of the regional combatant commanders has a SOF command element, its SOC. Central Command, the command with responsibility for the Middle East and Central Asia, has Special Operations Command Central Command or SOCCENT.[4] One change brought on by the war on terrorism is the effort to get SOCOM to take more responsibility for operations. Whether this effort will succeed remains unclear, since the regional commanders have tended to resist SOCOM taking the lead in operations. SOCOM exercises its service-like responsibilities by working with the service-specific SOF Commands. The Army Special Operations Command has responsibility for Special Forces, Civil Affairs, Psychological Operations forces, the Ranger Regiment and the 160th Aviation Regiment. The Navy Special Warfare Command has responsibility for the SEALs and their supporting boat units. The Air Force Special Operations Command has responsibility for the Air Force's special operations aircraft and its combat controllers and pararescuemen. Together, SOCOM and its subordinate commands take care of SOF-specific training and equipment, while the services provide to SOF what they provide to all personnel under their authority. For example, the Air Force buys aircraft, which the Special Operations Command then pays to have equipped as needed for special operations.

The various organizational and command relationships that govern SOF prepare them to carry out the following missions:[5]

Counterterrorism: offensive measures taken to prevent, deter, preempt, and respond to terrorism. These missions include intelligence operations, attacks against terrorist networks and infrastructures, hostage rescue, recovery of sensitive material from terrorist organizations, and nonkinetic activities aimed at the ideologies or motivations that spawn terrorists. These operations are generally cloaked in secrecy, so examples are hard to come by. One well-known foreign example, however, reportedly benefited from

U.S. counterterrorism expertise. Peruvian commandos rescued seventy-one hostages seized by terrorists from the Marxist Tupac Amaru revolutionary movement at the Japanese Ambassador's residence in Lima, Peru, in April, 1997.

Counterproliferation of Weapons of Mass Destruction: actions taken in support of DOD and other governmental agencies to prevent, limit, and/or minimize the development, possession, and employment of weapons of mass destruction, new advanced weapons, and advanced-weapon-capable technologies. An example of a counterproliferation operation would be stopping and searching a ship on the high seas suspected of carrying a weapon of mass destruction or material for such a weapon.

Special Reconnaissance: reconnaissance and surveillance actions conducted as special operations in hostile, denied, or politically sensitive environments to collect or verify information of strategic or operational significance, employing military capabilities not normally found in conventional forces. For example, in the first Gulf War, Special Forces were inserted behind enemy lines before the initiation of the ground war to analyze the terrain and soil conditions along the planned invasion route into Iraq. Navy SEALs also conducted offshore reconnaissance missions as part of a deception strategy to fix Iraqi attention on a potential amphibious invasion by U.S. Marines.

Direct Action: the conduct of short-duration strikes and other small-scale offensive actions conducted as a special operation in hostile, denied, or politically sensitive environments against targets of strategic or operational significance, employing specialized military capabilities. For example, during the Balkan conflict a SOF team destroyed a stretch of railroad tracks to prevent Serbian troop movements.

Unconventional Warfare: a broad spectrum of military operations normally of a long duration; predominantly conducted by, with, or through indigenous or surrogate forces. Unconventional warfare includes guerrilla warfare, subversion, sabotage, and intelligence activities. For example, in the first Gulf War, Special Forces trained 6,357 Kuwaitis, who formed an SF battalion, a commando brigade, and the Al-Khulud, Al-Haq, Fatah, and Badr infantry brigades.

Information Operations: actions taken to influence, affect or defend information, information systems and decision-making. An example of a SOF information operation would be a raid behind enemy lines to attack a vital communications link.

Psychological Operations: operations that convey truthful information to foreign audiences in an effort to influence their behavior and the behavior of foreign governments, organizations, groups, and individuals. For example, during operations in Afghanistan to topple the Taliban regime and run al-Qaeda terrorists to ground, Psychological Operations forces developed leaflets and radio broadcasts to weaken support for the Taliban and al-Qaeda. After the defeat of the Taliban, the objective shifted to building support for the interim Afghan Government led by president Karzi.

Foreign Internal Defense: actions of a foreign government to curb subversion, lawlessness, and insurgency. SOF's primary contribution to this interagency activity is to organize, train, advise, and assist host-nation military and paramilitary forces. For example, following the terrorist attacks on September 11 SOF undertook an advisory role with the Filipino military in their battle with the terrorist organization Abu Sayyaf Group.

Civil Affairs: activities involved in either establishing and conducting military government or civil administration until civilian authority or government can be restored or minimizing civilian interference with military operations and limiting the adverse impact of military operations on civilian populations and resources. For example, during the intervention in Haiti, Civil Affairs teams from the 96th CA Battalion assessed Haiti's creaking infrastructure, and Company A, 96th CA Battalion restored electricity to Jeremie, Cap Haitien, and other northern cities and towns for the first time in years.

It should be apparent from the above description of SOF and the list of their missions that SOF are complex and diverse forces. Part of what we discover in examining their experiences, selection, training, and history is how diverse they are, how many different kinds of missions political and military decisionmakers have called on them to undertake, how different are the orientations and skills of the different elements of SOF, and how political and bureaucratic pressures have shaped them over the years. Understanding this, we come to see that there is nothing inevitable or unalterable in SOF's current missions and organization. Might they be better focused and organized than they currently are to fight the war on terrorism, support conventional operations, and meet the future challenges of warfare? Which missions should they have and which should be passed on to general purpose forces? What are new missions that might emerge? The following pages provide the information to answer such questions and argue that some answers are better than others.

UNITED STATES
SPECIAL OPERATIONS FORCES

SPECIAL OPERATIONS FORCES AND THE WAR ON TERRORISM

THE PENTAGON, SEPTEMBER 11, 2001

A Special Forces colonel who was working in the Pentagon on September 11, 2001 describes what happened and reflects on the place of Special Operations Forces (SOF) in the U.S. military and the war on terrorism.

When the first plane hit the World Trade Center, I was discussing special operations actions with the Special Operations Division [the office on the Joint Staff that has oversight of Special Operations Forces (SOF) and their missions]. Like even the president, everyone in the office thought it was an errant pilot, a mistake. Looking back on it now, we did not consider this a military responsibility. FEMA [Federal Emergency Management Agency], FAA [Federal Aviation Administration], NYPD [New York Police Department], perhaps FBI, but not a military issue. I had sat in most of the CSG [Counterterrorism Security Group][1] meetings during the last year, and there was no real indicator of a threat to the United States, especially one so overt and simple. But when the second plane slammed into the World Trade Center, it was obvious that this was a deliberate attack on the United States. I was meeting with the Vice Director [of the Directorate of Operations, the office on the Joint Staff responsible for overseeing all military operations], going over briefing notes for a meeting on Bosnian war criminals, when the second plane hit. I began contacting the SOF community and gathering information that would be requested by the CSG or the vice chairman [of the Joint Chiefs of Staff (the chairman, like the Director for the Operations Directorate, was not in Washington on September 11)] in order to brief the Secretary [of Defense]. Information like Special Operations Forces readiness, locations of key forces and leadership, and opening a channel of communications with the Special Operations Command (SOCOM) [the military command with responsibility for SOF]. All this was SOP [standard operating procedure].

Forty-five minutes later or so, I located the Current Operations Director in the NMCC [the National Military Command Center in the Pentagon], to give him an update. The way I remember it, other than the two officers assigned to the NMCC, it was only him and me. We were talking about what the SOCOM was doing, what SOCOM's capabilities were and he gets a phone call. He hangs up and he says to me, "Hey, Bubba, one's coming this way." I remember thinking to myself, "Well, you've lived a good life." A sense of contentment came over me. What seemed like minutes goes by and all of a sudden the General says, "we were hit." The NMCC is well protected. I didn't feel it; I didn't feel anything. But we were standing together and he said, "I felt a change in the air pressure." He's a fighter pilot, so maybe that is where he gets it from, feeling the difference in air pressure. So, I immediately go out, outside the NMCC, and it's already full of smoke. There is just all kinds of havoc, the alarms are going off. I went back to my Office to make sure people are okay. Within the [Special Operations] Division, there were a couple officers and NCOs and we had a couple who were medically trained—emergency response guys, civilian contractors—and they wanted to go over to the other side of the Pentagon, the crash site, and assist. Knowing there would be casualties, I sent them over, after taking a complete head count. Then I went back to the NMCC. The Pentagon by this time was full of smoke; it was hard to get around; it was hard to see. By the time I got back to the NMCC, the Secretary [of Defense] and the Vice-Chairman [of the Joint Staff] were there. He was the acting Chairman, since the Chairman was gone. The Director [of the Joint Staff] was there and a whole host of other people. It was a pretty crowded room. I got SOCOM on the phone and we kept the line open as things developed.

The Pentagon had open communications with the FAA, with the Department of Justice, and others as they were trying to figure out what else was going to happen. At this point there was a huge amount of raw data coming in. I felt like we were living out... *War of the Worlds*. The data coming in led everyone to believe there were multiple attacks or potential attacks throughout the country. There were reports of planes not obeying the FAA [order] to turn around and clear the airspace. There were reports of planes on the runway reporting or signaling distress. It seemed as if there were about fifteen different events going on at one time, and I thought "this is a well-coordinated attack going beyond our [SOF] capability and other government agencies' [capability to respond]." But we stayed up with SOCOM, trying to keep them aware of what was going on and SOCOM stood everybody up [put everybody on alert], gathering the intelligence and waiting for guidance.

About a half hour after the attack, when things settled down a little bit, everybody was ordered to evacuate the [Pentagon]. I knew that the other shops [offices] under the Joint Staff were leaving, but somebody had to stay and help the senior leadership do what they had to do. So, I went over to the office and I said, "Listen, everybody is leaving the building; they're all evacuating the building because of the fire and the smoke, but we can't." I said, "Somebody's got to stay and help the Secretary and the Vice-Chairman." What I was asking them to do was to stay as long as they could. And they did exactly that. They stayed there, despite the smoke, the fire, the danger of further attacks. They were doing their jobs until the last minute, helping out. I was very proud of them; no one would have faulted them for leaving, but they stayed because they knew it was important.

One story tells you about the special operations ethos. When I went back to the office [of the Special Operations Division], I found an officer who had signed out and was on his way to his next duty assignment— and he couldn't wait to leave [his tour as a desk officer], just like most of them—who was trying to get into our secured area. He was wearing a breathing mask, one of those painter's masks, and trying to open the office door. He didn't know we had changed the code on the cipher lock. I said, "You should already be on your way to Hurlburt Field!" And he looked at me and said, "I thought you needed me." I wondered how he got into the building, decided not to ask, and said, "I really appreciate that but I think everybody's gone now." So, anyway, he left and I went back to the NMCC and we continued to filter through raw data and try to get the real scope of what had happened.

I am not sure if I went home that night. I don't remember. If I did it was very late, just to go home and shower and shave and come back. In fact that was a signal we wanted to send everybody. The Pentagon was obviously a symbol of our military strength. You just can't shut it down. So we went back; the next day everyone came in. This was a very dramatic time. I mean, you've got a new Secretary of Defense, the Chairman of the Joint Chiefs and the Director of Operations are out of the country, the building is on fire with hundreds of casualties, and the senior leadership is trying to do something never attempted since the Civil War, defend the continental United States while under attack. I was very proud of what I saw. It just amazed me how calm, collected, and directed everybody was, [with] not any immediate concern about their own safety. It was "how do we get the planes up to provide combat air patrols [over American cities]? Where are we going to position the ships? How do we help [rescue operations at] the World Trade Center? What about our own people, those in the Pentagon?" The NMCC was like a TOC [Tactical Operations Center], only this one was under attack. It was a very natural reaction to the events by the senior leadership. They were very directive, they were very focused and I will say I was impressed with the way they were handling the situation.

So, September 12 I worked out of my office providing special operations planning to the Joint Staff. The computers were up, the phones were up, the SIPRNET [classified Internet] and things like that were all working. We continued working contingency planning with SOCOM and also all the daily business too. You still had to do deployment orders to Colombia and the daily actions that you would normally do. It doesn't change. Probably 80 percent of our work was related to the impact of September 11, and 20 percent of it was doing the normal actions. But of course we were in a very hyper-secure environment. The building was being evacuated at least two or three times a day for the next couple of weeks, because somebody would get a call or they would hear a plane fly overhead—it would happen to be a military plane, but they would pull the alarm and the next thing you know everybody is running out of the building. You really had to wonder if you were safer inside the building than you were running out into the open courtyard. But the whole building was now reacting to what we would later know was the new way of doing business.

We started preparing military plans, knowing the president was going to call for some kind of response, and Afghanistan was the clear and obvious target. The Commander of SOCOM, of course, was very involved in the process, in presenting his plans, and [explaining] what SOF can do. This was the time for the Commander to look at the whole global network of terrorism, and SOCOM was called upon to develop those plans.

This direction came from the civilian leadership. They had probably a better appreciation, I would argue, than our military leaders did of the [difference between] special operations and conventional operations, particularly with regard to capabilities. Believe it or not, September 11 probably happened at an opportune time, because we had a new civilian administration on board, so they were still learning what the different capabilities were within the Department. So, instead of relying on preconceived notions of who does what, they were getting the textbook briefings about naval operations, army maneuver brigades, and special operations. In terms of special operations, senior leaders [had been] invited to Fort Bragg [before 9/11] and received capability demonstrations and briefings. So, the leadership had a clear, unfiltered view of special operations capabilities. This was the case with the Vice Chairman. Being an Air Force pilot, I don't think he had too much experience with special operations, but he was a very quick learner. The service chiefs—their perspective on special operations was already well honed from the Vietnam War and their experiences with SOF there. So, that's why I am saying that I thought that, other than the Vice Chairman, the civilians had a more unbiased view, and because of this I felt the senior [civilian] leadership fully expected the capability that they were shown. And the lesson is, if you say you can do unconventional warfare, you better be prepared to execute. And they would say, "that's what we have special operations [forces] for, so, damn it, they're going to do that."

Immediately after September 11, instead of getting into parochial arguments, things like "Well we've got a Marine Corps MEUSOC [Marine Expeditionary Unit-Special Operations Capable]; it has the words "Special Operations Capable"—why not send them?" It never got to that. There was never any of that discussion. It was a Special Ops mission. So, it was the civilian leadership that pushed for a special operations capability and wanted special operations involvement in the War on Terrorism. Truth be known, the military could have responded better, but I believe we were not used to such an aggressive style of [civilian] leadership and it took us a bit of time to adjust. The planning was very aggressive and the requirements went out immediately to the regional combatant commanders. They were the first to reply and provide a response to the SECDEF [Secretary of Defense]. Whether SOCOM is a combatant commander or not, we still have regional commanders out there who are responsible for those areas, so the messages immediately went out to them to develop the plans, identify the targets, and then we would apply the right resources to those targets. Meanwhile, SOCOM was given the responsibility of working on a worldwide counterterrorism plan. There was (at least at my level) very little talk of Iraq. [The talk was of] a global terrorist network and defeating this terrorist network, to include state sponsorship. But, again, the SOF focus was on the global network; any Iraq planning was done by another [non-SOF] office in the Joint Staff.

Given what we knew about this network and how we had to infiltrate this network, [we] required some new techniques, new tactics and procedures. [Secretary Rumsfeld] didn't think the military had them. In fact, we did but [in] very small [numbers]. He was very excited once he found out about this capability, and he wanted to expand those capabilities; but of course this could not be done immediately and would take years.

The planning for Afghanistan was going full bore in CENTCOM [Central Command, the regional headquarters responsible for Afghanistan] and the Joint Staff. My impression was that SOCCENT [the Special Operations Command in CENTCOM] was developing a very specific UW [unconventional warfare] campaign plan, right down to the doctrinal phases of a successful UW campaign.[2] I remember reviewing it, starting to get it around the Pentagon and Washington for approval. But of course there were also competing conventional military plans being worked at the same time. The optimist would say that "this gives the decisionmaker a range of options to select from." In the Pentagon and on the Joint Staff there is a "sister division" [to the Special Operations Division] called the Joint Operations Division, the JOD, and they handle all the conventional military planning. So, of course, they would be working the conventional alternatives to a special operations plan, likewise in CENTCOM. [It's] probably a good argument [for] why we should integrate special operations and conventional planners together, instead of separating them as we do now. I got the impression that the UW planning process was being received by the Commander of CENTCOM and his staff very favorably. I know it was also being responded to favorably within the Pentagon, particularly on the Joint Staff, given the difficulty of getting conventional forces into the theater. Couple that with what I mentioned earlier, about the senior leaders not being saddled with "negative baggage" about special operations, and you have the ingredients for a likely deployment of special operations in a lead role. A very, very rare combination and outcome, likely not to happen again, for a variety of reasons.

Once the decision was made to introduce special operations into Afghanistan as the lead military force, SOF responded well, linking up with indigenous rebel forces, grabbing HVTs [high value targets], preparing the ground for the introduction of conventional forces. SOF performed and became the darling of DOD and the American public. SOCCENT, I thought, had a very good plan. It was a very realistic plan. It spoke doctrinally about how an unconventional warfare mission was going to go and how long it was going to take, what those requirements were. I thought it was well received. I would argue that they actually used that plan in the initial days but there was always in the back of the [senior, conventional commanders'] mind "we are going to use this until the 10th Infantry Division can get there," and in fact that's when [the unconventional plan] unfortunately stopped and then it became more of a "occupied by mass" kind of thing.

[The military is] always going to tilt toward the conventional forces because they are represented in the Pentagon twenty-four hours a day and SOCOM really isn't. First, [SOCOM] is in Tampa and [its] lead representation in the Pentagon is an 06 [colonel][3] working for the Joint Staff. There was some friction [between SOF and conventional forces and commanders]. But I only remember one officer above the 06 level, one officer of senior rank, in a senior decision-making position, who made a comment, and he said he personally didn't agree with it [SOF growing beards and wearing Afghan hats to blend in with the population in Afghanistan]. He didn't think it sent the right message. Okay, we probably did ourselves some disservice in that regard too. Some of our guys took it a little too far, in the sense that you've got to know your audience and you've got to know your environment. What you wear in the deep woods is something different than you wear in downtown Kabul, you know what I mean? And if you don't make that differentiation then you are just pissing on your own boots. But that same officer had the influence to shut that down [growing beards and wearing Afghan clothes]. And he didn't because I think he understood that there was a capability [that was needed]. It was a kind of T.E. Lawrence relationship about these things. "We need you; this is the time we need you but as soon as it's done we will get rid of you." We conventionalized the effort after that, because I think it gets back to the relationship of SOCOM with the Joint Chiefs of Staff. Now that's two different organizations; two distinctive, different organizations. As long as the Joint Chiefs of Staff can influence the operational requirements, then you are going to have this conventionalization because that is who they represent [the services]. There is no SOCOM rep at the Joint Chiefs of Staff table, the tank.[4] Also, a lot of your combatant commanders don't believe that you need specially trained, specially equipped forces to do a special operations mission.

AFGHANISTAN, NOVEMBER–DECEMBER, 2001

A Special Forces captain, who was the leader of one of the first "A teams" to go into Afghanistan, describes his experience.

We were supposed to go into Afghanistan October 20 but there were weather delays. The pilots didn't think they could get in. So we actually went on November 1. It was a 6½-hour helicopter flight. We landed in the ... early morning hours [of] November 2. We were supposed to hook up with the Northern Alliance[5] commander in the region. He was one of the subordinate commanders in the whole alliance but in charge of this area. Some of his people were supposed to meet us. But nobody really knew the commander. We requested intelligence on him and they sent us stuff on a guy with a similar name but the meeting was set up through the Northern Alliance, so we flew in to meet up with his people. We landed at night and there was snow on the ground, which was cool. You know, we had done all these rehearsals to try and offload quickly because we were bringing in a lot of stuff. We took two bags of medical equipment, five parachute kit bags full of beans, five parachute kit bags full of rice, a couple dozen blankets, wool blankets because it's freezing, these guys are suffering 'cause they have no food, no blankets, no nothing, and they are trying to fight a war. And we had two kit bags full of medical supplies like bandages and stuff like that, that we wanted to give them right off the bat to establish that we understand their situation and get them strengthened up a little bit. So we rehearsed getting it off quickly but with the snow we just took the stuff on the bird [helicopter] and threw it on the snow, and because of the slope of the snow it just slid out of the way. We didn't have to carry it. Really, you could just kind of sling it, and it would slide down the mountain. So we got it off quickly and the helicopter got out of there and we took off. We're through and we were gone. And then we walked and walked and walked, all night.

Well the following morning, we hadn't been to bed yet, a big defection [from the Taliban] took place. All these bad guys were marched into a little courtyard. They all bowed and the commander's men had them under guard. They are drawn down on them [pointing weapons at the defectors] in this little courtyard and the commander brings out a video camera, which shocked the hell out of us. And he starts videotaping this defection and he is talking to them. They are standing there almost in a file and rank, and he is talking to them and I can't understand a word he is saying, and we don't have any interpreters and he is talking, but it is obvious that it's his deal. And everyone paid homage to the commander, the guy we were supposed to work with. They kissed his hand or bowed or whatever, in some way they paid him homage and then some of them, right there just picked up guns, right there on the spot. And this was hairy, like, holy shit, these guys just bowed three seconds ago and now because they promise to behave, they can carry guns? But these defectors were all Afghans. To the Afghans, this made sense. When they pledged their allegiance to [the commander] they meant it and most of them stayed with us all the way through the fight. This wasn't like [what happened later] at Mazar-e-Sharif;[6] those were foreigners. That turned out to be a perfidious surrender.

I was there for the initial surrender [of the al-Qaeda forces involved in the uprising at Mazar-e-Sharif]. The Northern Alliance commander I was working with, he and I went there [where the defectors were supposed to show up] about two or three in the morning. We got some intel[ligence] that five or six hundred were coming, and we moved first to the eastern edge of Mazar to see what the hell was going on, how they were surrendering or defecting. We knew from intelligence sources that nobody could defect or desert. Anybody that tried was killed, shot in the back dead. And the Taliban knew that Mazar-e-Sharif was the last holdout in the north. We understood it too and knew they couldn't afford to lose any forces. So, when the commander came in and said, "There's five or six hundred guys heading this way" nobody knew at the time exactly what they were coming for. The commander and I talked and our attitude was: Well, there's no way they could defect or desert. We know nobody can get out of there, let alone five or six hundred dudes with guns and weapons and trucks. We thought something's wrong about this, and so we picked up some guys and we went out there to the east side of town. And then this convoy of five or six hundred guys pulled up and stopped and said, "Send an emissary forward," saying "We want to defect." And the commander kicked into the Afghan military culture mode. My team was like, "Hey, we don't know the composition of the force but we do know the situation. And therefore, it's a ruse, at a minimum an opportunity to gather information on surrendering procedures, so they can be used against us in the future." Well, when the surrender went without a hitch, we said, okay. Well, it had to be [either] legitimate or an intelligence-gathering procedure, cause they actually did surrender. Pretty soon, it became clear that it was a ruse.

By the time of Mazar-e-Sharif [November 25, 2005] we were working well with the commander, but he was still responding in that Afghan way that didn't always make sense to us. At the beginning, when we first started, he didn't understand what we could do. He didn't understand the technology, what it could do. Neither did the bad guys. The commander realized that the Americans brought a lot of prestige, and for that we were good. And right off the bat, we started bringing in a lot of supplies, both lethal and nonlethal, and it's getting to be a tough time of the year, so the nonlethal aid was probably just as important as the lethal aid [ammunition, etc]. So, okay, great, we are very valuable, but in terms of this war-fighting shit, what are these Americans really bringing? My group commander warned me before I went into Afghanistan, they are going to look at you, baby-face captain, as some guy who's never been in war, and you need to be prepared for that. I don't think he was off base on that. I think the [Northern Alliance] commander kind of looked at it like, Okay, these guys are bringing me supplies, so I can do my thing. But then he saw what we could do. We had him look at a target through binoculars. And he says "Good target," and we say "No, no, keep looking, keep looking," and all of a sudden he sees this thing just go "Poof!" And he's like "Wow, you know these guys, these guys can do some good; they bring a whole new dimension to the battlefield!" He was right. A fortified target up a mountain or something and it would have taken forever to assault that location. But we could take it out like that; never even have to walk up that freakin' hill, let alone get a force large enough to accomplish that kind of assault. And now we can just plink it out of the way.

So it worked out. Where we were, it was clear what we had to do, how we had to get to Mazar-e-Sharif. That was the key in the north and it was clear what we had to do to get there. The Taliban had cities that were buffers around Mazar. We were going to systematically erode or exhaust that buffer backwards. So I told the commander there's a couple of things I need. (I was talking to him through an interpreter. The commander gave us one. The commander had a guy who spoke Russian. We also did the old pointy-talkie thing, and the little phrase books, you know, from DLI [Defense language Institute].) Anyway, I told him, I need someone who knows the places. I said, "I need to know what I am looking at." I needed someone who could tell me where the targets are, and we talked about that in a lot of depth. And hopefully, this will be someone who can speak either English or Russian (or actually at times English, Russian, French, or Chinese, because those were the four languages I had on my team, and Arabic. Probably after English, we had more Arabic speakers. But ironically nobody on the commander's force spoke Arabic. We didn't have an interpreter who spoke English at all, until the night before we entered Mazar). Then I said, "The last thing I need, I need to be able to get there." There were mines everywhere. So I needed an escort. And he said, "Okay."

Once we got to those locations, I split the team. Our teams' SOP was—you work this out in training—that I would take the junior weapons NCO (Non-Commissioned Officer), the junior Commo guy, and the senior medic, and the CCT [Combat Controller] with me. But I needed all the Russian speakers with me. That wasn't exactly standard for us, [but] I took all the Russian speakers, 'cause I was going to go talk to the guy that spoke Russian. That is how we split it up, and it worked out well. The AFSOC [Air Force Special Operations Command] combat controller was there too, which was great. Initially, we did not want an AFSOC guy. Traditionally, at least in my experience, and the experience of people I've worked with, we look at the AFSOC guys as kids, kind of liabilities. Because they don't have the maturity, because they come in to AFSOC a lot younger, whether they are PJ's [pararescue personnel] or STS [Special Tactics Squadron] or whatever. But this guy was great. He was mature, he was an E-6 [a senior noncommissioned officer], he was thirty-one years old, he was engaged [with the mission], he was laid back, but he was well trained; he had been around awhile and he fit right in real well, and he was in good shape. So, he was really, really an asset. Also, he brought another radio, which is a great radio. And it's great to have someone there that can talk to the plane, so you don't have to. Now, he did not understand UW [unconventional warfare] at all. But in fairness to him and to AFSOC that's not their job, to understand UW. It's his job to talk to airplanes. And that was great 'cause that is what I needed, and when things got a little hairy at times and we had planes stacking up, I felt confident that this guy is going to keep these planes safe; he's going to keep us safe [from the bombs of U.S. aircraft] and he's going to do the job. You couldn't ask for a better guy to control the air, but he didn't really understand this situation going on around him. But [even so, with him around] I have got another guy now that can do drop zones, do HLZ's [helicopter landing zones], and control drops and whatever I need to do. This guy can handle it, and he was good at what he did.

One [element of our split] team stayed, actually, not too far from the commander's command post and the rest of us went over to the other location. We talked by radio to establish priority targets. We both received information about various target locations and then we would swap the target information. I would say, "Okay, I got targets alpha alpha, zero zero one, through zero zero ten," and he's like, "Okay, I got zero zero eleven, through zero zero twenty," or whatever. Let's swap this and this. Lets prioritize these and renumber them and that's how we will take them down. The [Afghan] commander didn't get involved. He didn't meddle in how we were going to do it. I think it was because of the [technology] gap between us, and it was also respect, [since] it was kind of our show. We corroborated our information, and then our plan was to target the priorities. We set target priorities, to make those missions as valuable as possible. Other teams took different approaches, and I can't speak for their methodologies. But my particular team, we decided our methodology was going to be the way I described. We were not interested in dropping bombs on tanks, unless it's in an extreme situation. Even in one particular case where [the Taliban and al-Qaeda] fanned out and came after us with some tanks. We were confident that they didn't know where we were, and they were just kind of stumbling around. So, we asked for planes but we didn't call "in extremis" because there was no reason to waste the opportunity [on a tank that was not a threat]. [Instead,] I [was] going to take out one of the priority targets. And I think that really caused the rapid collapse. We went after foreign targets first because we recognized that the foreigners had all the experience and all the training and all the education. Chechens, IMU [Islamic Movement of Uzbekistan]—yeah, we finally got to take the gloves off against the IMU, the Pakis that had come over and the Saudis. Then after that we targeted Taliban leadership. This is not decapitation, we are not trying to take out one or two dudes and expect the whole thing to fall apart. But so many of the soldiers in Afghanistan were impressed into service and that was a potential recruiting pool for us for a variety of reasons. And if we could set the conditions so that they could have even a minimum opportunity to desert, if not defect, then we thought they would do it. So we targeted the leaders to give the soldiers a chance to leave. Also, we recognized how hitting multiple C2 [command and control] targets disrupted their C2, and since it was a very centralized army, that could be catastrophic for them. Of the enemy's elements of combat power, we chose to hit leadership with air assets.

One time we brought in aircraft to get a leadership target. It was a B-52. It bombed a chunk of land three kilometers long by one kilometer wide, and they missed. Didn't hit a damn thing. We blew up the desert, twenty-seven mark 82's [an air-delivered bomb] and we didn't blow up a damn thing but dirt. But still it looked impressive because this thing was on top of this mountain, it's way up above the valley. The whole arc went right up the side of the mountain; didn't hit a damn thing. But it looked—because this is a huge mountain—it looked spectacular. It was pretty cool, and you know what? Psychologically, it had to say to everybody in the valley, "holy shit, the rules have just changed." Another time, we were controlling some B-52's and they dropped. And the guys are waiting and they to talk to the pilots and say "We didn't see anything," and suddenly they hear boom, boom, boom from another direction and they look over there and they are like "Oh my God, you know we just destroyed some part of the village of aq Kopruk. We were supposed to drop the bombs over *there*, oh my God." Well, the commander jumps in the air, he throws his arms in the air, he's like "Alright!" He's happy and the controller is completely perplexed. He talks to the pilots. "How the hell did you drop those over there?" It turns out they accidentally punched in the wrong grid coordinates. You know, that is easy for them to say at 35,000 feet. For us down here, well that could be us [getting blown up] or hurting the local population we rely on. It turns out by the grace of God, and nothing less, the bombs just landed on another bunch of bad guys. And the commander knew about that target, too. He loved it. He thought it was great. We accidentally hit the wrong target but it worked. The probability of that...[shakes head].

You know this war was not won by the Air Force. The Taliban and al-Qaeda were killed by the Air Force but in a UW situation to drop the bomb, that's the easy part. The hard part is developing the infrastructure that facilitates knowing where the targets are, so you *can* bomb them. And that is what won the war. It's getting the targets and getting which targets, why this target or why that target and that's what makes it work. Riding around on horses, dropping bombs, I know that's sexy for the cameras and for the drama. But first of all we went on horses because that is all we had; we didn't have any vehicles in the beginning and some of those trails are not passable in vehicles. But basically if you did a relative combat power analysis between the two sides, the Taliban and al-Qaeda over here and the coalition on the other side, it wasn't just a lack of mobility assets that the Northern Alliance suffered from. One in three guys might have been armed. And when I say "armed," I mean like Ahmet shows up at the battlefield and he's got his AK-47 or he's got an RPG [rocket propelled grenade launcher], this is a great one, and his son is right behind him. He carries the RPG round and his youngest son is behind him waiting to see who dies first, because he will pick up what they drop. And that's kind of how we would go to battle, until we could bring in more lethal aid, ammo and weapons.

We didn't have any artillery. We had one piece when we got there, and it didn't work, and my weapons sergeant field-fabricated a firing pin to make it work. I don't even know what the hell he did, but he got the thing working. But close air support is not very close at this point. I mean most times [the aircraft] are dropping in excess of 25,000 feet. Our air defense assessment for the area was important to encourage the Air Force to come down a bit closer because you know we missed more often than we hit [when we bombed from high altitude]. The problem with that is you don't want to hurt any of the population, especially if we knew the population was on our side or could potentially be on our side. But we missed a lot with the JDAMs [Joint Direct Attack Munitions] to the point where we stopped using them. We really wanted to use the laser [laser device used to guide bombs to a target] and once we proved its capabilities, the commander wanted laser too, for the same reasons. I mean, he doesn't want to hurt the population either. But with the laser we now have a capability that can kill the bad guys with this air platform at sufficient standoff [so] that their otherwise superior combat power cannot kill us. And maybe the playing field was not even level anymore, now the sides were tipped to our advantage, once we began to work and gather information from the population, about where things were.

But in general it all worked. Once there was pressure in both valleys [where we and another team were operating] it really gave way. And once [one] valley went, then the [other] valley quickly followed, so they [Taliban/al-Qaeda] couldn't organize, while we ended up having a meeting between [the Northern Alliance faction leaders]. We got the factions trying to work together for the first time. By the end of November, I'd say after Kunduz [a town in northern Afghanistan] fell, we switched from an unconventional warfare operation to a counterinsurgency operation. And Kunduz marked that tipping point. That's why humanitarian assistance became very important also, because of the winter months coming on.

We had been thinking of [how to fight an unconventional campaign in Afghanistan] for a while. [My team] had deployments to Uzbekistan because we had a few people who spoke Russian on my team. In fiscal year 1998, CENTCOM [Central Command] assumed control of five former republics of the Soviet Union. They had not been formerly a part of the CENTCOM AOR [area of responsibility]. So, I was the first of four people, myself and three others, that were going to the 5th [Special Forces] group, who were all assigned to learn Russian because CENTCOM was going to pick up these five countries. At the end of 2000, a central Asian mission came to our battalion and the commander knew that my team wanted that and knew that we had at least one good Russian speaker and a couple other decent ones. Fifth group had called SWC [the Special Warfare Center, an Army Special Forces organization] and said, "Hey, we need some Russian-speaking guys now. Take X number of our Russian speakers, [plus] X number of our incoming assigned personnel and give them Russian. And make the rest Arabic or whatever." At that time, actually everybody was Arabic except for the four of us, so in that class all Arabic and four Russian. That's kind of how this whole Afghanistan thing gets started actually in 2000. Because my team begins to work with the Uzbek Army every month from December 2000 to August of 2001, except for I think two months. We worked with them in some way or another during that time; I think we had nine different deployments in that time span. We were training them in peace enforcement operations. We were working at platoon level and below. Actually, we did two things. We worked with mid-level leadership, teaching them how to do orders and planning. So we worked with headquarters staff and commanders and then we also worked with the platoon and below on patrolling techniques, you know, stuff that they would have to do in peace enforcement operations. And

Chapter 7 [the UN regulation governing peace enforcement operations] says you train for peace enforcement like you train for war. So we basically ran through small-unit tactics and sniper training. So we got a real good pulse on the situation. Our team room was plastered with information about the Northern Alliance and the Nationalist Islamic Movement.[7] Like all SF teams going into a new area, we really began to go over the areas of interest and areas of operations. There was a failed coup in Uzbekistan in August of 1999. The Islamic Movement of Uzbekistan kidnapped four Americans who were mountain climbing in the summer of 2000. And then we expanded our area of interest for this mission because we thought we should include Afghanistan.

I came home early from one of our deployments to Uzbekistan in August [2001] to get married. The team came back from the mission and we were going to stand down for the month of September and take a break because we had been working so much and deploying so much. I went on my honeymoon and then, boom—9-11 hit. I come back to my little bungalow—I can afford to stay in it because I got hit by a drunk driver. I chased her car down and I jumped on her car and she drove me like a quarter of a mile. And then the cops came and we settled out of court. This was in Atlanta in January of 2001, and I still haven't fixed my truck—Anyway, so there I am in my bungalow with my wife when 9-11 happened and I called my company commander as soon as I heard. When I called him, I had a copy of the *International Herald Tribune* in my hand and there's an article that Ahmed Shah Massoud was assassinated.[8] So they begin to earmark teams for a UW mission. There's this flurry of activity with everybody suddenly wanting an SF guy. I mean, every command wanted an SF liaison and, you know, 5th group of course being Central Asia and Middle East guys, we also got a war to fight. And we can't be giving out people to different units. The commanders were just fighting like hell to keep off all these requests after 9-11. My team has so much experience in Central Asia, the commanders are desperately trying to hang on to us for this UW mission. But at the same time, they are trying to balance everyone else's need for Russian speakers and whatever else they need, and they did a good job.

Finally, they put us in isolation[9] and that pretty much cordoned us off. At that point nobody knew exactly what we were going to do. I mean it was intuitive that we were going to Afghanistan. But nobody knew what the mission was. There is a million different things you are taught to do in that kind of situation. I did know that my Battalion commander had gone down to Tampa [the location of CENTCOM] to be a part of a planning cell. And the story was, the story I got through the rumor mill in September 2001, was that CENTCOM presented its plan [for Afghanistan] to the National Command Authority [the president and the secretary of defense]. And [Vice President] Cheney pushes it away and says, "Come back to us with a UW plan." And CENTCOM went back to SOCCENT and said, "What the hell is UW?" They [SOCCENT] were always understaffed, always under-resourced, nobody ever gave a shit about them, until they needed something that they couldn't figure out. So SOCCENT turned to 5th Group and said, "Hey, send us a UW planning cell" and that's why my [battalion] commander went to Tampa and he came back and said to us, "This is going to be a UW gig." But, you know, isolation was so professionally run, a lot of times we were almost complaining that we weren't getting enough information to plan with. In hindsight, though, I realize Headquarters didn't have information. The only thing I knew was that we were doing UW and, you know, that was all I needed to know at that point. That means the traditional seven stage model and that is pretty clear to everybody in SF. I knew the purpose was to support some larger conventional plan that they couldn't effect until after the spring thaw. They needed the UW thing to work until the conventional guys could come in and save us all. At the time we were kind of like, "Well, what makes them think this [UW campaign] won't work so well? 'Cause we think it's going to work just fine."

FORT BRAGG, NORTH CAROLINA, 2001–
SAN FRANCISCO, CALIFORNIA, 2005

A Special Forces Warrant officer[10] describes his efforts to develop some new technology for the war on terrorism.

I was in the same company in 3rd Group for fourteen years. It was the company that did surveillance and reconnaissance for the battalion. When a new company commander came, he asked me to make the company the best surveillance company in the military, to make sure that we had the best equipment, the right equipment to do the job. We looked at the Gulf War. We knew that a lot of the teams doing special reconnaissance got compromised. It turned out to be 70 percent—70 percent of the teams doing SR [special reconnaissance] got compromised! We tried to figure out why it happened. Typically, they were compromised by civilians. The teams had put their hide sites in areas where there were civilians. The reason they did this was that they had to get in real close in order to get the information they needed to complete their missions—because they did not have the right technology, they had to get in real close to their targets, and this meant setting up in areas where there were lots of civilians. So we needed better surveillance and reconnaissance technology to allow them to set up at a safe distance from the target.

I knew about Predator [a UAV or unmanned aerial vehicle] and I thought that it could be a platform that we could use. I knew about the [surveillance] technology that was available, and when I started to work with it and put it together it seemed to me that it could work with Predator. I got some support from my company but when I explained my idea and that the initial cost would be about $50,000, the commander told me that I should take [the idea] to one of the Special Mission Units [SMU],[11] since they were the ones that had all the money. So I decided to go to the military labs that were developing the UAV and show them what I had. I put the stuff in my car and just drove there. They were interested in it and worked on it with me. I met people from private industry there, and they wanted to work on it, too.

I deployed to Afghanistan in February 2002 with a prototype. I didn't operate it at first. The [SF] teams used it a couple of times but they couldn't get it to work. Finally, I told them that I could get it to work, if I went out with it. So I did and I was able to get it to work and it provided valuable information. We were able to see problems up ahead and get ready for them. We came across a compound and were able to determine that it was under friendly control before we reached it. We had real-time intelligence, surveillance and reconnaissance information with us in the field. We had audio and visual. Back in the JOC [Joint Operations Center],[12] they were seeing what we were seeing but we were seeing it a few seconds sooner. They couldn't figure out how we were doing what we were doing. They had the feed from the UAV but didn't know we had it right with us too. They would be getting ready to warn us about something, but we would already be reacting to it. When word got around about what we had, it created a lot of interest. The battalion commander was happy because White SOF [regular

SF units] had something that Black SOF [special mission units–SMUs] didn't have. Black SOF wanted it.

I returned to the States to continue to develop the technology. I wanted to get something that was handheld and incorporate more systems into the network. I started trying to work on it but I ran into some problems. I [had] enlisted in the Army with a recruitment deal but the Army didn't keep the promise they made and it was just a big struggle to get anything done. The [regular] Army was just too slow and bureaucratic. A lot of guys just putting in time. I was ready to get out but an old Sergeant who had been in SF told me to try that, so I did. It was great. I got to do things, I could get things done, do this, do that. I had a lot of responsibility. But [then] I ran into some problems with this [surveillance] technology [I wanted to keep developing]. They say SOF is the cutting edge, but it is not true. It's Black SOF that has the money, not the rest of SOF. And my commander was getting in the way. We didn't get along. I was pushing this hard, doing what I had to do to get it done and he didn't like it. He told me I wasn't working on it anymore because there were other things he wanted me to do, but higher ranking officers wanted it done, so I got to do it but [only by] working with private companies. Anyway, I am out of the active component now. I'm in the Reserves and still working this with private industry. The technology has continued to develop and there are now a number of units deployed overseas.

PAKISTAN, NOVEMBER 2001–MARCH 2002; IRAQ, MARCH–APRIL 2003

An Air Force major who flew special operations missions in Afghanistan and Iraq describes his experiences and reflects on the character of Special Operations Forces.

I was in an AFSOC [Air Force Special Operations Command] headquarters job on September 11. I think I flew the night before, so I was watching the airplanes hit the buildings at home on TV. I went into work and obviously everything was kind of paralyzed for a couple of days. I thought, you know, what are we going to do? What's going on? Everybody was [still] getting their wits about them. But AFSOC very quickly put together some forces. Very quickly started doing some forward deployment in anticipation of what was going to come next.

In that headquarters job, I was unique. [I was in one of] only two offices in the headquarters that required that you stay current and qualified in the airplanes. At the same time in the flying units, we had a manning shortage [of pilots]. [Prior to 9-11], a lot of great people ended up getting out and going to the airlines, so for better or worse—I know it was better for me—my flying skills [which I was able to keep up in my staff job] were more urgently needed than my staff skills in the immediate aftermath of 9-11. I really wanted to go fly. Our first wave of people deployed into Uzbekistan. Our unit was the first airplanes on the ground there, when they finally opened up. [I wasn't part of that but] two or three weeks later, we deployed to this exercise in Jordan. They told us to pack for six months because you're going to roll right from the exercise into something. We had our first group of guys go to Uzbekistan and I think it was November. Yeah, I think I was home for Thanksgiving but I was gone for Christmas.

Our unit went into Uzbekistan with army helicopters. They're the ones that showed up and provided the initial combat search and rescue capability that allowed the air campaign to begin. Eventually, our whole joint special operations task force, the gunships,[13] and everybody got into position. At that time of the year the weather was bad. So, my unit went from Uzbekistan to Jacobabad in Pakistan. It was the first week of December. At that point, [we] were a unit, we had our airplanes. We had Air force MH53's [long-range helicopters] there on station to do whatever; you know, all the different missions that came down the pike. Then we also supported the SMUs that were operating further in the country. When I compare [flying in Afghanistan] to what we did in [Operation] Iraqi Freedom, in Afghanistan flying was more of a SOF war. SOF was more on the point of it. And we did it. It was really gratifying [doing] all the different things that we trained to do. I remember being an instructor at the schoolhouse for three years telling students, "Hey, someday you may have to do this. That's why I am beating you over the head now. Someday you're going to have to land in the middle of the night, no lights, somebody's life's going to be at stake." All that stuff happened while we were there. It was the most gratifying flying we've ever been able to do as far as the high altitudes, and the rugged terrain. Helicopter aerial refueling missions were the norm, but we did a lot of other things as well. We did a lot of coalition support, we did a lot of foreign internal defense[14] missions, we set up FARP [Forward Area Arming and Refueling Point] sites along the border. We transported the equipment in that allows forward refueling areas in the border area. I mean obviously it was a very hot pursuit of UBL [Usama bin Laden] at that point. So we were in and out of little airfields along the border. We were in and out all over Afghanistan. We did a lot of direct action missions. They really stretched our capability but it was outstanding flying. We could take the helicopters from Pakistan, fly them into Afghanistan for direct action missions on these compounds. I mean, whatever intelligence [we had] to snatch and grab these guys was very perishable, so we had to plan and execute very quickly. Just the logistics of being able to do that in one period of darkness, as much aerial-refueling as the helicopters needed, was pretty amazing. We [the planes refueling the helicopters] were up [to the tanker aircraft] and down [to the helicopters], yo-yoing all night long, running through the mountains, following the helicopters.

These helicopters were in the air for twelve hours sometimes. From the time they cranked up to the time they finally got home, it was over twelve hours. And so they obviously needed a lot of fuel. The most complex of these missions involved three of our airplanes supporting eight or nine helicopters. We did five refuelings of the helicopters and we refueled a tanker three times ourselves. So you're running back and forth [from the tankers to the helicopters]. I mean [shakes his head] ... so the logistics, we were able to pull it off. I mean some of the targets were these mud adobe compounds at eight thousand feet up in the mountains, so the helicopters can't take in a full load of gas when they inserted the ground teams. They need to refuel every hour or so to keep their options open for emergency exfiltration of the teams. And they were able to grab up some folks. I don't know how many of them ended up in Guantanamo but several did. More than several. So, they had some pretty successful direct action missions.

We finally got to do exactly those things that we always saw on paper were our capabilities. We had the SMUs that called on us as needed for their refueling and it was on one of those missions that I had my fiasco of running an airplane into the side of a mountain. Long painful story there, but when you're dealing with those SMUs, the compartmentalization was so tight that we didn't get the information we needed [to plan the flight] until after we took off and there was a disconnect in the information flow so, you know, a little more information would have helped—and so a long painful story. Delays and delays [in the operation] and sunrise

coming [for surprise and security, the direct action operations were supposed to take place at night], having trouble getting fuel. Do we stop or
do I take them toward the objective? Cause I know the sun's rising, [so
we kept going towards the objective]. And it's in the middle of an in-flight
emergency because the helicopter's blades chopped off the [refueling]
hose. So, we're dealing with that emergency in the middle of coming
down a mountain valley at three in the morning. With the lack of a ter-
rain-following system [on the airplane], you know I got suckered into a
big snowy hillside that looked like a cut in the ridgeline and it ended up
being a shadow thrown on the side of the ridgeline. We ended up being
about 100 feet short [of clearing the mountain]. Airplane screaming at
full power. We had 46,000 pounds of fuel on board and bellied it right
into the snow. Nothing blew up; it hit the ground at 80 knots and luckily
everybody got out alive. Eight folks. Took us almost two hours to cut one
of the loadmasters out of the back. He was messed up pretty bad, but he
pulled through. We were lucky for that.

I thought that our training was outstanding for the operations we were
doing. We had been training to do the proper things, the blacked-out
landings, the helicopter refueling, and the formation flying that we did.
For a flyer, what you always wanted [is] to get the chance to put your
training to use. Afghanistan was all of it. I mean everything, every type of
utilization that we could be used for. I think we really used the airplanes
well. We really used the capabilities in a real rough area. I mean that is no
friendly place for any kind of machinery or anything else, so we learned
our lessons, high altitude wise. We've lost a lot of helicopters. We ended
up losing another MC-130[15] there, an MC-130H on a take off mishap.
You know, high altitude, seven or eight thousand feet at a little dirt strip
somewhere [and the pilot] ended up not having enough power to fly out
and the ground rose to meet him. So we lost a couple C130's. We lost a
lot of helicopters due to brown-outs [blowing dust on landing] and high
altitude stuff. It was basically the high altitude conditions that we were
unaccustomed to operating in, really pushing it to the edge of the envelope like that. But as far as the big picture of what we were doing there,
it was just fantastic flying and really purpose-built for our capabilities.
I mean, there was really nobody else that could do what we were doing
there. Nobody else could take helicopters and go into these eight thousand foot compounds and have really scary guys jump out right on the
porch. I mean there's no other force in the world that has these refueling

capabilities, the night fighting capabilities to be able to do that. Eight thousand feet at 2:30 a.m. Some really scary guys coming out of a helicopter in the middle of nowhere. I mean, we're hundreds of miles from anywhere. Any road or major city or whatever. So, it was really satisfying to be able to do what we do and provide that kind of capability. It was very soon after 9-11 [and] all of our fangs were still hanging out, knowing that we're refueling a helicopter that's got eight guys in it that they just snatched up from a compound. That's what we're here to do. You know, getting a little bit of payback. Getting a little bit of personal payback.

I missed the initial push to get into Iraq. Again, I had some head-quarters stuff to do. I ended up catching up with the unit in March, mid-March, 2003 for Iraqi freedom. So I was there when we started. You know in Afghanistan, before the ground operation had been set up, before the big Army came in, SOF was basically in charge. We had a pretty free hand to run around. I mean ours were definitely operations within a bigger campaign plan, but at least in Afghanistan—especially for the first month—there was nobody else there, so we were running around all over the place. And then in Iraq, obviously a completely different scheme of maneuver. We were a very small part. I would say we were definitely a subordinate part of the overall campaign plan, as it should have been with the objectives that we had there. We were able to do regime change in Afghanistan with a few hundred guys on the ground but I don't think that was really a possibility in Iraq. So, we [SOF] had the western desert, to find scuds, try to make sure they don't try to get Israel in the war, like we did before [in operation Desert Storm], and then as required the unique capabilities, apply them as required. We didn't fly nearly as much as in Afghanistan. It just wasn't as target-rich an environment as that. It just wasn't a target-rich environment for SOF. At least for our Air Force portion. I mean there were teams running around all over the place on the ground but as far as what I do, what my business was, it wasn't a huge demand for what we were doing.

There was one exception. We did one really high-profile mission. A big helicopter package. Just as the tanks were starting to roll through Kuwait, crossing the border, we flew three or four hundred miles deep into Iraq and took down one of Saddam's palaces. Again we supported the helicopters that went in to put the guys on the ground. They ran around, blew some things up, grabbed some stuff. I mean, I didn't think they expected to find him there but I think they got some computers, documents, and

whatever. But in a sense it may have been more of a psychological operation than anything else. You know, "we can go anywhere we want, any-
time we want, and there's nothing you can do about it." It was like fifty
miles outside of Baghdad. So, we were pretty far in there. We were able to
get a big package of helicopters in and out with no casualties. I mean, we
got shot at but nobody got hit. It was probably by far the most impressive
assembly of moving parts that I'd ever seen on a mission. In Afghanistan,
we were on our own. I mean as long as we deconflicted with the big blue
Air Force, the bombers and everybody. We actually talked to them once to
say, "Yeah, this is us. Don't have anybody shoot us down. Leave us alone
because we've got our mission to do." The particular mission in Iraq was
in a very high threat area. This mission had been planned for a long time.
We were the focus of support for that night. There were over ninety aircraft involved in it, with all the strike aircraft that were supporting us. We
had EA-6s up [electronic jamming aircraft], F-15s, F-16s [fighter aircraft],
and A-10s [ground attack aircraft] because, again when we're refueling
helicopters, I mean, we're at 110 knots, hanging on the propellers[16] at 500
feet above the ground way deep in bad-guy land. You're very vulnerable.
So, we had worked out this system where we had strike aircraft all over
us, covering us. A-10's in particular were assigned, maybe eight of them.
Two of them would be on top of us, doing turns at 1,000 feet, while we
were going down the refueling track with the helicopters. I could see
them the whole time we were in the refueling mode. The A-10's were
right on top of us. Two would be right on top of the target area taking out
targets. Two or four more would be orbiting above and then they would
rotate through as we [carried out the operation]. So, I think it was impressive, as far as the integration [with conventional forces] we always talk
about. Conventional wisdom is that SOF has a problem integrating with
other forces. We are often out on our own. I think that [this operation at
the beginning of the Iraq War] was a particular demonstration that we've
come a long way as far as integrating with other forces, at least in the air.
Because that was a truly impressive display and it went almost exactly
like we planned it. It was one of the things nobody expected. I mean, it's
the typical thing. We know it's not going to go exactly like we planned but
that particular one really did. There [were some] little sticking points here
and there—radio frequencies or not being able to talk to somebody when
you needed to or whatever—but as far as this gigantic conglomeration
of ninety aircraft all within the same area, at the same time, on the same

target, all there to support eight or ten SOF helicopters and to get us in [and out]. I think it was one of those CNN missions. I think they showed clips of it on CNN. But it just so happened to coincide with the night that Jessica Lynch got rescued. So that ended up sucking all the oxygen out of the psychological operations value of it, but it was still a display of incredible capability. I mean, again, there is nobody anywhere that came even close to attempting that type of a mission. You know if you just take it in the abstract and say "Okay we're going to go 400 miles into an enemy country with helicopters to put guys on the ground, stomp things, break things, let them take what they want and come back out again, right into the enemy's capital and come back out." I mean, that's really a pretty impressive thing, when you're looking at it in that way. But Iraqi Freedom went a lot quicker than any of us ever thought it would happen, as far as the regime falling.

For me personally, I always was just under a lucky star because in OIF [Operation Iraqi Freedom], just like OEF [Operation Enduring Freedom, i.e., the operation in Afghanistan], I had people all around me getting pulled into all these deployed staff jobs and headquarters jobs, but I managed to get a chance to go fly again with the unit. I was lucky enough to be in one of those two offices that had to stay current and qualified in the airplane and that gave me the chip to play this "Hey we're short on experience, so anybody can sit behind the computer and do schedules or whatever at the headquarters level. But we need guys down flying the planes that know what's going on." So I was able to work my way through that.

Getting into SOF was a choice. Upon graduating from Air Force Undergraduate Pilot Training [pilot basic training], I was given the opportunity to pick my assignment off a list and I chose to come to special operations C-130s. I was just bit by an aviation bug. I wanted to fly. *I wanted to fly.* And then when there were no fighters available on the list I got to pick from, it was just the hands-on aviation portion of special operations that really attracted me. I mean being able to take big ugly airplanes and do crazy things with them. That kind of really piqued my interest. You know C-5, C-141, now C-17 [all large transport aircraft], I mean, that's just mostly taking off, putting the gear up, you know, kind of a glorified bus driver. So I really wanted some sort of combat aircraft. There were no fighters available. There were no bombers either. I wanted combat flying, not trash hauling. C-130s had come through this evolution in the

Air Force. Anything with props [propellers], holy crap, nobody wants that. But [the feeling] evolved. When I graduated, C130s in general were very highly regarded because they were pilot flying airplanes and even in the non-special operations versions, you're still doing tactical airlift, which is going into dirt fields in South America, etc, which is exciting flying. So I think C-130s in general just operate at a level of "stick and rudder" satisfaction that just isn't around that much anymore in the Air Force, certainly outside of the fighter world right now. Plus the special operations mystique and everything thrown on top of it, I thought, hey, that'd be great. There was no bad side, no downside to it. But I think primarily it was that attraction to an airplane [that's doing something] other than flying from point A to point B.

Back in 1998 or 1999, all my friends said, "You're crazy for staying in [the Air Force]. Everybody's going to the airlines." Southwest was hiring. I mean it was literally just walking out the door [leaving the Air Force] and flying for an airline the next week. There was nothing to getting hired at the airlines at that time. And we just did the whole soul-searching thing. I just sat down with my wife and said, "You know, I'm really not done doing this yet. I really like doing this. It's fun." So, we had already made our decision to stay in at least until twenty years [a typical retirement point], maybe until twenty-five years. Airlines will always be there if you want to do that. It turned out that was a very fortuitous decision. [Of course,] it wasn't until 9-11 came around. In fact, three or four of the people, friends of mine, that I flew with active duty at the schoolhouse [pilot training], were begging their way back into the Air Force just to get a paycheck. So, I was already a company guy at this point. But, when you take a perfectly good airplane, there's nothing mechanically wrong with it, and just the situation put us in a place where I ended up having to crash land on the side of a mountain in the Hindu Kush mountains [in northeastern Afghanistan]—you know, you are girding yourself for this big investigation, the Safety Boards and all that goes along with it. And so, our commander came up and just said "Hey, well what happened? What's going on?" And you know some of the guys outside SOF whispered, "You know, maybe you should get a lawyer and maybe you should do this and God, maybe, you know," but then, on the other hand, he is the commander. He wants to talk about what happened. We sat down with six members of the crew (we were short the two guys that were hurt bad enough to where they airlifted them to Germany right off the bat) and told the commander what happened. We went through it very, very detailed, probably took 2 to 2 1/2 hours sitting around explaining exactly what we were doing, why we were doing it. And he just shook his head and went "Holy cow, you know, I don't think there was any negligence involved." And I'll never forget it. I didn't think he meant it, and he said, "Well, as far as I am concerned, as soon as you get your Safety Interviews over, get back in the airplane." I thought, "Yeah, right, like the Air Force is going to let me do that, you know there has got to be something going on here." So, we did our Safety Boards (it took like eight to ten days to get the Safety people from the States over to where we were), and they talked to our Wing Commander back in the States and three weeks later, it was "Here are the keys. Go out and fly." I mean, we did two sorties, just out and fly a milk run, and then one tactical flight into Afghanistan with an instructor pilot with me. It was a blacked out landing to Kandahar, in the middle of a dust storm and, okay, yeah, everything is still clicking, everything is still working, and I feel great. The same with the other crew members. They were all allowed to fly with an instructor once or twice. And then it was up to us and our commander, our local commanders. Personally to be treated that way, with that much respect and that much trust was something I did not expect in the wake of that accident. One of SOCOM's published "SOF Truths" is that "people are more important than hardware," and our commanders really lived up to that credo in our case. It was in combat, which makes it a different story. It was a unique set of circumstances that ended up in a national level mission. I mean it was an extraordinarily important mission, very last-minute again but a very high-value target. But the leadership's actions, that would only have happened in SOF; that would not have happened in the big blue Air Force. There would have been too much "Well, yeah, we know, but you know we just got to make sure." They got thirty to forty-five days to put [the accident report] together and then to staff it and send it around and get it crunched. So, typically I think it would be at least ninety days to six months before a crew involved in an accident like that would be allowed to fly again. And we were told just straight up "Hey, you guys are way too valuable to be sitting around doing nothing. We have looked at it."

Commanders are commanders. They have the authority. That really tweaked my outlook on things, as far as when I am in that position, hopefully, I can repay that favor. But they took a chance. I mean it took brass balls for this 06 [colonel] to say okay, go fly. If I had blown a tire, if

I had had any little mechanical problem, not related to anything, if I lost an engine, if say [I had] blown a tire on a runway somewhere. It [would have been] "What in the hell is this guy flying for while he's in the middle of a safety investigation for destroying an airplane?" Risk aversion is an institutionalized problem, especially in the higher levels of the military. But at least at that lower level, 06 command level, boy, they were with us a hundred percent and that meant a lot. I mean, that meant a lot. We had already lost a couple of helicopters by that point. And so they had developed kind of an outlook on how they were going to handle these things. And I know there was concern about a backlash or a chilling effect on the combat crews if you have them thinking "you go out and hack the mission, push hard, but boy if you screw up we are going to pound you." So I know that was a dynamic that was in play. But for us personally, I mean, I could not have ... I mean, I was just jaw-dropping happy that, holy crap, they let me fly and that was all I cared about. That, and that we didn't kill anybody. I don't have to live with that for the rest of my life. I was already kind of a "company" guy before. Now I am really a "company" guy, a SOF guy.

MAY 18, 2003–MARCH 2004, PSYCHOLOGICAL OPERATIONS IN IRAQ

A Reserve major who was in charge of psychological operations teams in Iraq describes his activities there and the relationship between Psychological Operations forces and other elements of the U.S. military.

We went to Iraq in April 2003. Our biggest obstacle was separating [differentiating] ourselves from CA [Civil Affairs]. In conjunction, [Psychological Operations and CA] are very powerful. We learned early on that CA developed a huge number of key contacts and key communicators in their areas of operation, whether they rebuilt schools, funded work projects, passed out food, or provided medical care. It was all good will that we could build on with the affected people. Generally, some sheikh, imam, or other local leader would take some amount of credit or pleasure in having the CA bunch do their thing for his people. When you combine this with IO [information operations] and PSYOP [psychological operations] messages, then you have a great opportunity to influence a great number of people. But CA is an interesting bunch. They are almost care-less about security and tactics. Maybe it was too many trips to the Balkans [a low threat environment] or not enough combat arms officers or NCOs present on their teams, but many of the CA units presented themselves as great targets to the insurgents. In two instances in two separate units, the CA teams were not allowed to go out or operate without us.

In any case, there wasn't a plan for how we would work. We found our-selves a job working with 2nd Armored Cavalry and then got picked up by 5th [Special Forces] Group. At first it worked well and then it didn't. And when it didn't, 5th Group ended up treating us worse than the convention-al forces. A new commander came in [to the 5th Group] who was more narrow. Our initial commander in 5th Group had utilized PSYOP and CA heavily in Afghanistan to great success. He understood our capabilities and was prepared to use us in Iraq. We had assigned PSYOP teams, TPTs [Tactical PSYOP Teams] to three of the ODAs [Operational Detachments Alpha, the basic twelve-man Special Forces (SF)team] with some real suc-cess. Before we could get fully operational, a new commander came in and began shutting everyone down across the board. The CA went away and we were severely curtailed in our activities. There was a definite im-pression that if you did not have a long tab [SF Tab on your uniform] then you were just part of the "help." The new commander was just focused on getting HVTs [high value targets]. But really, SF were not good at that. The SEALS were. That was what they were trained to do. SF wanted to own the battlefield but it was a detriment to have them going after HVTs because they did not focus on controlling the battlespace.

In Vietnam, SF were the biggest proponents of CA and PSYOP, but not in Iraq. We just did intel[ligence] for them because they were too high-speed to bother with that or didn't have the personnel to do it. We also worked with the Marines and the 3rd Infantry Division. We were in Sadr city. We got info[rmation] by trading info. We got actionable intel [intelligence that operational forces can act on] by telling people where to turn in unexploded ordinance and things like that. Once the media came in, this no longer worked as well as it used to because there were other sources of information, but until they got there we collected a lot. In Fal-lujah and al Ramadi, there was no media, so it worked well there.

SF looked at us as info dispensers, not as intel collectors. When we were attached to the 82nd airborne, (actually, to an armored brigade that was attached to the 82nd) we had language and country awareness that the conventional forces did not have, so we did intel. According to the Brigade S2 [intelligence officer] we collected 60 percent of their actionable intel. We met with the sheikhs and imams and the police chiefs and fire chiefs and influenced them. We looked for the key leaders, anybody that the masses turn to for guidance. If we influence them, then we influence a larger audience. The 82nd trusted us to do this. We got the 82nd's troopers to use loudspeakers and pamphlets. It doesn't take an expert to hand out paper. This is not doctrine, at least not now. But in WWI, everybody handed out leaflets, it wasn't just a PSYOPS mission.

Our greatest advantage was to be the liaison with the key leaders. If we don't do it, then you have some major doing it, who may be a great soldier but doesn't know about the culture and doesn't understand about talking to people, getting information, and influencing them. This was a significant issue in that many a maneuver or tactical commander wanted to put his own message out to the locals—often in direct competition or opposition to approved PSYOP and IO messages. In the areas where we enjoyed the most success, the local commander worked in conjunction with the PSYOP and CA team to present a seamless message and information campaign—typically letting PSYOP and CA be his voice to the local leadership and residents.

We had some language ability but we had an interpreter with every team. [Each tactical PSYOP team consisted of an E-6, an E-5, an E-4, and an Iraqi interpreter.] So, we would go and see the sheikhs and imams and drink tea and talk, talk about the economy, about politics, about our desires and messages. We didn't go in Bradleys [armored personnel carriers] and we didn't wear helmets and body armor in the presence of key leaders. They viewed the protection as an insult to them personally. We didn't wear it during meetings where we wanted the atmosphere to be nonconfrontational.

We worked in conjunction with CA at the tactical level, but there was no cooperation at the [brigade] level [or higher]. The tactical cooperation led to pacification and actionable intel. When we got out [of U.S. military compounds] and found out what was going on, then things went well. There was cooperation [between Iraqis and coalition forces]. In some areas PSYOP teams did not get out of the compound. They got no intel and had no impact on the area. If [some unit did not let] one of our teams out, then we didn't give them PSYOP teams. I simply did not have enough PSYOP to waste on a commander that did not use them correctly.

The [members of the] teams were prior service active duty, so they understood the infantry, but [being reservists] they had real-world experience as police, firemen, so they understood what was needed [in Iraq]. My soldiers and NCOs were used to dealing with people, students. This was a huge advantage over the active [duty] PSYOP. So, they [my soldiers and NCOs] could talk to the Iraqis. We also had interpreters living with us. We were the only unit that had interpreters living with the teams. So, we built rapport with the [interpreters] and learned from them. They taught us [Iraqi] customs and courtesies.

Being in PSYOP is hard because you can't measure the effectiveness of what you do. We were sitting around one evening and someone said "Let's put out an 800 number for reporting IEDs [improvised explosive devices]." We handed out leaflets with the number on it. We had 125 reports leading to defusing IEDs, 125 reports in 60 days. We pushed [gave] leaflets to squad level, so we could get more of them out. The al Anbar fire chief had his people out looking for IEDs and arms caches in cemeteries and mosques. So that worked and we could see that work. We also wanted to focus on who was making the calls [to the 800 number]. Turned out, it was women in the middle of the day. Concerned housewives. We didn't build on this enough, but we should have.

What the Army did not understand was that Iraqis were different. [The Army] looked at all Iraqis as the same. We didn't work with the separate groups or with females to encourage them to do things to protect their families. There was a disconnect between what happened on the ground and what got up to higher command. You can't just say that democracy is going to happen. [The Iraqis] did not necessarily know what [democracy] meant. So, we started a grassroots democracy effort but this was three months before the task force level started talking about it. The Sunnis weren't stupid; they knew they were a minority. So, with them, we talked about equality before the law—not one man, one vote. With the Shia [roughly 60 percent of Iraq's population], we talked about one man, one vote.

Working with the conventional military was not always easy. One commander ordered us to drive up and down the road with [our loud]speakers blaring so that we would get shot at and his guys could return fire. That was the last day we worked with him. We weren't going to be tied to doctrine. In the big Army, they are tied to doctrine so they were suspicious of us. We understood that we had to work out of our doctrinal role to be successful. Things that worked in the Balkans or during the first Gulf War were not going to work in Iraq and the institutional guidelines for PSYOP just plain sucked. "Go hand out leaflets and hope it all works out." Additionally, we all thought we could do a little more than what was expected of us. I had very intuitive, resourceful and creative NCOs and soldiers, more so than I ever had on active duty. I knew if I let them get creative, then they would be tremendously successful. I also understood that this creativity would not always be doctrinally or politically accepted by the big army.

But 1st ID [Infantry Division] trusted us because they got results. As long as we didn't get killed or kill others. This one commander [in the 1st ID] knew about insurgency and understood that SF worked in Vietnam until the big Army took over and he told us to go out and do what worked. We had been [in Iraq] seven months. We knew the customs and courtesies, we knew how to get around. We wore sterile uniforms and carried unauthorized weapons. We had much different roles [from the conventional forces], so by looking different, we reinforced our uniqueness.

We did not wear helmets when we talked to Iraqis. That was a sign of respect. Regular commanders had spent careers preparing to fight the Russians on the plains of Europe. They would not admit that they were fighting an insurgency. They were stuck in a thirty-year-old thought pattern. In many cases, PSYOP did not get to do anything interesting. But we could push hard to do things, and not be tied down by doctrine. We were reservists and it couldn't get worse than being in Iraq. We were away from our families, it was 120 degrees. There is nothing worse you can do to me [to punish me]. I told an O-6 [colonel] that, and what could he do but stare at me. Active duty PSYOP was not that flexible. If you found a commander that you could work with, you were alright and you could do interesting things.

PSYOP is the commander's voice to the locals. Now you have Army IO people running around. Since they were just staff people [did not have command over any forces], they wanted to take over PSYOP and CA and sitting in HQ [headquarters] they were telling us what to do, but they didn't know what was going on. They did not know what was coming up from the bottom. Maybe they had other intel from the strategic level but the IO guidance was not good. If we had followed it, we would have failed.

Most of the people I was with in Iraq got out [of PSYOP]. It was frustrating the way things were done and so people got out and are doing other things.

CIVIL AFFAIRS IN NORTHERN IRAQ, MARCH–APRIL 2003

A major in civil affairs describes his experiences working in Northern Iraq.

We started planning to go into northern Iraq in August 2002. Our mission was to support JSOTF-N [Joint Special Operations Task Force–North].[17] At that time, the only forces supposed to be going in [to northern Iraq] were conventional forces, the 4th ID [Infantry Division]. They stretched OPSEC [operational security] into planning for phase four.[18] This made no sense because in phase four we [U.S. or coalition forces] own the country, so who's the enemy they are hiding things from; but that's how they did it. You need to coordinate to get a unified restoration plan, but for OPSEC reasons there was no coordination between the 4th ID and CA [Civil Affairs]. This issue arose again when the 4th ID was denied entry to Turkey and the 173rd [Infantry Regiment] was called in at the last minute. The CA officer in the 173rd had been difficult to deal with on past peacetime operations. For reasons unknown to us [CA planners] there was no coordination between the 173rd and the JSOTF on CA responsibilities. CA operators went into Iraq with the JSOTF on March 25, 2003, as a planning staff to figure out where we needed to put our teams. But we even had some problems doing that. One of the Executive Officers [in the JSOTF] wanted the rest of the battalion headquarters company brought in instead of more CA. We only had one team in country and we wanted to get more in. Ultimately, it required the intervention by the Deputy Commander of 10th group [the SF group in northern Iraq] to get our CA teams on the ground. Most of our work focused on the Patriotic Union of Kurdistan sector until Kirkuk fell on April 10. We arrived in Kirkuk on April 13.

During this time there was a pissing contest between the JSOTF commander and the SETAF [Southern European Task Force] Commander that originated when combat operations spilled over into stability operations.

Essentially, the SETAF Commander would not let the Commander of the 173rd , an infantry O6 [colonel who worked for the SETAF Commander] be subordinated to the JSOTF-N Commander, a Special Forces O6. The 173rd assumed control of Kirkuk. Both they and an SF detachment from the JSOTF went into Kirkuk and set up on an airfield. They [the SF detachment] didn't want CA around because they wanted to hunt HVTs [high value targets] and they did not want to get involved in a humanitarian operation, so they sent us off somewhere else. They didn't want us getting in the way. We ended up down the road at the former headquarters of the Iraqi intel service. From our perspective the number one issue was reestablishing security in the city. The looting got so bad in Kirkuk that the 173rd finally ordered all the Kurd forces out.

As more CA and PSYOP were flowing in, we had about forty CA men and women at the CA Headquarters. To do our job we had to go out and move around at the expense of security at our headquarters, so we got the 173rd to send us a platoon to work as guards. The population was not out gunning for us. Some Iraqis did not like the fact that we were in the former intel HQ. Lots of bad memories. But they quickly realized that the place was under new management and accepted our presence. But looting was always a problem, so we needed security at our headquarters.

The culmination of all these factors, I mean no integrated plan, a combat-centric mentality, no command vision to do the right thing, all come out in this one example of trying to turn the water back on. The 173rd had contracted for water trucks to bring water into Kirkuk, but they looked like fuel trucks and so people were showing up with fuel cans and then putting water in the fuel cans because that's what they'd brought. The Iraqis did finally figure out that all we were passing out was water and brought the appropriate containers. The root problem was all the city wells required pumps and there was no electric power. All the power workers were home protecting their houses rather than going to work because of the looters. So we needed security at their homes. But the 173rd did not want to supply the security. They were looking for HTVs and weapons caches. The 173rd commander in charge of Kirkuk didn't know anything about the infrastructure in Kirkuk and had no plan. We gave the JSOTF a breakdown of all the infrastructure, but whether or not that was forwarded to 173rd I don't remember. If it was, there is no indication [that] at the time they acted on our findings.

On April 15, [2003], we, just CA, met with the Northern Iraqi Oil Company vice president and other senior officials because they controlled the power station. They spoke good English and we explained the situation. We learned that the power station was a pair of state of the art computer-managed GE turbines. Ironically, the morning of the day we showed up at the oil fields, the three control computers were stolen. Just up the street from the power station, the 173rd was protecting the 1950s vintage refinery on the field but the refinery just makes fuel for running the oil company equipment, not for export. The managers gave us all the detail on the infrastructure and who the authorized employees were to get on the facility. The managers told us that the housing areas were at risk and all their employees were home protecting their houses. They said, "If you provide some security, people will come back to work. Without the computers we need to get the workers back at work in order to run the turbines manually." We told the 173rd that we needed security for the housing areas. The 173rd said that the refinery was the priority and that that was what they were going to protect. Finally, the managers got volunteers to come in and get some power going.

While we were working out the details for employees to get access, the vice president [of the Northern Iraqi Oil Company] told us that they had explained everything to some lieutenant colonel. Nobody in the 173rd or the JSOTF knew who this officer was. Turned out he was a Corps of Engineers guy working for the 4th ID. He had been the point man for 4th ID's plan to secure the oil fields under the original [restoration] plan. He had a whole team of petroleum engineers with equipment and everything required to cap wells and assess infrastructural damage, and this was the first time we had heard about it. As far as we knew, since August of 2002, we were supposed to be the lead planners for infrastructure. So, once we made face to face contact with each other, I got this lieutenant colonel spun up on the oil field and we turned it over to him. The 173rd was hunkered down on the Kirkuk airfield, destroying weapons caches, guarding the roads into the city, but not doing much else with respect to stabilizing the situation. Maybe they did not have the resources, but the impression they projected was more a lack of desire.

A significant limitation to executing any quick solution to the water problem or any other problem is funding for civil affairs. Although the JSOTF Commander had some funds for immediate impact projects, larger projects or more expensive small projects required State Department funds. Although we met with the State Department DART [Disaster Assistance Response Team] prior to deployment and even notified them that the JSOTF would stage in Romania and not Turkey as originally planned, they still went to Turkey. The DART teams were then stuck in Turkey with the money and we were in Iraq without cash. When I left Iraq in late April [2003] the DART teams were still stuck in Turkey.

I'll make a final comment on the direct action mentality in SOF. Several of the ODAs in our area were given the task of blowing up caches. There were anti-aircraft positions all around the oil field. One morning while surveying the security fence with the Iraqi oil company guys we hear a huge explosion. We thought it was bad guys but it was SF. When we talked to them we found out that they were going around Kirkuk destroying military equipment. The possible consequences of spiking guns on an operational oil field never crossed the team leader's mind. I pointed out that the guns they just blew up were 200 meters from a 1 million cubic foot liquefied natural gas storage tank, but they didn't get it. They were just following their orders. They got fixated on going after the target and they forgot about the environment they were operating in.

We had one project: to get the water running, and that was what we had to go through to get it done.

PHILIPPINES, FEBRUARY–JULY 2002

In response to the terrorist attacks on September 11, the Pentagon launched Operation Enduring Freedom (OEF). The best-known part of this operation took place in Afghanistan. OEF, however, had other components. A Special Forces lieutenant colonel describes the role of Special Forces in OEF–Philippines.

I was with 1st Special Forces Group. The Commander of SOCPAC [Special Operations Command Pacific] and the Commander of 1st Group decided to use some counterinsurgency models taught at the Special Operations program at the Naval Postgraduate School to help develop an assessment and a plan that would be used for combating the Abu Sayaf Group [ASG][19] on Basilan Island in the Philippines. Abu Sayyaf was using Basilan Island as a haven, and had a strong presence on the island. The ASG murdered, raped, and kidnapped people on Basilan continuously.

We used a triangular COIN [counterinsurgency] model on the island that depicted the relationship between the people on the island, the government of the Philippines and Abu Sayaf. This model, as well as several others, allowed us to develop a plan that efficiently used all our resources to expel the ASG.

By applying all the elements of national power, the DIME model [diplomatic, informational, military, economic elements of national power], to each leg of the triangle, we were able to develop an assessment tool that was distributed and used by all the ODAs on the ground. The results of the assessment tool allowed us to tailor resources as needed to each village for maximum effect against the ASG. What do they [the local people] really need? What's more important—roads, schools, security? What's really going on in each area? When we dug a well, or helped improve a port facility, we really knew where and how it needed to be implemented for the greatest effect. This was not a drive-by assessment, this was an assessment that asked the structurally correct questions—as shown by the COIN models—of the men on the ground. The key was that these assessment questions were answered by the guy on the ground who becomes intimate with the local area he operates in. It's the guy on the ground, not the headquarters, who has the answer to how resources should be applied in his area of operations. The ODAs on the ground were the perfect tool to conduct the assessments, and were then able to provide exact recommendations of how to apply resources in their area to fix the problem. Their recommendations used all the elements of national power and discussed how these resources could best be tailored for implementation on their piece of turf. The guy on the ground knows the answers. It is the job of the headquarters to ask him the right questions. The models allowed us to do that.

Once you have established a baseline with the first assessment, and the operations, training, and resources indicated by the assessment begin to be executed, after a time you can reassess in the same areas, and use the feedback to tweak your resource allocation.

The baseline was what we developed with the assessment tool, and with the assessment tool we were able to ask the right questions, so we could get relevant ground truth and properly resource needs on the ground. Because of the great work by the ODAs conducting the assessments, it worked well. We could look at each area on the island and figure out which resources to apply, and how to apply them. With the ODA reassessments, the process is dynamic and able to adjust to changing conditions on the ground.

The results of the assessment tool weren't all carrots. It included both carrots and sticks. Unfortunately, due to some of the rules of engagement, we were only permitted to operate as advisers to the Philippine military at the battalion level, except for a few weeks when we were permitted to accompany the Fils [Filipinos] on company level operations. However, this will likely be the case in most countries, because unlike early Iraq or Afghanistan, when a state system is intact and the turf belongs to them, they are not about to have Americans roaming free over their terrain. That being the case, I think we'll see many more operations like OEF-Philippines on Basilan in the future as the GWOT [Global War on Terrorism] progresses.

We had the support of the [U.S.] Embassy [in Manila] and [a SOF officer in the embassy] had constant interface with Embassy personnel in Manila, but on Basilan it was our ODAs and the Filipinos. The bottom-line to the entire operation—the COIN models, the assessment, the ODA-driven resourcing—is that it worked. We had leadership at the JTF [Joint Task Force] and the ARSOTF [Army Special Operations Task Force] that understood we must operate through, by, and with the Philippine people and military, and the ODAs drove the train from the ground up via the assessments. When everything was said and done, the U.S. forces departed the island, the Philippine Army was able to cut its presence down to a comparative handful of the troops they had on the island at the start of the operation, and the ASG had a dramatic—and to this date continuous—reduction in the numbers of murders, rapes, and kidnappings that they conduct on the island. The ASG lost Basilan. While there are many other problems throughout the Philippines, and the ASG is alive in other areas, our mission was to drive them from their Basilan island haven, and the JTF and 1st Group worked through, by and with both the Filipino people on Basilan and the armed forces of the Philippines, and we accomplished the mission.

2

SELECTION AND TRAINING

LIKE MOST MILITARY PERSONNEL, Special Operations Forces (SOF) spend much of their time training. The end of the Cold War, which brought SOF new opportunities for deployment, did not change this. The war on terrorism has. The heavy involvement of SOF in the war has understandably decreased time for certain kinds of training.[1] Still, as we shall see, some SOF units aim for a training and deployment cycle that keeps them in training of some sort for as much as two-thirds of the time. This devotion to training is essential to maintain the skills that allow them to do their jobs. Since they spend so much time at it, to understand SOF, one must understand their training. Before they get to training, however, SOF personnel must first become members of SOF. "Selection" is the process by which this happens, the process by which the various special operations forces choose those who serve in their ranks. Understanding this process allows us to understand what SOF think they are and aspire to be. Selection and training reveal the character of SOF and the differences among the various units that compose these forces. As the first SOF "truth" is that the "central defining quality of SOF has always been its distinctive personnel," selection and training is the proper place to begin to understand SOF.[2]

SOF select their members, but only from among those who volunteer. The volunteer character of SOF bears on an issue that has been controversial, which needs to be addressed before we set out to describe their selection and training process. The underrepresentation of minorities in SOF has raised concern in some circles. Although Hispanics and other minorities have been "proportionately represented or overrepresented" in Army SOF, in other SOF forces minorities, especially blacks, are under-represented.[3] Several factors affect minority willingness to volunteer for SOF. For example, minorities tend to lack role models—minority officers or enlisted personnel—who are in SOF and can inspire others to join. According to one study of the issue, perceived racism in some SOF organizations may also be a problem. Finally, minorities tend to join the military with a view to learning skills that transfer well to the civilian job market. As someone said in a focus group convened to discuss minority attitudes to SOF, "What are you going to do in civilian life—put on your resumé that you can kill a man with a spoon?"[4]

Could these barriers to better minority representation in SOF be removed? Of the three barriers, the third—minority interest in military service as civilian job training—is not one the military or SOF can address. The second—a perception of racism in some SOF units—may have been an artifact of the period in which the surveys documenting this perception were conducted. At the time they were being done, a racially based crime and a racially based incident had recently occurred at a major SOF installation, Fort Bragg, North Carolina. In addition, a newsletter appeared at Fort Bragg at the same time, published by a group calling itself the Special Forces Underground, which mimicked the anti-government rhetoric of the militia movement and to some also had a racist slant. Investigations of these incidents revealed that SOF personnel were not involved in the racially motivated crime; the incident—painting Swastikas on doors—was apparently the work of a Black SOF sergeant. Because of the association of Fort Bragg with SOF, however, these episodes may have created or helped to create the perception that SOF were racist. In any event, the Army and Commanders at Fort Bragg took steps to deal with the problems on the post and with the surrounding civilian community, and no further problems have been reported.[5] It may also be the case that the association of a prominent retired SOF officer, Bo Gritz, with various extreme right and racist organizations has also unfairly tarred SOF.

This leaves the first barrier to better minority representation in SOF—lack of role models. This barrier would disappear if there were more minorities in SOF. Insofar as the problem here is not perceived racism or interest in acquiring skills that can be transferred to the civilian economy, what other factors have hindered recruitment of minorities to SOF? For one thing, more minorities than whites have had difficulty meeting the required score on the Armed Services Vocational Aptitude Battery, a standardized test given to all recruits.[6] Minorities, particularly blacks, also have more difficulty than others in passing the swimming qualification for SOF. "Research and anecdotal evidence suggest" that this problem results from urban geography and socioeconomics. Blacks tend to grow up in places where access to public pools or other swimming areas is limited. Consequently, black children and their families do not tend to see swimming as a recreational activity or a competitive sport, so that blacks end up with less skill in swimming. There is also some evidence, albeit controverted, that there are physiological differences between blacks and others that make blacks less adept swimmers.[7] SOF have taken steps to prepare all volunteers to meet the various initial physical requirements for entry into SOF, including swimming, since it is in SOF's interest not to lose an otherwise qualified recruit because of an easily remediable deficiency. Beyond that, removing physical and aptitude test barriers to better minority representation in SOF would require lowering the requirements for entry to SOF. Neither white nor minority military personnel when questioned in focus groups have approved of such a solution.[8]

In one respect, however, owing to the demand for more Special Forces (SF) in the war on terrorism as well as to increased retirements, SF have already changed, if not lowered, entry requirements. Younger, less experienced personnel can now try to join.[9] If the requirements can be changed to get more personnel into SF, why could they not be changed to increase the pool of minority applicants? Would this not also be a way of addressing SF's additional manpower requirements?

In the first place, when it decreased what we might call the experience requirement, SF increased other requirements. Less experienced soldiers have to score higher on standardized tests than their more experienced colleagues. The higher standardized test score is apparently required because, in order to compensate for the lack of experience, SF gives less experienced soldiers more training to bring their skill levels up to those that more experienced soldiers possess. All other entry qualifications, including the swim test, remain in place because, presumably, they do help select the people with the physical and mental skills that SF need. Thus, while SF would argue that it has not lowered requirements for entry, standards in the various SOF forces do remain an issue, especially since SOF are under pressure to increase their numbers.[10]

Although, on balance, it may not have lowered entry requirements, SF has changed them. Two consequences follow, one bearing on the issue of minorities in SOF and another on the character of SF, an issue we will address later. Any change of entry requirements will inevitably establish cleavages in SOF between those who entered under the more rigorous standards and those who entered under the more relaxed ones. If the performance of those admitted under the less rigorous standards matches that of those admitted under the older, more rigorous standards, we should expect the cleavage to disappear over time. In this case, any disruption to SOF efficiency and effectiveness would be temporary. If a change were made to increase minority representation in SOF, and especially if it were a change that appeared to lower standards, the cleavage between those who entered under the older requirements and those who entered under the newer ones might form along racial lines. The consequences of this for morale and effectiveness would therefore likely be worse and might well renew the perception of racism in SOF, itself a barrier to better minority representation.

The gain, some might argue, would be permanent, because a more diverse force would be better able to carry out the SOF role of working with military personnel and civilians from other cultures. This argument is not compelling for two reasons. First, although many different kinds of SOF, like other military units, may work with people of other cultures, not all SOF have such work as their primary mission. Second, and more important, for those who do (Special Forces, Civil Affairs, and Psychological Operations personnel), there is no evidence that matching racial or ethnic backgrounds makes that work easier. Being able to speak the local language is important for SOF, but looking like the locals is not, at least for SOF who work openly as Americans. As for cultural affinity with the locals, there is no reason to believe that anyone raised in the United States will share cultural traits because they share ethnic ancestors. The only justification for changing or lowering requirements to produce a more representative SOF, therefore, is that this will have somehow a beneficial effect on the civic and political life of Americans.

A similar argument would apply to women in SOF, although this case is different in important ways, one of these being the ban on women in combat units. Women do serve in Civil Affairs and Psychological Operations units, for example, because these are not combat but rather combat support units. As many have noted, however, in a war like Iraq and even more so in the insurgency that followed, the distinction between combat and noncombat units and areas has become less evident. Should, therefore, women be allowed in all SOF units? As with minorities, there is no compelling evidence that having women in SOF units would make those units better able to carry out their missions. Given prejudices around the world, it might even be the case that having women in SF A-teams, for example, would make it harder for the teams to accomplish their training mission. Where their gender might most plausibly be thought an advantage (civil affairs and psychological operations), women are already present. If as a result of the evolution of warfare, or of American mores, the general prohibition on women in combat is removed, the question would still remain of the physical requirements for SOF. It is certainly possible that a woman would be able to meet these considerable requirements with sufficient training or the help of modern science and technology, which SOF themselves hope to enlist to improve their own physical performance. (One woman did apparently graduate from the SF qualification course in the early 1980s, one presumes without the aid of modern science or technology.)

Technology could certainly conquer nature in this case, but insofar as women were successfully redesigned to meet requirements set for men, they would cease to be women and, therefore, it would no longer be a question of women, at least as we currently know them, joining SOF. If the redesign did not remove the sexual attraction between men and women, the argument would then turn on the effect of mixing the sexes on small teams operating for long periods of time in remote areas. Of course, the situation here is not comparable to the mixing of the races, with which the military has generally succeeded over the last fifty years, since sexual differences and resulting problems and conflicts are natural in a way in which racial differences are not. Whether one acknowledged that those sexual differences were natural or insisted they were merely cultural, one might still argue that for the sake of equality (no military reason suggesting itself), they should be overcome through habituation. One may reasonably doubt, however, that habituation will overcome sexual attraction, although some might argue that it has not been given enough time to do so. But why should the effort be made, especially at the risk of military effectiveness? Again, as with minorities, the conclusion we reach is that the only justification for lowering or changing standards to make SOF more representative or diverse is that this will somehow benefit not SOF or the military but American society at large, or at least those individuals who for whatever reason fail to meet the current standards set for entry to SOF.

In the 1990s—when the U.S. military and SOF were involved in humanitarian assistance, disaster relief, and peacekeeping operations, and wars seemed unlikely—it was easier to think of the military's place in our larger political life as a more important consideration than it seems to be several years into the war on terrorism. Military effectiveness, particularly in the missions that SOF carry out, seems a higher priority now than it was before September 11. The role of SOF and the military more generally in our civic and political life remains an important issue, of course, if less decisive than it was.

Those who meet the minimum qualifications for SOF volunteer for a variety of reasons. If you ask a special operator why he wanted to join one of the special units, the answer typically has something to do with the challenges associated with such forces. SF personnel often say that they were in a conventional Army unit and doing fine but felt they wanted something more. Perhaps the soldiers they worked with were not as committed as they were or as driven to excel. Perhaps the work they were doing was not as challenging or as interesting as they had hoped it would be. Some, like the warrant officer working on new reconnaissance technology who described his efforts in chapter 1, chafe at what they feel are the overly bureaucratic ways of the regular Army.

One also often hears from SOF about a special operator whom they met and came to admire or who encouraged them to apply to SOF. A fair number of those who seek to join SF are attracted by the independence that SF soldiers enjoy. In the regular Army, they may have come into contact with SF and been impressed by their freedom to act and the responsibility given even to junior officers and noncommissioned officers (NCOs). A desire to test oneself and to take one's infantry skills to a higher level motivates many who join the Rangers. A similar motivation apparently is at work in those who have volunteered for the new Marine Corps Component of the Special Operations Command, MarSOC.[11]

Pilots who volunteer for special operations, whether in the Air Force or the Army, also tend to say that they wanted more challenging or interesting work—they did not want to end up just "hauling trash" (cargo)—or wanted to improve their skills as a pilot. The Air Force pilot whose interview is in the previous chapter expressed these views, for example. For SEALs, combat controllers (Air Force personnel who work in combat to direct and control air traffic), pararescuemen (Air Force personnel who parachute in to rescue downed pilots), and special operations weathermen (Air Force personnel who collect environmental data from denied areas) who, unlike other special operators, often come to special operations right from college or enlistment, a primary motivation is the challenge rather than any dissatisfaction with military life as they have already lived it. For all those who volunteer, there is the allure of an elite unit and the pride of making the grade. The SOF colonel we met in chapter 1 who was in the Pentagon on 9-11 briefed high ranking civilian officials during his tour there. He used the phrase "feeling the magic" to describe the aura that surrounds SOF.

> When I would give briefings on classified special operation missions to [civilian officials] they would almost be excited. They were part of something special. So, they would ask questions, like if we told them we were parachuting into the Indian Ocean, the question would be "from how many feet?" If you would say "full weaponry," they would say "what kind of weapons or what kind of rounds or how many rounds are they taking?" Getting down to that combat level, I would call that "feeling the magic;" everybody wanted to feel the magic of SOF.

The magic is particularly associated with the special mission units (SMUs).

Working against the "magic of SOF" is the notion that joining SOF hurts your career. An officer describing how he ended up in SOF in the mid-1990s remarked that his immediate superior told him not to join SF because of the adverse consequences for his career. The officer joined anyway and described his superior's concerns as a myth. What his superior officer was referring to was that historically, past a certain point, the promotion prospects of a SOF officer diminished significantly. This occurred because the conventional forces dominate the U.S. military. The officers who rise to the more senior positions in the military, where they became responsible for ever larger numbers of subordinates and more important pieces of the military—armored divisions, fighter wings, carrier battle groups—thus need to know about and to come from these big pieces, from the conventional units that make up the core of the military. From the perspective of conventional forces, SOF is a marginal or peripheral activity. SOF personnel were thus not as "promotable" as other officers. In principle, this promotion logic, if you will, still applies today. Yet, its effects have been mitigated since the the 1980s, when, in response to changes in the threats that the United States faced as well as to civilian prompting, the U.S. military gave SOF a more institutional-ized existence. For example, the Army made SF a branch (1987) and set up an Army Special Operations Command in 1989.

In the Army, a career branch is a recognized military specialty, in which a soldier can serve for his whole career. The branch has a bureaucracy of its own and an established place in the Army bureaucracy. Those who belong to a branch thus have standing in the Army and are less likely to be overlooked when it comes time for promotions. They also get advice and support in managing their careers. Civil affairs and psychological operations have recently become branches. With the establishment of the Army Special Operations Command, SF officers and others in Army SOF had a better opportunity to rise to senior ranks. Similarly, the in-stitutionalization of SOF in the other services created pathways to se-nior rank and bureaucracies to manage and oversee the SOF promotion process. The United States Special Operations Command (established in 1987), headed by a four-star general, provides additional senior ranks open to SOF officers, as it has assumed the responsibility of monitoring promotion rates for SOF across the services. Recently, SOF promotion rates have been comparable to non-SOF rates and in some cases better. If promotion remains an issue, it is with regard to the differences, or at least perceived differences, within SOF. Personnel involved in the direct action missions of SOF (personnel in the Rangers or SMUs, for example) are promoted to the most senior command positions in SOF more read-ily than personnel involved in other SOF missions. In any event, most SOF acknowledge that no one joins SOF or should join SOF because they are looking for a good career.

SELECTION AND QUALIFICATION

Minimum requirements for entry and retention differ among SOF units. Because SF teams often undertake missions that are politically sensitive and conduct them unaccompanied by the higher ranks of commanding officers, SF requires mature soldiers who can operate responsibly on their own. Therefore, it seeks more experienced officers than do other special units. In practice, this means that the most junior SF officers are cap-tains, officers in their mid to late twenties, who have some experience in the military. Other SOF units, whose principal function is combat, utilize younger officers. The officers who are the combat leaders in the Rangers come from the combat arms within the Army; the youngest are at least first lieutenants, who have successfully lead platoons before joining the Ranger regiment. The most junior SEAL officers are a grade and sometimes two grades more junior than SF officers and have less experience in the military. Some may have come directly from College Reserve Officer Training Programs. Air Force special operations pilots and navigators, and their Army colleagues, are most often captains and majors who have significant flying experience, while officers who join pararescue or combat controller units are younger, more like SEAL officers. Officers specialize in psychological operations and civil affairs as captains or majors. The special mission units attract officers from a variety of military specialties and backgrounds. All officers have college degrees.

The minimum qualifications for enlisted personnel also differ depending on the special unit. Again, because of the nature of the operations that SF undertake, SF enlisted personnel are more senior than in other special units. Enlisted personnel in SF have been typically sergeants, with at least seven years of service when they join. As noted above, to meet the demands generated by the war on terrorism, SF changed this requirement after September 11, accepting less experienced soldiers, in hopes of increasing the pool of soldiers from which it could draw. Similarly, Army personnel from outside SF can now volunteer to join the one active-duty Civil Affairs unit. The Marine Corps intends to staff its Foreign Military Training Unit, which will train foreign military personnel, with sergeants,[12] since the foreign training mission requires a level of maturity and interpersonal skills that combat does not. Ranger enlisted personnel do not have the same grade requirements as SF for the same reason. SEALs do not need any prior military experience, and anyone currently serving in the Navy may apply to be a SEAL. Reportedly, 30 percent of recruits come from those already serving in the Navy; 50 percent from enlistees who join with the idea of becoming a SEAL; and 20 percent who enlist and then decide to become a SEAL.[13] Like SEALs, combat controllers, pararescuemen and special operations weathermen do not need prior military service. Volunteers for MarSOC can come from anywhere in the Marine Corps but will be screened to ensure that they possess "the right combination of maturity, character, experience and skills to accomplish SOF missions."[14] Most PSYOP personnel enter the Army directly and are relatively young. In contrast, enlisted personnel who join

Civil Affairs units generally have had about ten years of prior experience in the military. Again, as is the case with other SOF, this is changing as the demands of the war on terrorism have led the Army to increase the number of CA personnel. Some senior noncommissioned officers choose Civil Affairs as their final tour before retiring because it allows them to deploy and remain active without incurring the degree of physical stress that an SF deployment imposes on its personnel. Enlisted personnel must have high school degrees. Some have college degrees or some years of college education. To qualify for SOF, enlisted personnel must also meet minimum score requirements on various standardized tests administered by the military. These minimum scores vary among the special units but are typically higher than for most other jobs in the military.

In addition to the requirements just mentioned, to qualify for SOF both officers and enlisted personnel must have no disciplinary problems on their records. This is a change from the World War II era, when, as we shall see, commanders who had been asked to contribute troops to special units often sent troops with discipline problems. Dumping those who had been insubordinate into special units may have reinforced the long-standing belief of conventional military personnel that special units lack discipline. But this reputation also comes from the fact that unconventional forces do break the rules. Fighting unconventionally requires this. World War II era commanders may have thus felt justified in sending rule-breakers to the special units. Not only did it get rid of their discipline problems but it sent people not overly committed to the rules to units that were supposed to break them. Of course, not all SOF break the rules. Since their reestablishment in the 1970s, the Rangers have developed a reputation as the most disciplined, if not regimented, unit in the military. Nor are all the rules that SOF do break the same. Most appropriately, SOF break the rules by which *the enemy* lives and fights because the surprise this generates helps compensate for the fact that SOF are often outnumbered and outgunned by the enemy. If surprise prevents the enemy from putting superior numbers or firepower in the fight, then SOF rule-breaking gives them an advantage.

Rule-breaking, however, is not just a case of breaking the enemy's rules. Achieving surprise or some other advantage may also require breaking the rules by which the U.S. military fights. Fighting according to these rules is part of what the enemy expects of U.S. military forces. If SOF did things the way conventional forces did, they would not only cease to be special or unconventional but also would be doing things that the enemy had come to expect. That would diminish surprise and thus their advantage. Again, in deciding whether this rule-breaking is good or bad, the question is which American military rules or expectations are broken. If they are tactical standard operating procedures or doctrine, this may not objectionable, if the rule-breaking results in success, because it is understood that SOF are unconventional forces. But what about breaking rules in order to be in the position to innovate tactically? The Warrant officer in chapter 1 who created a technological innovation did this by ignoring standard operating procedures and by pushing ahead, in some instances over the objections of his commanders or in spite of their expressed priorities in a way that could be considered insubordinate. The Warrant officer did nothing illegal or immoral, but his actions certainly might be thought to violate good military discipline and order, precisely the sort of thing for which conventional officers have criticized SOF. For his part, the Warrant came to SF and stayed precisely because SF gave him the independence to deviate from standard operating procedures. This is not to say that he carried on *against* orders. At key points, as he noted, officers, including a general officer, approved and supported what he was doing. But he did proceed with a degree of independence that would be unusual in a conventional unit and did not sit well with at least one of his SF superiors and, again, might well appear unmilitary to those in conventional forces.

The Warrant officer's bending, or breaking, of rules achieved a significant amount of good not only in improving SF's ability to capture and kill its targets but in protecting civilians who might otherwise have been hurt inadvertently in the process. In this case, the envisioned end justified the means he used, in part because the means were only unusual from the military point of view, rather than illegal or immoral. To what extent, however, can ends justify means? Following the disaster at Desert One, the Army established a unit to provide support for its counterterrorism force. The intent was certainly good, but the Army eventually had to shut the unit down because of financial improprieties, some reportedly linked to the later Iran-Contra scandal.[15] At least initially, the more lax accounting rules that the unit used were justified by the importance and urgency of the work it was doing. To cite another example, what do we make of the fact that the Navy charged four SEALs with abusing detainees in Iraq? Could the urgency of stopping terrorist campaigns ever justify such abuse? The French faced a similar question in Algeria. The use of torture there helped discredit the French cause in France and around the world. But is it only a question of what works politically?

At some point, those involved in special operations, both civilians and military, high- and low-ranking, must ask such questions because they are inseparable from special operations. For the moment, the more immediate point is twofold: those who are inclined to stretch rules or do not mind doing so may find special operations attractive; and SOF and ultimately the American people have an interest in encouraging such rule-stretching because special operations require it. Because special operations require rule-stretching, selection and training, the entire conduct of SOF must encourage it. At a promotion ceremony after the Gulf War, a senior SEAL officer praised the SEAL he was promoting for taking the initiative while he was on patrol to get into the war just as it was beginning, when from another perspective what the officer did could have appeared a reckless and self-interested (getting in the fight increased his promotion chances) disregard for the spirit (but not the letter) of his orders. Clearly the Naval Special Warfare Command appreciated the officer's initiative and rule-stretching. A similar point emerges from the experience, related in chapter 1, of the special operations pilot who crashed his plane. An organization that must take risks to succeed cannot conduct itself in such a way as to discourage risk-taking.

Yet there are limits. As SOF must wink at the stretching and even breaking of rules, it must at the same time breed special operators who know which rules can be broken or stretched and, perhaps most important, when this is permissible. Similarly with risk-taking: at some point it becomes reckless, and officers and enlisted SOF must understand when they reach that point. Both SOF officers and enlisted personnel receive training that bears on these issues, and officer education addresses professional ethics. Perhaps the most important constraint in this regard, however, is the ethos among team and crew mates. Because they depend on the members of their small teams and crews for their lives and the success of their missions, special operations personnel consider trust in their colleagues to be critical and consequently demand integrity from them. This constraint, however, applies most forcefully within a team or crew, which may not use the same principles to judge integrity as the public at large, the conventional military, or even other special operations units.[16] To some degree, the constraints of team or crew ethics may carry over to other relationships and activities. At least, there is no evidence that SOF have more disciplinary problems than conventional units. On the contrary, one often hears from those in SOF that one thing that encouraged them to volunteer is that those manning SOF units are typically more "squared away" than those in conventional units. SEALs and some other special operators once had and to some degree still have a reputation for drinking and rowdiness, but such activities are less winked at than they were. In general, SOF do try to live up to the motto of "quiet professionals."

Ultimately, in a business where rule-bending is needed, nothing can replace the judgment and example of leaders at all levels of command. Throughout the military, personnel rise slowly through the ranks, taking on ever greater responsibilities so that their judgment can be seasoned, tempered, and evaluated; for it is upon this judgment, particularly in unconventional operations, that success depends. And not just tactical success. The integrity of SOF personnel is essential in establishing the trust between SOF and conventional military leaders and political decisionmakers that must exist if these leaders and decisionmakers are going to allow SOF to use their capabilities most effectively. Precisely because SF, for example, operate beyond the immediate reach of senior commanders, these commanders and their political superiors must trust them not only tactically but morally and politically as well. This is a critical issue for the command and control of SOF, to which we return in chapter 7. SF must bend or break rules to succeed, but success requires knowing *which* rules can be broken, and *when*. Throughout SOF and not just in SF, a major purpose of selection and training is to produce SOF with seasoned judgment.

Whatever brings officer or enlisted personnel to the conclusion that they would like to join SOF, they can volunteer, if they meet the minimum qualifications and are willing to go to jump school (if they are not already airborne qualified). In the past, selection criteria for psychological operations and civil affairs were minimal, but this is changing. Once selected, personnel begin their initial training. For officers in civil affairs and psychological operations, this means language training, regional studies, and training in their respective specialties. The Psychological Operations Orientation course covers such things as target audience analysis and testing to evaluate the effectiveness of a given psychological operation. The officers also learn about Abraham Maslow's theory of a hierarchy of human needs. According to this theory, the primary human motivation is need, and humans seek to satisfy basic needs (food, security, acceptance) before trying to satisfy other needs (knowledge, self-actualization). Enlisted personnel receive the same training as officers but do not do any regional studies. Civil affairs officers go through a course now more than twice as long as it once was that provides an introduction to the purpose and methods of civil affairs, leadership training, and an extensive and realistic field exercise. They also learn the rudiments of the assessments they do of physical and civil infrastructure, using United Nations templates, since this is what the nongovernmental organizations that they often work with use. For some of this training, officers and NCOs work together. The NCOs also have their own course. Officers also take regional-studies courses and do some language training. As with initial language training for psychological operations officers, the aim of the language training is to get students to a 1 on a 0–5 scale, in which 5 is fluency and 3 is professional competence. Reserve officers and enlisted personnel, who make up the vast majority of Psychological Operations and Civil Affairs forces, are now supposed to receive the same training as their active-duty colleagues.

Air Force pilots who volunteer for special operations receive that assignment on the basis of the good of the service. If they are good pilots with substantial experience and have no problems on their records, they may be assigned to one of the special units without an additional selection process. Once assigned, they undergo training on the aircraft they will fly, either a helicopter or a fixed-wing aircraft. In addition to learning the capabilities of their special operations aircraft, they must learn to handle the requirements that make special operations special. They must learn to operate according to precise schedules and to push themselves and their aircraft beyond what pilots in conventional units would do. For example, the pilot who described his experience in chapter 1 crashed because he was trying to support a mission of high importance conducted in response to perishable intelligence. Planning was necessarily hasty, schedules tight, flying conditions not the best; but he and his crew pressed on. Training must not only give pilots and crews the skills to fly such missions; it must also prepare them to withstand the pressure that accompanies them.

The selection process for the Army's 160th Special Operations Aviation Regiment is similar to the process that Air Force pilots undergo. Experienced pilots who volunteer must pass a week-long assessment that includes standard military physical fitness tests, as well as evaluations of their emotional suitability. A panel reviews the records of the volunteers and their performance during the assessment week. Once part of the 160th, pilots undergo intensive training in the special techniques that the

Regiment uses. For enlisted personnel, this training lasts several weeks; for officers, several months.

The selection and initial training processes for psychological operations, civil affairs, and Air Force and Army aviation special operations personnel are similar in that they do not test the physical endurance of applicants. This is because in the duties these personnel perform, physical endurance is not critical. Certainly one should not underestimate the physical toll of flying for long hours hugging the ground; nevertheless, the principal stress that pilots face is mental: maintaining focus in a blizzard of information and instantly making the right decisions. Their training shows whether pilots have these mental skills, as it takes pilots through exercises that mimic the stress of actual operations. Similarly, for psychological operations and civil affairs officers, the key to success is not physical endurance. Rather, a flexible approach to problems and skill dealing with people are what matter most.

This lack of emphasis on physical stamina is not characteristic of all SOF selection processes, of course. Officer and enlisted volunteers for the Rangers, for example, go through a selection process of several weeks that tests them physically and psychologically. Once in the regiment, this evaluation continues. At any time, they can be removed from the regiment for failure to meet standards. If enlisted personnel want to stay in the Rangers, they must early in their time in the Regiment pass Ranger school. Ranger school is a four-phase process. The first phase is physical conditioning so rigorous that injuries occur, and students sometimes do not perform well enough to remain in the selection process. Harassment of students is also a significant part of the first phase. Along with the required physical exertion, this harassment puts the students under enough stress to test the limits of their endurance. The next three phases put the students through a variety of small-unit and light infantry operations, including airborne (parachute) and air assault (helicopter) operations. Students operate in three different environments: mountain, swamp, and woodland, taking turns leading small units, as well as planning and conducting patrols and assaults in difficult environments, with insufficient sleep and food, and at a rapid pace. The conditions in which the students must operate are severe and dangerous. According to the Government Accounting Office, fifty-six Ranger students died in the selection and qualification course between 1952 and 1997.[17] When four students died of hypothermia in a Florida swamp in 1995, both Congressional and Army investigations ensued, followed by remedial actions. These occurrences testify to the physical demands of the selection and training process through which students pass to earn the right to wear the Ranger tab on their uniforms. The justification for this severity is that it approximates the conditions in which Rangers operate when engaged in a real mission. So arduous and realistic is Ranger training that it has become a rite of passage even for military officers who are not part of the Ranger Regiment. Promotion is more likely if an officer has qualified to wear the Ranger tab.

Ranger school combines selection and training, but its principal purpose is selection. Air Force pararescuemen and combat air controllers go through a similar process. Pararescuemen go through an intense period of physical testing early in their training cycle that serves to select out those without the physical and mental stamina to succeed. Those who pass this portion of the training go through an array of courses covering military and medical skills that they need to do their jobs. Combat controllers receive much of their training before they go through their physical ordeal, since those who do not pass the physical screening still have aircraft control skills that the Air Force can use. The combination of military and physical training that the combat controllers receive—including airborne jumps into water, rappelling, and fast roping—allow them to go into combat with the SOF they support. Much the same holds true for SOF weathermen. SOF weathermen first receive extensive training as meteorologists. Those who fail any portion of the physical training, such as airborne school or advanced skills training, can be sent back to the regular Air Force to perform a more traditional meteorological job.

Ranger selection also resembles SEAL selection, which takes place in two phases, Basic Underwater Demolition/SEAL Training (BUD/S) and the SEAL Qualification Course. BUD/S itself has three phases: physical conditioning, dive training, and land warfare. The first phase is an endurance test to determine how much punishment an individual can take without giving up and to show those who do not give up that their limits are beyond what they imagined. In addition to performing calisthenics and running, candidates exercise with telephone poles and must stay afloat in a pool with their hands and feet tied. They also spend a lot of time wet, cold, and covered with sand. The most grueling part of the first phase is the infamous "Hell Week," during which instructors push the candidates relentlessly, demanding physical exertion almost without cease for five days. (During Hell Week, the instructors work in three shifts around the clock.) Among other things, the candidates must carry rubber boats wherever they go, even through the obstacle course. Candidates get only a few hours of sleep during this ordeal. They spend so much time in the cold and wet, moving in and on the sea, that candidates often shiver uncontrollably and come to the point of hypothermia. Instructors and medical personnel monitor the candidates to prevent this from occurring but, as one now retired SEAL has noted, medical supervision "allows current BUD/S instructors to safely take the trainees a little closer to the edge"[18] than they did when he went through the training.

In addition to physical exertion and pain, Hell Week consists of two other things: team work and competition. The candidates operate, as SEALs do, in small teams. The instructors divide the candidates into small-boat teams, consisting of an officer and enlisted personnel. Each team has its own small inflatable rubber boat. This is the boat that is the nearly constant companion of the teams during Hell Week. The exercises, such as the obstacle course that must be completed while carrying a rubber boat, require teamwork. Hence, even as the candidates suffer individually, they must function as members of a team. Second, the teams and individual candidates compete with each other. Instructors focus the attention of teams and candidates on who wins and who loses. They do this not only verbally but also by giving the winners a small reward, such as a few minutes to rest between drills and exercises. Sometimes they get a bit more. By the last day of Hell Week, one member of a team observed by a reporter developed a leg injury that effectively disabled him. His team would not leave him behind, however. They held him up, even though they were in almost as bad shape as he was, as they moved along a beach carrying their rubber boat. Falling further and further behind the other teams, they risked having to repeat this particular exercise or spend additional time in the sea. Finally, it was clear to the instructors that the injured candidate could not go on; he would fail to complete Hell Week and would be unable to continue the SEAL selection process. At this point the instructor announced that the candidate was done, and so was the team. Having come in first consistently all week, the team was allowed to finish Hell Week a few hours early.[19] This episode distills the aim of Hell Week and the first phase of BUD/S: to push men beyond the limit of physical endurance and yet expect them to function as a team to complete their assigned task. Attrition is high: reportedly, the average "washout" rate is near 79 percent;[20]

"near 40 percent is the highest portion of one recruiting class to make it through Hell Week in SEAL history."[21]

Physical exertion continues after the harrowing of the first phase of BUD/S, but in subsequent phases it is more for the sake of conditioning than testing. In the second phase, the candidates learn to be divers. They learn how to use and maintain scuba gear and do practice descents in a dive tower. They also learn how to navigate underwater and perform practice dives by night as well as day. At one point during the second phase, they must restore their ability to breathe and operate underwater after an instructor has "rearranged" their dive gear. The phase closes with a long ocean swim.

The third phase of BUD/S introduces the candidates to land warfare. They get the gear they need to operate on land (for example, rucksack, sleeping bag) and time to break it in, in some cases by exercising while carrying it. The SEAL candidates also learn patrolling, ambushing, reconnaissance, and other small-unit tactical skills. They practice these skills in repeated exercises, planning how to solve tactical problems they are given and then operating according to their plans. They also do a lot of shooting, with pistols, rifles and other weapons, and compete against each other in shooting matches. They take a demolition course, learning among other things how to make improvised explosive devices and use them in an ambush. In the course of their training, SEALs fire 850,000 rounds and detonate 5,500 pounds of explosives.[22] They also practice moving from the sea to the land to begin operations.

Following the completion of BUD/S, the candidates go to the Army's airborne school at Fort Benning to learn military parachuting. After completing this school, the candidates report to SEAL Qualification Training (SQT), the second step in the process of becoming a SEAL. Enlisted personnel go directly to SQT, while officers go to leadership training before going to SQT. This training includes everything from spending time with SEALs recognized as superior leaders to learning the details of the various administrative procedures that the military bureaucracy requires. The officer training also includes instruction in firing range and dive safety and participation in Survival, Evasion, Resistance and Escape (SERE) School, a brutal and realistic re-creation of the prisoner of war experience that also includes training in how to avoid capture and how to link up with rescuers.

One SQT began with an instructor saying in part "we are warfighters; you are preparing yourself for combat. Think about it. If you are not here to prepare for combat then get the hell out. Don't waste our time. This is a school for warriors, and we are training for war."[23] SQT is about learning the skills necessary to fight, win, and survive. It is training, but it remains selection. Candidates are graded on written and field tests and have to meet certain physical conditioning standards. If they do not make the grade, they are asked to leave. They may also be asked to leave for failing to show the proper attitude, which includes commitment to team work. The training itself includes land navigation, combat medical care, close quarter combat, urban operations, marksmanship with a variety of weapons, demolitions, tactical movement, and combat swimming operations (navigating under water to a target and disabling or destroying it). For much of this training, the individual candidates work as and compete with one another as individuals. But almost every segment of training concludes with an exercise in which the candidates must operate as a team, with command of the teams rotating among the officers. If the candidates make the necessary grades in all of this training, they become SEALs. Those who do then head to Alaska, where they learn rock climbing and how to operate in cold weather. With the completion of this training, the new SEALs report to their first assignments.

As the SEALs were told at the beginning of SQT, SEAL selection and training aims to produce warriors, men who can get up close to the enemy to kill or capture him or destroy or disable his ships and other equipment. Selection seeks to pick out those who will never give up, those who are intensely committed to enduring any hardship to complete the mission. The training that is part of selection seeks to give such men the skills they need to accomplish their missions, no matter what the obstacle or the conditions they need to overcome. The Department of Defense defines special operations, in part, as operations that differ from conventional operations in degree of physical risk, operational techniques, mode of employment, and independence from friendly support. These bland words barely suggest the danger and difficulty of such operations or the combination of determination and lethality necessary to succeed at them. SEALs are selected and trained to possess such characteristics. They aspire to possess them so thoroughly that they define the standard of excellence for such special operations.

Like SEAL selection and training, the SF equivalent puts more emphasis on physical endurance than does the selection and training of personnel in psychological operations, civil affairs, Air Force special operations,

and Army special operations aviation. SF selection includes a psychological test, but this is designed to weed out the unfit rather than predict who
will finally qualify as SF. SF selection proper begins with a program called
the Special Forces Assessment and Selection (SFAS) course. SFAS is a
test of a candidate's ability to withstand mental and physical stress. With
regard to physical stress, it is a less intense version of BUD/S but contains
many of the same components. Selectees must complete timed land navigation courses of increasing length, doing so alone and with increasingly
heavy packs. This physical stress must be borne without any indication of
whether the candidate is succeeding or not, an additional burden of ambiguity and mental stress. Physical trials also include an obstacle course,
a swim assessment (50 meters in battle dress uniform and boots), timed
runs, and small unit tactics. The small-unit tactics test leadership and the
ability to operate as part of a team, as well as physical skills. Recently, SF
selection has put more emphasis on trying to assess the judgment of candidates and their ability to influence others, a critical skill when SF work
by, with, and through indigenous forces to achieve their objectives.[24] If a
candidate shows that he has the ability to operate effectively while under
significant mental and physical stress and possesses sound judgment and
a talent for influencing others, then he is allowed into the next phase of
the Special Forces Qualification Course (SFQC).

The SFQC, which is both a qualification and a training course, has several phases. The first phase focuses on the common skills that all SF need.
These include expertise in land navigation, small-unit tactics (patrolling,
ambushes), demolitions, and a variety of tactics and techniques peculiar
to special operations. The purpose of the first phase is to select and train
individuals who can survive and operate in a harsh environment, on their
own if necessary. The next phase focuses on the specialized skills that
make up the SF detachment. Officers take leadership training; enlisted
personnel go to separate schools for medical, engineering, communications, and weapons training; and Warrant officers go to their own school.
The Warrant officers, who achieve this rank after successful careers as SF
sergeants, represent the continuity on the team, remaining with their "A"
team longer than other personnel. They are supposed to be the reposi-
tory of tactical and technical knowledge and the hard-earned wisdom that
comes from experience. The enlisted personnel who take medical training
achieve a level of skill unsurpassed among military medics. The engineers
become proficient in a variety of construction and demolition techniques.

The communications personnel learn how to establish communications using a variety of radios, antennas, and other communication devices, including satellites. The weapons personnel become proficient in the use and maintenance of an array of American and foreign weapons. It was such a weapons expert, described by the SF officer in chapter 1, who fabricated a firing pin to get a Soviet artillery piece working again during the fight against the Taliban. This specialty training produces personnel who can come together in a typical SF "A" team, containing an officer, a warrant officer, two communicators, two weapons experts, two medics, and two engineers, as well as an intelligence sergeant and a team sergeant. This structure allows the team to split into smaller teams, each with all the expertise of the larger team, just as the officer in chapter 1 described splitting his team. Ideally, members of the team have been cross-trained so that they develop expertise in more than one skill. Such a team should have the skills in their specialties and in advanced small-unit techniques and tactics to survive and operate effectively behind enemy lines for prolonged periods under austere conditions. Throughout these early phases, rigorous physical conditioning continues, as do field exercises, both of which test the drive and endurance of candidates. Language training also occurs, as does SERE training.

The SFQC culminates in a field exercise, in which the skills of individuals come together in an "A" team that plans and carries out operations. This final phase of selection and training culminates in an exercise known as "Robin Sage." In this exercise, an "A" team plans to train a guerrilla force and then must execute its plan by infiltrating into a remote area to link up with a guerrilla leader, win his confidence, and train and prepare his men to carry out operations. Throughout this exercise, the "A" team is subjected to a good deal of physical and mental stress. They operate at night, in all sorts of weather, in difficult terrain and without sufficient rest. They operate against role players who do not make things easy but who generally respond realistically to the efforts of the team. If the team offends the guerrilla leader or his men or fails to convince them of its own competence and professionalism, then the guerrilla leader and his men will prove reluctant students, just as they would in a real situation. Constantly under the gaze of evaluators, the students are continually in situations in which there are no obvious right answers. In one exercise observed by a reporter, the guerrilla leader summarily "executed" one of his followers.[25] Should the team ignore this, break off contact and end the mission, or give the leader a lecture in human rights? What are the costs of continuing or ending the mission? Demonstrating sound judgment in such cases and in others that are more simply operational, under the pressure of operational requirements, in a harsh and demanding physical environment, generally with insufficient information and too much fatigue, is the core of Robin Sage. If the leaders and the team demonstrate the judgment and other skills that SF need, they are qualified to join an SF detachment.

SF and SEAL selection and qualification both emphasize physical endurance and the willingness to persevere against unyielding circumstances, but they differ in emphasis. Dealing with a guerrilla leader, as SF must do, is not a question of physical endurance. More precisely, it is not a question *only* of such endurance. Tolerance of ambiguity, adaptability to the unexpected, and the ability to influence and persuade are also necessary. Perhaps the guerrillas offer food the sight and smell of which is repellant. To refuse, however, would give offense. Perhaps getting to the guerrilla camp requires overland maneuver along treacherous paths with guerrillas you have just met. Or perhaps to accomplish your mission, you must use local forms of transport unfamiliar to you, such as horses. The guerrilla leader will certainly ask for more money and weapons than you can give and may want training that is not appropriate for his men. Somehow you must work with him, win his confidence, and steer him in the right direction. Dealing with these kinds of situations, in climates where cold or heat, humidity or dryness, or lack of oxygen from altitude are themselves taxing, requires something of the adaptability, interpersonal skills and seasoned judgment that psychological operations or civil affairs officers require, as well as something like the physical endurance and warfighting skills that characterize SEALs.

The Department of Defense defines special operations, in part, as operations "conducted in hostile, denied, or politically sensitive environments ... through, with, or by indigenous or surrogate forces." These bland words barely suggest the danger and ambiguity in which SF operate or the combination of determination and adaptability necessary to succeed in these operations. SF are selected and trained to possess these qualities. They aspire to possess them so thoroughly that they define the standard of excellence for such special operations.

Having examined the SOF selection process, and particularly the process for selecting and initially training SF and SEALs, we can return to an issue that we mentioned earlier: the changed entry requirement for SF that allows younger, less experienced personnel to join. The additional training that SF provide these less experienced soldiers may raise their skill levels to those of more experienced soldiers, but it will not give them the experience and judgment of these older soldiers. Only time can do that. Since the maturity and experience of SF soldiers is particularly relevant for the unconventional warfare mission of working with, by, and through indigenous forces, this change in the entry requirements represents at least a relative depreciation of that mission. It moves SF in the direction of the SEALs, who are primarily a direct action force, and who therefore have traditionally accepted less seasoned personnel. Other evidence of this change is the increased emphasis on warfighting and the warrior spirit in the SFQC.[26]

TRAINING

Once the students have completed their initial training successfully, they are qualified to join their SOF organization. For several of these organizations, the intensity of training does not diminish following qualification.

The training that a SEAL gets as he moves through the selection and qualification process is, in a sense, his basic training. When he joins a team, he deepens his basic skills and acquires the experience that makes those skills even more valuable. SEALs train and deploy on a two-year cycle, divided into four six-month periods. Only one six-month period is a deployment; the others are training. (Since 2001, deployments have been more frequent, although the SEALs want to return to one deployment every two years.[27]) The first six-month period begins after the team returns from a deployment that has kept them away from their training base and homes for six months. The first training period consists of professional development and individual training, as well as time for SEALs to take leave and get to know their families again. SEAL teams require their members be expert in different skills. During the individual training period, SEALs polish these skills. For example, a SEAL might recertify himself as a jump master so that he can run his unit's parachute training. SEALs may also acquire new skills in this period, learning how to use unmanned aerial vehicles, for example.

Unit-level training is the second six month cycle. At this stage, the individuals that make up a SEAL platoon (two or three officers and fourteen enlisted) come together and work on their tactical skills, going through many of the exercises they performed as part of their qualification training. Among other things, they work on camouflage, concealment, land navigation, patrolling, ambushes, surveillance, beach reconnaissance, tracking, construction of sites in which to hide to observe the enemy, demolition, taking down special targets such as oil platforms, and boarding and searching ships. And they spend a lot of time shooting. Periodically they engage in an exercise to integrate these skills and build teamwork. They do all this in a variety of environments. They practice and exercise in the sea, of course, but also in desert conditions. Sometimes a platoon will spend more time in a desert environment if on its upcoming deployment it will be operating in the Middle East.

In addition to sharpening skills and learning to operate, platoon training also serves to make the platoon a team. Much of the platoon training takes place in remote areas away from families and the rest of the world. In a sense, the platoon has only itself to rely on, and its members, some of whom may be on their first assignment after the selection and qualification process, must learn to work together. Platoon training is in effect a shakedown cruise designed to find out if any of the members of the platoon do not function as required or have problems fitting in. The platoon needs to know these things before it deploys. Platoon leaders watch for problems during training, as do those who are in charge of the training.

It would be wrong, however, to speak of platoon training as only a shakedown cruise. More important is its effect in building up the platoon's camaraderie and the sense of belonging that develops among platoon members. The simple recitation of what the platoons do in training does not capture the effect the training has on the individuals who go through it. Like selection, ongoing training demands an extraordinary investment of time and energy. The greater the investment in getting in and keeping up to standard, the more one is committed and the harder it is to leave. This is not just a question of psychic accounting, of sunk costs holding one tight to an organization.[28] Camaraderie and bonding, the inevitable byproducts of spending so much time together doing difficult things, are inducements to stay. Pride in being part of an elite unit is also important. This pride is built in part through competition among individuals and platoons.

The final six months of the training cycle is squadron integration training. The squadron is a SEAL team augmented by boat crews (who handle the special boats that SEALs use to attack their targets), communication specialists, explosive ordinance and intelligence personnel, and linguists. The purpose of this last phase of training is to integrate these different elements so that they can function together effectively and to make final preparations for deployment. These final preparations include training and planning specific to the area where the SEAL squadron will deploy and the particular missions it will undertake there. With the conclusion of this phase, the Squadron begins its six-month deployment, after which it will begin the training cycle for its next deployment.

The Ranger and SF training cycles are shorter than the two-year SEAL cycle, which reflects the deployment cycle of the Navy's combat ships. The Ranger and SF cycle is a year. In other respects, however, the training cycles are similar. Rangers and SF engage first in individual training, then in small-unit training (squads and platoons or "A" teams). Rangers also train as battalions, which are made up of three companies and a headquarters company. (The Rangers are in the process of adding support personnel and functions, so that their support will be organic to the regiment.) There are three battalions in the Ranger regiment. The training cycle allows one battalion or its companies to be deployed or to be ready for deployment, while the other two are in different stages of recovering from deployment and training up for the next one. Like the SEALs, both the Rangers and SF engage in exercises so that teams, companies, and battalions can integrate skills and prepare for the various missions that they will have to conduct when deployed. These exercises and the entire training cycle build skills but also build cohesion, integrating new personnel and commanders.

Marines in the MarSOC will go through the training that all Marines go through. In addition, the Marine Special Operations companies, the fighting units of the MarSOC (four or five of which will make up each of the two Marine Special Operations battalions in the MarSOC), will receive training in special operations tactics, techniques, and procedures. The Foreign Military Training Unit will also receive specialized training, since its cadre "must develop the art of salesmanship, negotiation, and becoming a confidant to" the leadership of those they train, skills not part of normal Marine training. To deliver this training, the MarSOC will contain its own trainers and do its own training.[29]

One difference between SF on the one hand and SEALs and Rangers on the other is that not all SF training can be completed in training facilities. More than either Rangers or SEALs, SF carry out their missions by working with indigenous forces and personnel. While training in the United States with role players can provide some preparation for these missions, it is critical to their readiness that SF get opportunities to work with indigenous personnel. (The Marine Foreign Military Training Units are likely to discover the same requirement.) To this end, training monies pay for SF to deploy to work with other forces, on the understanding that the primary benefit of such training deployments accrues to SF. In the 1990s, for example, humanitarian de-mining gave SF teams an opportunity to get into countries and to know foreign forces and conditions they might not otherwise have had. De-mining is not an SF mission; but the principal purpose of these deployments from the SF perspective was not de-mining but the chance to work with foreign forces and personnel, learning about countries or regions where they might some day have to carry out their principal missions. During the Clinton administration, some friction developed with civilian officials in the Defense Department over the issue of humanitarian de-mining because they, unlike SOF, were primarily concerned with the humanitarian benefits of de-mining. In the second Bush administration after 9-11, friction developed with civilian officials in the Defense Department over de-mining missions because the officials wanted SOF on missions to kill terrorists. Despite the different political starting points and agendas, the one thing that remained constant was the failure to understand SF's indirect approach to conflict and the connection between that and the training deployments to foreign countries that SF undertake.

Ongoing training for civil affairs and PSYOP personnel differs from the training cycles of SF, Rangers and SEALs for several reasons. While CA and PSYOP personnel operate in teams, their skills are more individual than team skills. The skill of one CA soldier, for example, may be all that is necessary in a given situation. This is less likely to be the case for SF, Rangers, or SEALs. This means that CA and PSYOP units have less need for the integration of skills that other SOF achieve by training together. In addition, since most CA and PSYOP capability is in the reserve component of the military, CA and PSYOP active-duty personnel have deployed since the end of the Cold War more frequently than SF, Rangers, or SEALs, which makes training more difficult to schedule. CA and PSYOP training is in effect always on-the-job-training.

One thing that all SOF have in common, along with the U.S. military generally, is a well-honed system of self-criticism and evaluation that informs training and leads to something like continual improvement. First, of course, trainers evaluate trainees. As we have seen with the SEALs, this is often done in an environment of competition among individuals and teams. Throughout SOF, the trainers are SOF personnel who have been with SOF teams, platoons and aircraft and are typically going back to them. The trainers thus infuse training with operational experience and have a personal stake in making sure that only the truly qualified end up in the operational units. But trainees also evaluate the training they receive. Since most of the trainees who go through the training cycle have operational experience, this evaluation is worth more than many student evaluations.

The system of self-evaluation goes beyond evaluation feedback in training. The squadrons, teams, and other units that are deployed learn in the course of their deployments about what works and what does not. This information travels to the trainers and others in SOF formally through "lessons learned" reports and informally through word of mouth. Trainers adjust training accordingly. As we have noted, the SEALs and SF and other components of SOF are small in number, which facilitates informal feedback from the field. In addition, more so than the conventional forces, except in time of war, SOF are almost constantly deployed and operational, which means that formal and informal feedback systems get constant exercise. The result is a system that perhaps better than any in the military lives up to the U.S. military's admonition that success comes from training as you fight.

The success of this training regime was evident to at least one SF officer who fought in Afghanistan.

What we did [going into Afghanistan and hooking up with an indigenous force] ... in some ways the whole thing was so textbook. I remember I came back to America, [the Special Warfare Center (SWC)] called and said, "Hey, we want to know what's wrong with [the training]. How can we fix it?" The whole team said "man, don't fix a thing. It's so spot on." I mean from the viewpoint of my experience, it was just like [training]. I got out of the helicopter [in Afghanistan]. I walked all night long until I met [the guerrilla leader]. The only difference is that the trainers [gave me a hard time getting] on the [guerrilla] base. In Afghanistan, [the guerrillas] didn't. And I told [SWC] that. I said, "So many things were so well constructed in training." [Afghanistan] was like the training except it was real, even what we did [in training], certain vignettes that were culturally specific to Afghanistan, like inter-factional tension, violence, competition, those kinds of things.

PSYOP may be an exception to this training standard. Psychological operations is an inherently ambiguous business, at least more ambiguous than the kinds of operations conducted by SEALs, SF, and even CA. It is easy to assess whether a SEAL team has seized an objective or taken a prisoner with an acceptable level of casualties. SF teams must deal with ambiguity when dealing with guerrilla leaders, but ultimately the guerrillas that SF train either turn into an effective fighting force or fail to do so. CA work is complex and, as with the work of SF, interactions with people from different cultures and backgrounds can be quite ambiguous. Yet, ultimately, either the lights go back on or they do not, the water runs or does not, the judicial system functions or it remains ineffectual. PSYOP success is harder to measure. Sometimes PSYOP can achieve definite results, especially when the pain that the U.S. military can inflict supports the PSYOP message. Leaflet drops warning about B-52 raids produced surrenders in the first Gulf War. But often, when the issue is more complex, it is hard to judge whether PSYOP worked or why it did. If attitudes change or do not change in Afghanistan or Iraq, for example, should PSYOP be praised or blamed? Polling, when it can be done, can help determine that attitudes have changed but will not necessarily provide decisive information concerning the role of PSYOP in bringing about that change. In any event, PSYOP personnel typically do not have the expertise to conduct such polling. For these reasons, feeding lessons learned into training is harder for PSYOP than for other components of SOF, although the PSYOP community continues to work on improving its measures of effectiveness.

Differences in the effectiveness of feedback systems is not the only way that PSYOP selection and training differs from that of other SOF. Because it deals with human attitudes and motivation and is directed at people in foreign cultures, PSYOP is arguably the most complex work that SOF does. Yet the PSYOP selection process results in a cadre of enlisted personnel—the people who do most of the work—of which 90 percent have only a high school education.[30] Few of the enlisted or officers who join PSYOP have any background in communications or the media. As we have seen, relative to the work that PSYOP must do, training is minimal. It also contains remarkably little about human psychology. The training and the most recent version of PSYOP doctrine discuss Maslow's hierar-chy of needs, as we noted, but research has almost universally failed to find empirical support for Maslow's theories. They turn out not to be good guides to human motivation.[31]

Language training is also minimal for PSYOP. In a sense, this is un-derstandable. To use a foreign language effectively in PSYOP requires a native capability, or close to it. Anything other than the most simple messages will suffer if not delivered in idiomatic language. It is prob-ably not cost effective for the military to invest what would be neces-sary to develop fluent speakers for PSYOP. Translators suffice, as long as those developing or reviewing the messages understand the culture that will receive them. The active-duty PSYOP unit employs a cadre of regional experts but it would be better if PSYOP personnel were better at languages, both to assist them in understanding their audience and to supervise those preparing the messages that PSYOP units disseminate. Language is more important for SF and CA, who must work with and among indigenous forces and people and therefore should be able to communicate effectively with them. Although the SF community con-stantly tries to increase it, the language proficiency of its personnel is not as good as it should be.

CONCLUSION

When it comes to selecting and training to shoot and kill, SOF estab-lish the state of the art. When it comes to selecting and training for cultural sensitivity and communication, it does not. For example, no one in SOF spends an amount of time learning languages and cultures comparable to the time SEALs spend learning to shoot. What should we make of this?

To begin to answer this question, we need first to consider that selec-tion and training reveal the heterogeneity of SOF. The different selection processes seek individuals with different skills and abilities and the train-ing process reinforces these differences. There is some overlap among SOF, but the differences are striking. SEALs and Rangers focus on de-veloping proficiency at bringing force to bear on a target directly. SEALs focus on tasks specific to small teams such as special reconnaissance and capturing high-value targets, while the Rangers focus on missions (such as airfield seizures) that require larger units. SF have the widest array of missions, but their special contribution is bringing force to bear indirectly by working through and with indigenous forces. PSYOP and CA also work indirectly on the enemy, but they do so without using force at all. Indeed, their functions are wholly different from what one normally thinks of when one thinks of military force. In working with indigenous forces, SF also do something different from general purpose forces. Yet in working with indigenous forces, SF must be prepared to use the same small-unit military skills that SEALs possess. In bringing force to bear directly, SEALs and Rangers are most like general-purpose forces. As far as their skills and capabilities are concerned, what distinguishes them from general-purpose forces is often a matter of degree, not kind. Similarly, what distinguishes Air Force and Army special operations aviators from other Air Force and Army aviators, what makes them "special," is principally the degree to which they possess certain flying skills.

If skills, abilities, and missions differ among SOF, it might be that what SOF have in common are certain attitudes. For example, we earlier discussed a willingness to bend rules and improvise. But as we also noted, Rangers, because of the kind of work they do, adhere strictly to the rules. SEALs, too, follow standard operating procedures and tactics in their operations, for much the same reason that Rangers do. Emphasis on improvisation is probably more characteristic of SF and is also a way of life for CA, in this case particularly because of a lack of resources and the restrictions that mark much of their work, as we saw in chapter 1 in the case of CA efforts in Kirkuk. A sense of being part of an elite unit might be something that all SOF have in common; but such a sense or feeling is stronger in some kinds of SOF than in others. It is most keenly felt by special mission units, SEALs, Rangers, Air Force and Army pilots, SF, pararescuemen, combat controllers, and SOF weathermen—perhaps in that order. PSYOP and CA, on the other hand, do not share the same cachet.

The differences between PSYOP and CA and other kinds of SOF that are revealed when we look at SOF selection and training suggest that the U.S. military values some SOF capabilities more than others. Hence, SEALs shoot with a very high level of accuracy, while SOF language speakers rarely achieve real proficiency. If we review the history of SOF, we see that such disparities are not a recent development. For this reason and others that will emerge, reviewing the history of SOF provides a necessary perspective for understanding these forces.

3

HISTORY

ALTHOUGH SPECIAL OPERATIONS FORCES (SOF) as we now know them came into existence only in the 1980s, the U.S. military has throughout its history developed special or unconventional units—out of necessity and most often reluctantly. In the seventeenth and eighteenth centuries, the tree-covered, hilly, and mountainous terrain of eastern North America created the possibility of warfare different from the kind carried out by military forces on the plains of Europe. In addition, the presence of tribal societies between the outposts of two competing nation-states meant that warfare with conventions entirely different from European warfare was likely to flourish. Finally, the political principles of the British and even more of the Americans emphasized suspicion of standing professional military forces as a tool of tyrannical rule and upheld the importance of militia and armed citizens. From these varied circumstances and influences emerged mixed units of colonists and friendly Indians who fought hostile Indians during King Philip's War (1675–1676) and the series of French and Indian Wars stretching from 1689 to 1763. In the final war of this series, known as the French and Indian War (1756–1763), Robert Rogers organized and led a small group of frontiersmen, Rogers' Rangers, against the French and their Indian allies. The Rangers, who were paid by the British and supported British operations, operated from a camp near the edges of British settlement, from which they would penetrate deep into enemy territory to scout and harass.[1] Rogers also led his Rangers in an attack on the Abenaki Indians at St. Francis, in Canada, an attack that has traditionally received credit for removing the Abenaki as a threat to British settlers.

Units like Rogers' Rangers saw less use in the Revolutionary War than they had earlier, but some units, such as the one led by Francis Marion, did use guerrilla tactics to harass the British in the southern theater. Specialized units in the Revolutionary War also included Knowlton's Rangers and Whitcomb's Rangers, whose principal function was to gather intelligence by patrolling near enemy positions. More than Rogers' Rangers had been, these units were integrated into the regular Army they supported. Washington's Continental Army strove to imitate professional European forces, which had come to include a variety of light forces supporting the more heavily armed regulars who stood in line to receive enemy fire and discharge their own. It was the regular forces, whether light or heavy, that carried the revolutionary cause during the War of Independence, although the myth of irregulars, citizen soldiers, harrying the British remained a powerful prop of American democracy.

By the end of the eighteenth century, American military experience included specialized units operating under the direct command of conventional forces or on their own, either in support of conventional forces or, in some cases, as an independent force serving a strategic purpose. The raid on the Abenaki Indians by Rogers' Rangers is an example of such an independent strategic use of a special unit. However they were used, the specialized units were both volunteer and professional, and on occasion they included mixed units of colonists and indigenous people. These are all characteristics of special operations forces that recur in the American military experience. Also evident by the end of the eighteenth century was another recurring theme: some tension between conventional and unconventional forces. The Continental Army, for example, aspired to European standards in tactics and conduct. Washington concentrated "on opposing regular British and German units in a formal battlefield context."[2] Irregular or militia forces found it difficult to stand in the open and face the fire of British regulars. Other specialized units that operated outside the "formal battlefield context" were suspected of indiscipline.[3]

The tension between conventional or professional soldiers and irregulars continued into and heightened during the first half of the nineteenth century, as part of the Jacksonian revolution in American life. Andrew Jackson, an amateur soldier himself, in fact came to prominence as the leader of a volunteer militia force that won the Battle of New Orleans in 1812, showing apparently the superiority of hardy, unschooled citizen-soldiers to the professionals of Great Britain. Jackson again led companies of volunteers in his campaign against the Seminoles. Similar organizations formed to fight Indians as settlement spread west. This was the origin of the Texas Rangers, for example, who later served in the war against Mexico as scouts and guides. The romantic allure of the volunteer irregulars suffered during the Civil War, however, as such units became infamous for the destruction of civilian property and life.

The military that emerged from the Civil War was perhaps even more committed to professional standards in operations and conduct than its prewar version had been and looked to European forces, particularly Germany's, as a model. Unfortunately, for the professionals, the principal task of the post–Civil War military was not to fight the organized professional armed forces of another nation-state but to chase and subdue tribal societies across a vast expanse of territory. The distance between preferred and actual operations led historian Robert Utley to speak of the paradox that "the army's frontier employment unfitted it for orthodox war at the same time that that its preoccupation with orthodox war unfitted it for its frontier mission."[4] Under the leadership of a succession of Civil War generals, the Army never developed any doctrine or specialized units for fighting the Indians but instead fought a conventional war against them, using its superior resources to wear down the tribes. Some generals did develop unconventional approaches, but their fate is instructive. George Crook, for example, used mule trains to increase mobility and employed large numbers of friendly Indians to fight hostile Indians. In using Indians in this way, Crook was foreshadowing the Special Forces discipline of unconventional warfare, which works "by, with, or through indigenous or surrogate forces" to achieve U.S. objectives. It was this kind of warfare with which Special Forces achieved success after 2001 in Afghanistan and the Philippines. Crook was also inclined to negotiate as he pursued and fought with his Indian opponents. Crook had some success with these methods, but they were heterodox. Never enamored of Crook's approach, Philip Sheridan, who had observed the Franco-Prussian war from the German side, relieved Crook of his command following setbacks in his efforts to subdue the Apaches.

By the end of the nineteenth century, the American military had become more professional, more committed to the conventions of military organization, operations, and conduct characteristic of the premier military forces of the day. This professionalism allowed little if any room for the volunteer or specialized units that had appeared regularly up to the time of the Civil War. This pattern continued when the Indian wars came to an end and the U.S. military found itself involved in a series of colonial police operations or small wars that were, like the Indian wars, not its preferred kind of fight. As it had during the Indian Wars, the military developed no specialized forces to fight its colonial struggles. Instead, it used the forces that it had, which were designed for conventional or large-scale military engagements. Communications at the time were such, however, that commanding officers in far-flung conflicts were not burdened by overly strict control from central military authority. Commanders had room to exercise initiative. Some adapted tactics to the conflicts they actually faced. For example, Merrit Edson, fighting the original Sandinistas in Nicaragua in the late 1920s, worked with the indigenous Miskito Indians to improve the operations of his small force. Edson enjoyed greater success than his predecessors or successors, who ignored the indigenous people. In the Philippines, the Army succeeded against the insurgency that followed the Spanish American war but, again, successful operations depended on the initiative and skills of individual officers and not on the U.S. military as an institution responding to this unconventional threat. As these colonial policing efforts were winding down, the Marine Corps codified some of the lessons it had learned in a *Small Wars Manual*, developed in the 1930s and published in 1940, but these colonial policing engagements otherwise left little mark in doctrine and none in military organization.

In the midst of these colonial engagements, the U.S. military participated in World War I. This conflict did produce a specialized unit, an ancestor of forces now part of current Special Operations Forces (SOF). In order to build and maintain support for the War, Woodrow Wilson established a Committee on Public Information. One journalist working on this committee, Heber Blankenhorn, believed that information or propaganda directed at enemy soldiers might persuade them to surrender and help shorten the war. When the Committee on Public Information refused to take on this task, Blankenhorn contacted a friend in the military and ultimately persuaded the Army to set up a Psychological Subsection in the Military Intelligence Branch in February 1918. Blankenhorn was put in charge. He and his staff did not deploy to France until July 1918, in part because the military did not see information or propaganda efforts as its responsibility. Support from civilians in the War Department finally got Blankenhorn and his unit to France, where they began dropping leaflets on the enemy. In carrying out this work, the psychological section met with indifference or hostility from military officers, who did not see the value of these efforts or believed that, by consuming precious resources, they detracted from the war effort. Blankenhorn constantly struggled to get planes for leaflet drops, for example. Ironically, none other than Billy Mitchell, after telling Blankenhorn that propaganda had no place in combat operations, threatened Blankenhorn with a court martial if he did not stop trying to get pilots to drop leaflets. Blankenhorn and his staff persisted, however, and some anecdotal evidence suggests that the leaflets did help produce surrenders. One student of Blankenhorn's efforts argues that the Army's first psychological warrior succeeded despite "the general indifference toward unconventional warfare displayed by combat soldiers and their hesitancy, if not outright refusal, to consider its use in support of operations."[5]

The indifference that Blankenhorn's efforts elicited was clear when the war ended, for the War Department immediately disbanded the psychological operations office. This was part of the larger postwar demobilization and a political necessity. Propaganda fit uneasily with American notions of limited government and freedom of the press. Accepted grudgingly as a necessity during wartime, the War Department could not abide a propaganda function during peacetime. Yet, also at work in the decision to disband the psychological operations office was the sense, expressed by Mitchell, that psychological or propaganda operations were somehow not work worthy of real soldiers. Lingering questions about the effectiveness of psychological operations also contributed to the decision to get rid of them. Finally, the resource issue worked against such operations. Most in the military thought that its limited resources should be spent to support conventional operations. In all these respects—propriety, effectiveness, efficiency, professionalism—Blankenhorn's efforts produced reactions and criticisms that have continually accompanied special operations and the forces that carry them out.

By the time the Marine Corps published the *Small Wars Manual*, it had decided to bet its institutional life on opposed amphibious assault, a mission entirely different from small wars. Following World War I, when military planners thought about the possibility of war with Japan, they realized that the Navy would have to seize islands to use as naval bases. This gave rise to a new mission for the Marines but also to the need for military units that could clear beaches of obstacles placed to impede assaults. The Navy therefore established demolition teams, which eventually were called underwater demolition teams (UDTs). Following the assault on Tarawa, where heavy casualties resulted from ignorance of water depth and conditions on the approaches to the beaches, these Navy teams also got the mission of hydrographic reconnaissance. The Army, too, recognized the need for units to assist in amphibious assaults and trained its own personnel in these new military skills. Early in this effort, there was even a joint Amphibious Scout and Raider School that trained both Navy and Army personnel. These units assisted in assaults across the Pacific as well as in the Mediterranean and Atlantic theaters, including the Normandy invasion.

World War II saw the development of other specialized units. Merritt Edson organized and led a Marine Raider battalion, one of four that the Corps organized during the war. Edson won the Medal of Honor for his defense of a critical ridge overlooking the airfield at Guadalcanal. The Army revived the Rangers, initially in part to provide a leavening of experienced fighters to the unseasoned recruits that would make up the mass Army of World War II. Ultimately, the Rangers did fight as units, distinguishing themselves not only at Pointe du Hoc, during the Normandy invasion, but in the Mediterranean and Pacific theaters as well. To improve its intelligence in the Pacific, the Sixth Army organized the Alamo Scouts, who conducted reconnaissance of Japanese forces and installations and carried out other activities, such as establishing coast-watcher stations and organizing indigenous forces to fight against the Japanese. They also liberated a number of Allied prisoners of war (POWs) and supported the 6th Ranger Battalion in its successful mission to liberate over five hundred Allied POWs from the Cabanatuan camp in the Philippines. The 5307 Composite Unit (Provisional) (Merrill's Marauders) operated behind Japanese lines in the China-Burma-India theater, seizing a critical airfield and tying up large numbers of Japanese troops. The First Special Service Force, consisting of American and Canadian personnel, fought in the Aleutians and in Italy, where it helped lead the breakout from the beach at Anzio and then worked with tanks to clear German positions on the right flank of the drive toward Rome.

Through the prompting of a civilian, Assistant Secretary of War John McCloy, the War Department slowly revived psychological operations. In 1940, the Army had only one officer with any experience in these activities. When it recalled Blankenhorn to active duty, he found himself involved in the same battles for resources he had fought decades before and the Army even more resistant, in his opinion, to psychological operations than it had been in World War I. Initial Army efforts in psychological warfare included establishing its first tactical radio teams and the publication of a psychological warfare training manual.

World War II called forth three specialized units that had not before appeared in the U.S. military. The Army Air Force (AAF) put together special units, often specifically designed to support land-warfare special units. For example, in 1943, the AAF organized the First Air Commando Group to support the British Army's Chindit raiders, whose mission was to penetrate into Burma behind Japanese lines as part of the Allied effort to recapture northern Burma and open a supply line to China. To accomplish this important strategic task, the AAF put together a composite force consisting of fighters, bombers, transports, gliders, and the R-4 helicopter, the first production single-rotor helicopter, which made the first casualty evacuations in 1944 during fighting in Burma. On March 5, 1944, the First Air Commando Group carried the Chindit raiders over 200 miles into enemy territory in the "first night aerial invasion of enemy territory."[6] The First Air Commando continued to support and resupply the raiders during their operations in Burma and evacuated over two thousand soldiers. Despite its effectiveness, the unit received some criticism. A visiting conventional officer "complained that [the Commando Group's] men were 'nothing less than a mob' and that no two men wore the same uniform, while almost all were growing beards."[7]

Civil affairs was the second new specialized activity developed to meet the demands of Allied operations in World War II. By the time the war started, the U.S. military had governed territory from the Rhineland through the Caribbean to the Philippines and beyond to China but had never seen such government as an inherent part of military activity. The military focused on the fight, not its aftermath. A focus on the requirements of fighting was not the only reason that the Army neglected government in the territories it occupied, however. Just as important was the sense, which it shared with civilians, that military government violated fundamental principles of American political understanding. Americans did not consider it proper for military forces to have political authority. The military never prepared to govern, therefore, since involvement in political matters was both a distraction from its principal task and at least vaguely un-American. The consequence, at least in the case of the military's government of the Rhineland following World War I, was, in the words of the colonel in charge of this effort, an occupying Army that "lacked both training and organization to guide the destinies of the nearly 1,000,000 civilians whom the fortunes of war had placed under its temporary sovereignty."[8] As World War II progressed, it became evident that the need for military government and its complexity would be much greater than in the previous World War.

Even before Pearl Harbor, the Army had begun to consider the question of military government and to discuss training options. It established a Civil Affairs School at the University of Virginia in April 1942, but the personnel, operations, and plans divisions in the Army staff objected to assigning officers to civil affairs when there was training to do for the expanding Army. In the Army's view, civil affairs was not a priority. Officers were eventually assigned, however, although the quality of students remained a concern. The Army also worked to identify other officers and civilians who had the special skills that civil affairs called for. The Army's thinking about civil affairs revolved around a simple distinction between short-term and long-term requirements. The Army believed that it must have governing authority in the short term, during what it called the period of "military necessity" ("so long as there is a danger of the enemy continuing or resuming the fight"), but that during this time it would need the cooperation of civilian agencies. In the long term, the Army believed that it should turn over governing responsibilities to civilians. The Army was prompted to publish its views and distribute them to civilian agencies, which it did in September 1942, because these agencies were expressing interest in the government of occupied territories. The Army's effort to forestall the civilians ran into the opposition of President Roosevelt. Apparently prompted by New Dealers, including secretary of the Interior Harold Ickes, who feared that the Army was promoting imperialism and employing too many Republicans at its Civil Affairs school, the president declared in October 1942 that governing occupied territories was "in most instances a civilian task."[9]

The invasion of North Africa, November 8, 1942, led to a test of civilian control of civil affairs in military areas. President Roosevelt had made the State Department preeminent in purely civil matters, but General Eisenhower still reported that it felt as if he were spending nine-tenths of his time on political and economic issues. He also thought that the president's decision had created divided authority. A general sense developed in the government that civil affairs efforts were insufficiently coordinated in North Africa. By November 1943, the president had changed his mind and acknowledged that if civil affairs, particularly the distribution of relief supplies, were to be handled efficiently and effectively, the military would have to do it. Although the military accepted this responsibility, it did so reluctantly and still planned to turn over civil administration to civilians as soon as possible. In principle, this remained the policy of the U.S. government as well. Shortly after V-E day, both the secretary of war and President Truman announced that the War Department would transfer responsibility for civil administration to the State Department, but neither State nor any other civilian agency had the resources to take on these responsibilities in Europe, Japan, and several other locations around the world. In early 1946, the State Department insisted that the War Department continue to administer civilian areas.[10]

In addition to these overt special forces, during World War II, for the first time, the United States made extensive use of covert special operations. These were run through the Office of Strategic Services (OSS), established in June 1942, which worked for the Joint Chiefs of Staff. These special operations included intelligence gathering, black propaganda (information purporting to come from the enemy), and support to resistance groups. (The OSS also included an intelligence analysis office.) As part of its intelligence gathering function, OSS inherited espionage activities from the military. It also received from the military responsibility for military psychological warfare, a kind of warfare that, as we have noted, the military did not much care for. Once it transferred that function to OSS, the Army shut down its own psychological warfare staff office, while the JCS forbade OSS from doing psychological warfare in any theater and gave the authority for such warfare to the theater commanders. After psychological warfare showed its worth under Eisenhower, who valued it, the Army reestablished a central staff office for this activity late in 1943. OSS also provided support to indigenous resistance movements in Axis territory, parachuting its personnel in to occupied areas to help lead guerrilla efforts against the Germans and Japanese. In the European theater, the Army Air Force set up special units to support OSS missions. Aircraft from these units flew at night and at low altitudes and also landed at improvised landing fields in occupied territory.

Although Eisenhower valued at least some covert activity, others did not. Both General MacArthur and Admiral Nimitz banned OSS from operating in their theaters, while Latin America was the FBI's preserve. Information operations in Latin America belonged to a special committee headed by Nelson Rockefeller. OSS also had no role in intelligence operations in the United States. Perhaps the most important restriction placed on OSS came about when the State Department and the military succeeded in getting President Roosevelt to decree that OSS would not have access to the most sensitive intelligence gathered during World War II—the decoded intercepts of Japanese and German communications.

The range of special operations carried out by the U.S. military in World War II is striking. They included raids to free prisoners, reconnaissance deep behind enemy lines, strikes at strategic targets, reduction of coastal defenses, work with indigenous forces, night flight operations, beach reconnaissance and demolition, and espionage in civilian clothing. These varied operations served one of two purposes. They either supported conventional operations (e.g., beach clearance to assist an amphibious assault) or strove to achieve a larger strategic effect (e.g., the operations of Merrill's Marauders in the Burma theater). All of these special operations were done with only rudimentary selection procedures to identify the men and women (in the case of the OSS) who carried them out and with training that was also often rudimentary as well. In fact, for many of the raider or ranger units, training consisted of several weeks of intense physical activity that built the endurance and esprit de corps of those who survived it rather than imparting any special skills. Units like these were really elite infantry, taking infantry skills (land navigation, patrolling, marksmanship) to new levels rather than developing and using special skills. The Army Air Force units that supported these special operations also tended to be elite units, that is, units that carried to a higher degree of proficiency skills that were part of regular Air Force units. The UDTs and OSS espionage efforts were examples of units that developed skills not normally resident in the military.

That many of the special units in World War II could be best described as "elite" explains one of the problems that these units encountered. Many in the military disliked elite units. The Army faced an enormous task in building a force large enough to fight a two-front, global war. To accomplish this task, the Army focused on producing standard units from raw recruits. Those responsible for this training and unit formation saw siphoning off men for special units as a distraction and a waste of resources on units whose missions regular infantry units, they believed, could accomplish. To the degree that the men who went to the special units were the most motivated or aggressive, unit commanders were worried that this would degrade the units they left, a longstanding concern about elite or special units.[11] Counteracting these views was the notion, mentioned earlier, that the Ranger units could serve as training units from which soldiers could return to their original units with increased skills and esprit, a function that Ranger training still performs in the U.S. military.[12] Also counteracting the dislike of elite units was the recognition by officers, often at higher levels of command, that there were missions that standard units either could not perform or were less likely to perform successfully.

Developing units for special missions, however, led to another problem: what do you do with the unit when the mission is over? After the First Special Service Force took out batteries that threatened the beaches during the invasion of southern France, the unit guarded the right flank of the invasion force and ultimately ended up guarding rear areas, missions that did not require an elite or special unit. The fate of such units was often worse. Typically, once the units had completed their special mission, conventional commanders put them in the line with regular units, where their lack of firepower put them at a disadvantage. In these cases, the units often suffered serious casualties. To prevent this, commanders sometimes gave the elite units additional firepower in the form of artillery or coupled them with tank units. This gave the units more firepower but also made them more conventional. Often, to make up for their personnel losses when they were used as regular line units, the elite or special units were given insufficiently trained recruits, which rendered the units incapable of performing the special missions they were originally designed to carry out. In one case (Cisterna, in Italy), the use of Ranger battalions without proper reconnaissance led to the units being surrounded and destroyed by more heavily armed German units. These problems arose in part because the special or elite units went to war without doctrine explaining what they could and could not do to guide conventional commanders. But it was also the case that the commanders of the units and the men who filled them were eager to fight, and in their eagerness they were not always careful enough about which fights they got in. At various points in the war, either because of the number of casualties suffered or lack of suitable missions, senior officers disbanded special or elite units.

As soon as the war ended, the military disbanded all of these units, except for the UDTs, a small number of which the Navy kept in service. President Truman also disbanded the OSS in September 1945, sending its analytical function to the State Department and its clandestine capabilities to the War Department. While the analytical function found a home at State, where it continues to function, the covert capabilities became orphans, living with uncaring military step-parents. These activities were uncared for because in the American tradition they were seen as acceptable, as a perhaps unavoidable necessity, only in wartime and initially the U.S. government thought that the end of World War II had ushered in a period of peace. The assumption of a clear distinction between peace and war was typically American, part of America's separation or hoped for separation from the *realpolitik* of Europe, in which war is only the sharpest manifestation of the constant conflict and competition between sovereign states. In addition, the military viewed covert operations as incompatible with military professionalism and overt psychological warfare as less important than real soldier skills, even though Eisenhower had praised the effectiveness of psychological warfare at the end of the war.[13] Consequently, the military devoted only limited attention to psychological warfare and surrendered covert operations as soon as it had the chance, much as it had surrendered them to the OSS earlier. In January 1946, President Truman created the Central Intelligence Group (CIG). By the spring of 1946, about six months after having received it from the OSS, the War Department transferred the responsibility for covert activity to the CIG. With the passage of the National Security Act of 1947, this activity went to the new Central Intelligence Agency (CIA).

The CIG and then the CIA came into existence as a response to events overseas. By 1947, communists had taken over Poland, Hungary, and Romania and were attempting to take over Greece, while continuing pressure on the government of Turkey. In response, President Truman announced in March 1947 what came to be called the Truman Doctrine, which committed the United States to supplying military aid to countries under attack from communists. Other problems had emerged in Europe. The economic and political situation in France and Italy, both with large communist parties, looked bleak. Fears began to mount that the communists might win elections in 1948 (communists were already in the cabinets of both countries; in France, the Minister of Defense was a communist). In response to this threat, in October 1947, Secretary of State George C. Marshall announced a program of economic aid for Europe, a program that came to be known as the Marshall Plan. In September, the Soviets had established the Communist Information Bureau or COMINFORM, which included communist parties in both Eastern and Western Europe, launching it with a bellicose speech by the Leningrad party boss.[14] Events outside Europe, for example, in the Philippines, where a communist insurgency was underway, also caused concern in the U.S. government.

One of the first reactions to the emerging Cold War was renewed interest in psychological warfare. About a month after the COMINFORM meeting, the Army representative to the State-Army-Navy-Air Force Coordinating Committee (SANACC), a forerunner of the National Security Council, sent a memorandum to committee members approving plans developed by the committee for the establishment during wartime of a National Psychological Warfare Organization. This interest in psychological warfare grew out of the limited activities that the military continued after the war. For example, the various psychological warfare offices overseas turned to the task of informing and shaping opinion in Germany, Austria, Korea, and Japan, printing and distributing newspapers and magazines and running radio stations and movie houses. In the United States, the Army formed an experimental "Tactical Information Detachment," performed some studies of psychological warfare, and did some planning for its use in wartime.

In addition to approving a wartime psychological warfare capability, the Army representative to the SANACC also argued that the "events of the past few months" suggested the need to consider "as a matter of urgency" the "desirability or necessity" of "deliberate coordinated" psychological warfare in peacetime. The Director of Central Intelligence seconded this motion a few days later in his own memorandum to the SANACC. A few days after that, the Secretary of the National Security Council forwarded to Secretary of Defense Forrestal "a very persuasive and accurate appraisal of the need for psychological warfare operations to counter Soviet-inspired communist Propaganda, particularly in France and Italy."[15] This renewed interest in psychological warfare, however, ran head on into the effects of demobilization. In a memorandum to the under secretary of State, the SANACC reported that "the Department of State and the Military Establishment have no funds appropriated for psychological warfare purposes" and that "no psychological warfare specialist reserves exist within the Military Establishment or the Department of State."[16]

As the SANACC's planning effort continued, much of the military's time and energy for psychological warfare was spent answering two questions. The first was where the truncated psychological warfare capability should reside. Two possibilities existed. It could reside in military intelligence, where it had been during the war, or in the office responsible for plans and operations, where, as an operational activity, many thought it more properly belonged. It was finally assigned to operations and plans toward the end of 1946, although some associated functions remained with other offices. This question having been answered, the larger question of the role the Army should have in psychological warfare opened in 1947 with the appointment of Kenneth C. Royall, a retired World War II general, as the secretary of the Army. Royall was skeptical of psychological operations, as were a number of high-ranking officers and civilians. Throughout this period, Royall and other civilian secretaries of the military departments argued that the military should not be involved with psychological warfare during peacetime because it would inappropriately involve the military in political matters, a domain where the military also lacked the necessary subtlety to operate effectively. These civilians also argued that the question-able morality of psychological warfare would adversely affect the image of the military, if its participation in this activity became known.[17]

Two of Royall's deputies disagreed with him, however, and worked with like-minded officers, including Lieutenant General A.C. Wedemeyer, the Director of the Office of Plans and Operations, where the responsibility for psychological warfare now resided, to give the Army a psychological warfare capability. In his memoirs, published in 1958, Wedemeyer argued against slaughtering the enemy, which he called the standard American and British approach, as the only way to fight a war. The failure "to use political, economic, and psychological means in coordination with mili-tary operations" had prolonged World War II, he contended, and increased Allied casualties. These views were clearly consistent with Wedemeyer's earlier action in support of psychological warfare. One of Royall's depu-ties, who worked with Wedemeyer, was William H. Draper, another World War II Army general, whose responsibilities included the occupied areas, where Army psychological operations were continuing. The other official was Gordon Gray, who had only a limited experience in the Army dur-ing the war. In an effort to change Royall's mind and preserve the Army's psychological warfare capability, Draper commissioned a study by a civil-ian consultant that described what the Army was already doing in psy-chological warfare. This report was passed to Royall. Apparently it helped persuade him that the Army should have some capability in this area, for he agreed, in 1949, toward the end of his tenure, that the Army should establish a psychological warfare branch. Royall stipulated, however, that a civilian within the department should have ultimate responsibility for this activity. Wedemeyer was not happy with this arrangement, fearing that it would compromise the military chain of command, but he accepted it and psychological warfare found a precarious place in the Army.[18]

Not everyone was happy about the revival of psychological operations, especially in their covert form. Secretary of State Marshall opposed them. His opposition or, at least the State Department's, appears to have derived from sentiments similar to those then present in the military. Psychological operations, especially covert psychological operations, should they come to light, were incompatible with diplomacy and therefore potentially damaging to the Department's efforts. The NSC staff made psychological operations more palatable to the State Department by dividing the government's information activities in two, calling the overt component that accompanied U.S. foreign policy "foreign information activities" and the covert component "psychological operations." Consequently, National Security Council document 4 (NSC 4), "Report by the National Security Council on Coordination of Foreign Information Measures," (December 17, 1947) put the secretary of State in charge of providing policy for and coordinating America's overseas information efforts. NSC 4-A gave the CIA authority to carry out "covert psychological operations abroad."

The CIA ultimately defined these operations as "all measures of information and persuasion short of physical in which the originating role of the United States Government will always be kept concealed." NSC 4-A granted this authority to the CIA subject to the approval of "a panel designated by the National Security Council," which would include representatives from State, the Joint Chiefs of Staff and the military services. This approval process was to make sure that the CIA carried out covert psychological operations "in a manner consistent with U.S. foreign policy, overt foreign information activities, and diplomatic and military operations and intentions abroad."[19] Based on this division of responsibility and with this oversight and its new resources, the CIA conducted covert operations in support of democratic parties in Italy. In the election of April, 1948, the Christian Democrats won 48 percent of the vote, giving them control of the government. The outcome of the elections established covert operations as an important weapon in the Cold War.

As the covert psychological warfare apparatus took shape in the U.S. government, the military was at best a reluctant and hesitant participant in any kind of psychological operations. We have already recounted the Army's institutional indifference. The situation was not much better in the other services. In 1949, only the Air Force had an office devoted to psychological warfare, which was supposed to develop plans and policies and consider logistical requirements. The Navy was in no better shape than the Army. The Joint Staff did establish a component to meet the support requirements that it felt would follow from the establishment of a covert capability in the CIA, but it otherwise dealt with psychological warfare issues by creating ad hoc groups. A high-level planning group on the Joint Staff expressed concern about this state of affairs, arguing that the Joint Staff's ad hoc response had resulted in its interests being inadequately represented in the interagency discussions that led to a peacetime psychological warfare capability. The planning group recognized that part of the problem was a fundamental difference in orientation between State and Defense. Defense believed in long-range planning, while State did not. The State Department felt that "political contingencies were so variable and intangible that long range political plans were impracticable, if not impossible." This difference led to frustration and misunderstanding on the Joint Staff that no amount of staff structure would have overcome. But many of the Joint Staff's responsibilities could have been handled more effectively with more staff. Proposals to augment staff to meet the full range of requirements associated with psychological warfare ran into objections from the Services, however. "A year of wrangling" passed before the Joint Chiefs approved an organizational design.[20]

The difficult birth of a peacetime psychological warfare capability is most apparent, however, in the Army, where the greatest responsibility lay. When Secretary of the Army Royall consented to the Army having a psychological warfare capability in 1949 this did not lead immediately to anything. Royall's successor as Secretary of the Army was Gordon Gray, one of the subordinates who had worked to change Royall's views about psychological warfare. Now in a position to support this capability, Gray exerted pressure on the Army staff, as did Gray's successor, Frank Pace. Yet, in the summer of 1950, fifteen months after Royall had first authorized a psychological warfare branch, the Army was still trying to identify the personnel spaces to fill it. The Army had no schooling underway in psychological warfare and only a handful of people qualified to conduct it. Pace's insistence that the Army staff do something, along with the outbreak of the Korean War, finally led the Army to create in January 1951 the office that Royall had originally authorized. It was no longer a branch but a special staff office, the Office of the Chief of Psychological Warfare.[21]

The creation of the psychological warfare office did not resolve the Army's difficult relationship with this unconventional capability. In his meetings with the Army's Chief of Staff, secretary Pace continued to insist on the importance of psychological operations, calling them "the cheapest form of warfare." He inquired directly of General Matthew B. Ridgway in Korea about his ability to conduct such operations. Meanwhile, the general in charge of psychological warfare, Robert McClure, warned his staff at their first meeting of the prejudice that existed in the Army against their activity. It was not seen as the work of a true soldier, he told them. Because of this prejudice, officers were reluctant to become involved with psychological warfare. During the war in Korea, McClure repeatedly complained, as Blankenhorn had in the First World War, that the Air Force was not making sufficient aircraft available for leaflet drops. Like Blankenhorn, McClure also had to deal with Army officers who did not see the value of psychological warfare. His efforts to assist the Far Eastern Command in establishing its psychological warfare office were blocked by the Army Staff's operations office. Some of these difficulties were the result of personality clashes and the aggressiveness with which the new office pursued its responsibilities, but the major problem was the belief in the Army that psychological operations took more time and money than they were worth. Yet, despite all of the obstacles, by the early 1950's, the Army, and the military generally, did have for the first time offices devoted to psychological operations, which had become and remain to this day permanent features of military organization and operations.[22]

The Korean War helped revive not only psychological operations but special operations more generally. Both the Army and the Navy infiltrated Koreans into the North to gather intelligence and disrupt enemy operations. The CIA carried out such operations as well. The Air Force supported the Army by establishing composite wings as it had in World War II but, in the event, conventional Air Force units flying standard aircraft provided infiltration support. The Navy's UDTs had little to do in the war, since except for the landing at Inchon amphibious assault was not a significant element in the fighting. The UDTs did help with the infiltration of Koreans into the North and also pioneered a new mission by conducting raids from the sea instead of just reconnoitering beaches and clearing obstacles. The Army deployed radio and leaflet teams to conduct psychological operations. Civil affairs had little role to play in the war, since the South Korean government continued to function throughout. The Army also revived the Rangers, deploying seventeen companies of the elite infantry to the Korean peninsula, where they conducted raids behind enemy lines or reconnaissance missions close to enemy positions. They also functioned as shock troops, assaulting particularly difficult points in the enemy's line. They suffered high casualty rates in these missions, as they had in World War II.

While special operations were part of the Korean War, they were not an important part. To some extent the military appears to have conducted them as a reflex response, as part of the effort to do everything that could be done to win the war but without sufficient attention to the likelihood of success or their place in some overall strategy. For example, during the war it became clear that virtually all of those infiltrated into the North would be killed, captured, or compromised, yet the missions continued. They did produce some intelligence. Special operations led to the discovery of masses of Chinese troops moving into Korea weeks before they attacked, for example, but MacArthur refused to believe what the special units reported. The CIA continued to conduct infiltration operations as well, but the military and the new agency never coordinated their efforts. The military also failed to support adequately the special operations it conducted. During the first year of the war, Air Force pilots who flew missions to support these operations did so as an additional duty, flying at night after having flown their usual missions during the day. The UDTs took on a raiding mission but the Navy did not train or equip them to do so. The Army did specially train and equip Rangers but then allowed them to be used inappropriately by commanders, who often stuck them in the line to plug a gap or take a difficult enemy position. All in all, special operations achieved little in Korea. The Ranger companies were disbanded in August 1951, although fighting continued for almost two years more. Ranger training continued in the United States, but only to help build infantry skills for soldiers in conventional units, the mission with which the Rangers had begun World War II.

Confusion about and lack of support for special operations in Korea reflected confusion in the military generally about what special operations were for and which units should carry out which missions. Were Rangers elite infantry, shock troops to be thrown against difficult enemy positions, or were they best used for reconnaissance of enemy positions? But if for reconnaissance, was it to be near the front lines or in the enemy's rear areas? But if they could penetrate rear areas, should they not carry out strategic strikes rather than reconnaissance missions—or could they do both? And what about training and working with indigenous forces in guerrilla warfare operations against the enemy in support of conventional operations, one of the missions carried out by the OSS in World War II? As the war in Korea ground on, officials debated these questions in Washington. Based in part on the experience in Korea, the debate concluded that regular infantry could have done most of what the Rangers did, that working with indigenous forces behind enemy lines was a useful mission (it promised to inflict damage on the enemy but limited the risk to U.S. personnel), but that the Rangers were not the force to carry out that mission (they did not have the language skills to operate deep behind enemy lines). Consequently, the Rangers were disbanded to make room within personnel ceilings for a force that could lead guerrilla operations behind enemy lines.

The task of developing this capability fell to General McClure, in charge of psychological warfare in the Army. The military placed the guerrilla warfare mission under psychological operations because these operations were understood at the time to include such guerrilla warfare, along with subversion, sabotage, and raids. All of these activities were intended to influence the will of an opponent to fight, as much, if not more than, his ability to fight. McClure in turn called on a veteran of the OSS, Colonel Aaron Bank, to lead the new guerrilla warfare unit. In June 1952, Bank became the first commander of the 10th Special Forces (SF) Group, located at Fort Bragg, North Carolina, where it was part of the newly created Psychological Warfare Center. The mission of the 10th Group was to organize and direct guerrilla warfare behind Soviet lines in the event of war in Europe. Its inspiration was the fifteen-man OSS teams possessing a variety of skills that had carried out a similar mission in Nazi-occupied Europe. Staffed by former OSS men and European émigrés who spoke a variety of languages fluently, the new unit set about developing the skills to support guerrilla warfare.

The new CIA was doing the same thing. The agency had inherited the OSS capabilities that the Army had spurned and so was in direct competition with the new Special Forces. In principle, conflict might have been avoided. The agency had a covert mission that it conducted in peacetime, while SF prepared for wartime. As a practical matter, however, this distinction made no sense. If the war came, would the agency and SF both conduct guerrilla warfare behind Soviet lines? This threatened redundancy and possibly conflicting operations. Would the CIA prepare the battlefield, so to speak, in peacetime and then turn over its partisans and organization to SF? This suggested a possible loss in efficiency and effectiveness when the guerilla warfare mission was most important. SF and the CIA did not resolve this conflict; no higher authority intervened. As a consequence, the CIA did not share intelligence with SF. In addition, SF had conflicts with the Air Force, which claimed that its wartime experience supporting special operations gave it a claim on the special warfare mission that SF thought was its own. Finally, as the 1950s progressed, SF distinguished itself from psychological operations, which slowly lost their all-inclusive character. Many in SF favored dissociating themselves from psychological operations because of the stigma these operations carried. The conventional Army, whose support SF needed to thrive, disdained psychological warfare as unworthy of a real soldier. SF did not want their own efforts seen in the same light.[23]

In the 1950s, SF faced an unfriendly environment. With the advent of the Eisenhower administration in 1953, the United States adopted a strategy of massive retaliation. The strategy called for the use of our nuclear arsenal to respond to threats. This was an effort to provide national security without bankrupting the United States, since nuclear weapons were cheaper than standing forces. In this strategy, it made sense to cut resources from the conventional forces, particularly the Army, and give them to nuclear forces. Such a restricted budget environment was a difficult one for a new force that many Army officers did not deem necessary. In part they did not think it necessary because they considered guerrilla war to be a smaller version of conventional war. If it was, then any infantry soldier should be able to take care of it. This undercut support for SF, whose existence hinged on the idea that guerrilla warfare was a special mission, for which special training was necessary. SF did deploy, for example to Laos, to help train indigenous forces but it remained unappreciated by the Army. The Army's first worldwide Combat Arms Conference in 1959 did not discuss special operations or unconventional warfare. When the Army created an official pedigree for SF in 1960, it traced its roots to such units as Rogers' Rangers, the First Special Service Force, and other elite raiding organizations, which had little or no connection to working with indigenous forces, rather than to the OSS, which did.

The strategy of massive retaliation made sense only on the assumption that the United States would use its nuclear weapons even when national survival was not at stake and that an opponent could not seriously damage the United States by fighting small wars where the use of nuclear weapons as a response would seem particularly disproportionate. Leaders of the Army thought neither of these assumptions valid. Army Chief of Staff Maxwell Taylor put his objections in writing when he left office. He argued that the United States would not in fact use its nuclear arsenal when anything less than national survival was at stake, and that the United States therefore needed a military able to respond to a variety of threats. His analysis matched the thinking of the Democratic candidate for President in 1960, John F. Kennedy, who upon assuming office changed America's defense strategy to "flexible response." Under this strategy, SF got a prominent role, since the strategy identified Marxist insurgency as a threat to the United States and SF as the force best suited to meet it. This mission was not what the Army had created SF to do, of course, but counterinsurgency, as it was called, was a mission that the new administration, from the president down, was willing to support.

The level of support the administration gave to the new mission of counterinsurgency showed how seriously the president and his advisers took it. The president spoke about it in public on several occasions, including a speech before a special session of Congress and another at West Point. The National Security Council issued a series of Action Memoranda on the subject. The administration set up a special high-level cabinet group to focus on counterinsurgency and several other lower-level interagency groups. The president met with the Joint Chiefs of Staff and sent memoranda to Secretary of Defense McNamara on the subject. The president's chief advisers also gave speeches and wrote articles on insurgency and counterinsurgency and visited military installations involved in the new mission to underline the importance that the administration attached to it. President Kennedy himself visited SF headquarters at Fort Bragg to review what SF was doing. Altogether, the administration's guidance to the military on what it wanted it to do in counterinsurgency was both emphatic and detailed.

The administration's efforts had some effect. The Army created another SF group, which focused on Vietnam, and a senior staff position to oversee counterinsurgency efforts. It wrote doctrine for counterinsurgency and increased the instruction in counterinsurgency in its schools. The Navy changed its UDTs into SEAL (Sea-Air-Land) teams, codifying and supporting the increased missions that the UDTs had taken on during the Korean War, and, in response to the administration's urgings, adding the mission of working with indigenous forces. The Air Force, which throughout the 1950s had provided support to SF and the CIA through several special operations units, responded to the administration's guidance for an effective counterinsurgency capability by reestablishing the composite air wings it had used in the World War II. Whereas in the early 1950s Air Force interest in special operations had appeared to the Army to threaten its turf, in the early 1960s, the Army's interest in providing air support for SF and other special operations appeared to the Air Force to threaten its turf. Eventually a rough compromise was reached in which the Army focused on supporting special operations with helicopters, while the Air Force used fixed-winged aircraft.

Although the Army and the Air Force eventually reached a workable compromise when it came to counterinsurgency, the military and the administration never did. The Kennedy administration called for the military to consider counterinsurgency, and unconventional warfare generally, to be as important as conventional warfare, and to organize, train, and equip itself accordingly.[24] The military never came close to accepting such an equality. Most of the change to accommodate the emphasis on counterinsurgency was superficial. Most Army doctrine and practice remained unchanged. Senior Army leaders disparaged counterinsurgency. As for the Navy, the changes it made were more a ratification of developments that the UDTs had been undergoing, which made them a raiding as well as reconnaissance force, than they were adaptation to the demands of counterinsurgency. All the services remained focused on a possible big war in Europe against the Soviet Union.

The failure of the U.S. military to take counterinsurgency seriously occurred not only at the strategic level, where it was defensible, but in Vietnam itself. Perhaps the best example of what happened to the counterinsurgency effort there is the saga of the Civilian Irregular Defense Groups. As part of efforts underway to increase the security of the South Vietnamese population, an Army officer working for the CIA came up with the idea of having U.S. forces train and advise Montagnards, tribal people living in the highlands of Vietnam. Trained and armed, they could protect their villages from the Vietcong. In the fall of 1961, SF began training and supporting the tribesmen, in a program run by the CIA. The units of tribesmen were called Civilian Irregular Defense Groups or CIDGs. In their support of the CIDG effort, Special Forces aimed at the insurgency's social-political center of gravity by winning the loyalty of the villagers. For example, they conducted medical assistance in the villages and included in the program other civil affairs activities, work with the United States Agency for International Development, and psychological operations. Working in the CIA program, supported by the agency's flexible and militarily unorthodox supply system and its money, Special Forces had control of its resources (people, time, money) and the latitude and flexibility to develop its counterinsurgency practices. While not without problems, the program succeeded. After reviewing CIDG activities in Vietnam in early 1963, the Special Assistant to the Chief of Staff for Special Warfare Activities reported that "the CIDG program holds the key to the attainment of the ultimate goal of a free, stable and secure Vietnam. In no other way does it appear possible to win support of the tribal groups, strangle Viet Cong remote area redoubts, and provide a reasonable basis for border patrol."[25]

The Army soon brought to an end the autonomy of SF in the CIDG program. As more villagers joined and the area under control of the South Vietnamese government increased, the CIA requested more SF. The more SF involvement in CIDG grew, the less the Army liked it. The Army leadership disliked having U.S. forces involved in operations that did not fit their strategy of engaging and destroying the enemy. They also disliked the fact that the CIDG program allowed military forces to operate outside the control of the regular military command structure. Secretary of Defense McNamara concurred with the Army leadership and decided to put the program under military control. On July 1, 1963, with the end of the CIA's logistic responsibility for the program, all control passed to the U.S. Military Assistance Command, Vietnam (MACV). From that time on, the U.S. Army assumed complete responsibility for SF activities in Vietnam.[26]

Once control of the CIDG program passed to the Army, operational control of SF detachments was transferred to MACV, which had little experience in counterinsurgency and used SF and the CIDGs in support of conventional operations and strategy, leaving population protection to the South Vietnamese Army. Village defense became less important, for example, as the CIDG training camps turned into bases for offensive strikes against Vietcong. With the assumption of the South Vietnamese border surveillance and control mission in 1963, the responsibilities of SF shifted further away from pacification and population security operations to missions viewed by the military hierarchy as more appropriate to and reflective of conventional Army doctrine. One consequence of this, in a now familiar pattern, was that CIDG units were used, in effect, as regular troops, a role for which they had not been trained.[27] To address this problem, the Army began organizing the CIDG as a more conventional force. They established a standardized table of organization and equipment for a CIDG light guerrilla company in an attempt to "standardize" indigenous forces for better pursuit of the Vietcong.[28] This completed the process of conventionalization, turning the CIDGs from a force focused on the counterinsurgency mission of protecting the population from Viet Cong and North Vietnamese attacks and intimidation to the conventional task of closing with and destroying enemy forces.

The indigenous units organized by Special Forces in Vietnam killed a lot of Vietcong, as did the raids and ambushes of Navy SEALs. Subordinate as these were to the strategy of attrition the U.S. military pursued, that was their purpose. But as with the strategy they served, these "kills" were to no avail. This is the story by and large of all special operations in Vietnam. They were all absorbed into a conventional effort that, for the critical years of the war, followed a strategy of attrition that was unlikely to produce success. For example, the Army organized some Long Range Reconnaissance Patrol (LRRP) units, eventually brought together as a Ranger regiment, that carried out missions in support of conventional forces similar to missions carried out by scout and raider units in World War II. Civil Affairs and PSYOP units also operated largely in support of conventional forces but were not seen as an important component of the military's activities in Vietnam.

The same ineffectiveness characterized the covert operations carried out in Vietnam by the Military Assistance Command Vietnam-Studies and Observation Group (MACV-SOG).The special operations assigned to the group included infiltrating personnel into North Vietnam to collect intelligence and carry out sabotage, attempting to limit the movement of materiel and people on the Ho Chi Minh trail into South Vietnam, and constructing an elaborate effort to deceive the North Vietnamese into thinking that there was a resistance movement operating in the North. As in the Korean War, virtually all of the infiltration efforts failed. A principal reason for the failure was that the infiltrators were supplied by South Vietnamese organizations the Viet Cong had penetrated. The deception effort did cause the North Vietnamese some concern, as did interdiction

efforts along the Ho Chi Minh trail, but neither of these operations affected the ability of the North Vietnamese to pursue their war aims. Despite
the undoubted bravery of the men who carried out the covert missions
and the tactical innovations they produced, covert special operations in
Vietnam were no more successful than their overt counterpart.[29]

Although the overall strategy in Vietnam was bad, this was not the only
reason for the ineffectiveness of special operations there. In response to
civilian pressure and a sense among civilians that somehow SOF were a
panacea,[30] SF grew rapidly from 1961 to 1966, adding three groups and
increasing their numbers sixfold, from 1,800 to 10,500.[31] To allow this
growth, the Army lowered standards for entry into SF. Rapid expansion
diminished quality and, more important, along with subordination to
the conventional military, made SF a more conventional force, a force
inclined like the conventional military to see its principal role to be closing with and destroying the enemy. A senior officer who observed SF in
Vietnam in the 1960s reported that some SF officers did not fully understand the difference between the requirements of counterinsurgency
(population protection) and unconventional warfare (training indigenous
people to attack the enemy).[32]

In its efforts to recover from Vietnam, the military came to blame the
vogue of counterinsurgency for many of its problems there. If only the
Army had been allowed by the politicians to fight its kind of war, the
outcome would have been different. Because counterinsurgency came to
stand for civilian interference in the war, and SF and SOF generally were
the forces most closely associated with counterinsurgency, they received
an inordinate share of the blame from the conventional military for the
failure in Vietnam. The fact that in the eyes of the conventional military, SOF had received an inordinate share of fame and publicity during
the war also contributed to their postwar neglect.[33] The LRRPs virtually
disappeared early in the post-Vietnam drawdown and Civil Affairs and
PSYOP forces were also cut drastically, as were SF themselves, which
went from seven groups to three. The number of SEALs was cut in half,
while the Air Force put in the reserves or eliminated most of the units
that had supported special operations in Vietnam.

During the 1970s, the military, in particular the Army, was refocusing
on the conflict with the Soviet Union, a conflict in which SF and unconventional warfare did not have a big role. In addition, certain activities
carried out by SOF in Vietnam strengthened the traditional view that spe-

cial units tended toward indiscipline or to flout the standards of military professionalism. The work of personnel from special units, particularly the SEALs, in the Phoenix program, an intelligence and targeting effort directed at the Viet Cong cadre, which was accused of carrying out assassinations, was one reason for this view. The charge of indiscipline was also given currency by the case of Colonel Robert Rheault, a commander of the 5th Special Forces Group in Vietnam, who was accused, along with several of his men, of murdering a Vietnamese double agent. For a variety of reasons, then, the 1970s were a period of decline for Special Operations Forces.

The low esteem in which the Army held SF manifested itself in a plan to revive the Rangers. The Chief of Staff of the Army, Creighton Abrams, believed that the United States needed a rapid reaction force to meet contingencies around the world. The hijacking of four airplanes to Jordan in 1970 and the attack on Israeli athletes at the 1972 Munich Olympics by Palestinian terrorists, as well as the worldwide alert of U.S. forces that accompanied the Yom Kippur war in 1973, suggested the need for such a force. Abrams believed that the 82nd Airborne Division, for example, could not mobilize quickly enough to serve as a quick reaction force, while SF could not mobilize enough people to fill this role. Abrams's solution was to reconstitute the Rangers. For Abrams, the Rangers also solved two other problems. First, the Marines were claiming to be the country's quick reaction force and the Army was in danger of losing that mission unless it developed a new rapid response capability. Second, Abrams, the last commander of American forces in Vietnam, did not like SF. The reconstituted Rangers could take Green Beret missions, which had grown to include such traditional Ranger missions as raids, reconnaissance, and target acquisition, thus justifying further cuts in SF numbers. Discussions among the Army's leadership gave the restored Ranger regiment the traditional Ranger missions of raids and reserved training foreign forces for SF. Civilian pressure had pushed the Army to cut Ranger force strength to make way for SF. In the aftermath of the war in Vietnam, the Army was now able to cut SF to make room for the Rangers.

Shortly after the agreement among Army leaders distinguished the roles of Rangers and Special Forces, another debate over roles emerged. The terrorist attacks that convinced Abrams that the United States needed a quick reaction force, convinced General Edward Meyer, then Deputy Chief of Staff for Operations, U.S. Army Europe, that the United States needed a force to counter terrorists. Meyer, who was concerned with more than just a force to fight terrorists, believed that the whole assortment of unconventional missions needed attention; but he focused on countering terrorists as the activity most likely to win acceptance in the Army.[34] Following his tour in Europe, Meyer joined the Army staff as the Deputy Chief of Staff for Plans and Operations. In that position, he oversaw the creation of a unit that could carry out an array of special missions, among them rescuing hostages being held by terrorists.

Two different already existing units in the Army argued that the new unit Meyer wanted was not necessary. The Rangers believed that the hostage rescue mission was theirs. Rescuing hostages required raiding techniques, and raiding was what the Rangers did. SF also claimed the mission. SF had conducted a raid at the end of the Vietnam War (Son Tay) to rescue POWs. Although the raid recovered no POWs (they had been moved), it went off flawlessly, showing, in the opinion of SF, that they were up to that sort of mission. Ultimately, Meyer and his supporters prevailed. Influenced by the example of the Israeli and German rescues of their citizens at the Entebbe airport in Uganda (1976) and in Mogadishu (1977), respectively, and President Carter's interest in those rescues, the Army agreed to establish the new special mission unit, which it activated in November 1977.

The new hostage rescue unit received its first big test in 1980, when it participated in the effort to rescue the Americans held hostage by the Iranians in Tehran. Although the hostage rescue unit was a permanent unit, the rest of the forces involved in the rescue attempt were brought together from the various services just for this mission. Marine pilots flew Navy helicopters and had to coordinate with Air Force pilots. This ad hoc arrangement was how the U.S. military had always met the need for forces to conduct special operations. This time, the effort ended in disaster. At the rendezvous point inside Iran, Desert One, the commander of the rescue attempt decided to call it off because several of the helicopters on the mission had suffered mechanical failures, leaving the rescuers without sufficient airlift to complete the mission. As the remaining helicopters and aircraft prepared to return to their starting points, a helicopter and aircraft collided causing an explosion and fire that killed eight. Celebrating a victory over their superpower rival, the Iranians later broadcast pictures of the ruined aircraft and charred remains of the crew members.

SOF as we now know them emerged from the ashes of Desert One. The official report on the rescue attempt concluded that had it failed not because it was infeasible or too complicated. It pointed instead to such things as the number of helicopters used, aspects of command and control, and concerns for security that prevented a full-scale rehearsal. It also noted that the forces used were an ad hoc collection rather than a permanent Joint Task Force. Such a permanent task force would have allowed the rescuers to focus on the details of the rescue mission rather than on cobbling their force together and attending to the unavoidable administrative and logistical matters that accompany even an operation of such importance.[35] The failed rescue convinced SOF and the U.S. military generally that special operations could no longer be carried out by ad hoc organizations. It also convinced them that special operations had to be joint, that training and operations had to unite SOF from all the services. The commitment to special operations carried out by permanent joint organizations manifested itself first in the establishment of a joint special mission unit dedicated to counterterrorism and eventually in the development of the Special Operations Command (SOCOM).

The failure at Desert One also prompted the Army to attend to its special operations aviation capabilities. The result was the establishment of the 160th Aviation Battalion in 1981. The 160th was put together with components from a variety of aviation units and specialized in low-level and night time helicopter operations. Since its establishment, it has supported SOF in all their major deployments. In 1990, the Army designated the unit the 160th Special Operations Aviation Regiment.

The failed rescue mission had a broader effect. It helped defeat President Carter and bring Ronald Reagan to office. The Reagan administration focused again on confrontation with the Soviet Union and on terrorism as one of the principal ways that the Soviet Union was attacking the United States and its allies. This focus on the Soviet Union and terrorism helped spur interest in SOF. The Republican platform in 1980, for example, called for their revival. At the same time, outside the administration, the failed rescue effort became one of the principal pieces of evidence used by SOF's supporters to argue that this component of America's military forces needed attention. These supporters consisted of former SOF officers serving in the Pentagon and on Capitol Hill and several civilian staff members on important Senate and House committees and in the Pentagon. Together they began a campaign to get SOF the resources and organizational structure they felt these forces needed. Ultimately, they persuaded a host of influential Senators and Congressmen to support SOF reform efforts. This level of support was necessary because although the administration emphasized the importance of terrorism and other unconventional warfare missions (counterinsurgency and support for insurgency chief among them), the Department of Defense continued, in the eyes of the reformers, to neglect SOF. The bureaucratic inertia of the Services and the Pentagon trumped the concern expressed in the Republican platform and by some of the Reagan administration's officials. For example, Congress provided money for aircraft to support special operations, but the Air Force reprogrammed it for fighter aircraft. In addition to this neglect, the invasion of Grenada (1983) to rescue medical students and oust a government friendly to Cuba added impetus to the effort to reform SOF. Operations in Grenada revealed deficiencies in SOF equipment, misuse of their capabilities, command and control problems, and limits to the military's ability to operate jointly.

In response to the pressure from the reformers, the Pentagon established the Joint Special Operations Agency in 1984. This did little to satisfy the reformers, however, since the agency did not have direct control of any SOF. The reformers ultimately introduced legislation in both houses of Congress to address the problems they believed existed with the nation's SOF. After the Senate and House compromised on their separate proposals, the SOF reform legislation became law in 1986. The legislation, known as the Nunn-Cohen amendment, established SOCOM, with a four-star General in charge, bringing SOF from all the services under one command. In addition, it gave the Command its own line in the defense budget and the authority to develop and acquire SOF-specific equipment; specified what missions constituted special operations (direct action, strategic reconnaissance, unconventional warfare, foreign internal defense, civil affairs, psychological operations, counterterrorism, humanitarian assistance, theater search and rescue,[36] and other activities that the president or secretary of defense might designate); established the Office of the Assistant Secretary of Defense for Special Operations and Low-Intensity Conflict in the Office of the Secretary of Defense, to provide civilian oversight of the Command and its budgeting and acquisition activities; created a low-intensity conflict board in the National Security Council; and required the appointment of an assistant to the president for low-intensity conflict.[37]

The Reagan administration, bowing to pressure from the Pentagon and reluctant to acquiesce readily in such a sweeping Congressional redesign of the executive branch, opposed the legislation and implemented it slowly. It did set up SOCOM (activated April 1987) but in Tampa, Florida, far from the Pentagon. It delayed nominating an assistant secretary for special operations. Congress ultimately had to step in and resolve this problem. Neither the Reagan administration nor its successors ever set up a functioning low-intensity conflict board in the NSC or an adviser to the president for this kind of conflict. Additional legislation was necessary to implement SOCOM's acquisition of SOF-specific equipment.

The administration's opposition to Congressional plans for SOF and its reluctant implementation of the Nunn-Cohen amendment was based on its judgment that SOF were receiving sufficient support and did not need the special arrangements that the law required. In its defense, the administration pointed to the fact that the budget for SOF had increased over threefold between 1981 and 1987, from $441 million to $1.6 billion.[38] The reformers responded that most of the increase in SOF resources had gone for capabilities useful in conventional conflicts. While important, these were, in the reformers' minds, not the only or the most important conflicts the United States would face.[39] Some reformers even believed that unconventional conflict—insurgency, terrorism, guerrilla warfare—would determine the winner of the Cold War. This was the most fundamental disagreement between the administration and the reformers. The administration did not accept the reformers' argument that unconventional threats were the most important threats the United States faced. Therefore, the administration disagreed with the judgment of Congress that unconventional conflicts and SOF were more important to the national defense than the tanks, aircraft carriers, and fighter jets that the military preferred to buy.

As it turned out, the administration was more right than Congress. The Cold War ended on terms favorable to the United States without the increased capabilities that Congress wanted having had much effect. SOCOM eventually came to include Army Special Forces, the 160th Aviation Regiment, the Navy SEALs, Civil Affairs and Psychological warfare units, the Rangers and the Air Force's special warfare units. Yet, the Command and the other reforms Congress mandated had little effect before the Soviet Union started to implode. Operations to support insurgency against Russian-backed forces in Afghanistan and to counter Marxist insurgencies in Central America contributed to the defeat of the Soviet Union, the former perhaps significantly, but by themselves would not have brought about this defeat. On the other hand, absent American involvement in these unconventional conflicts, it is possible to imagine a combination of Soviet economic and social incompetence, NATO cohesion, Western economic expansion, and technological advances in America's military capabilities dooming the Soviet Union. The Cold War was won by a system that the reformers believed was incompetent to handle America's security, not by the innovation they worked so hard to bring about.

If they did not help win the Cold War, the reformers' efforts, along with other changes, such as SF becoming a branch in the Army (1987), did improve the readiness of SOF and its standing in the military. Not long after its activation in 1987, SOCOM and its forces were showcased in several operations. SOF performed well in an extended series of small engagements against Iranian forces attempting to disrupt shipping in the Persian Gulf in late 1987 and 1988, and shortly thereafter, in Operation Just Cause where they spearheaded efforts to depose Panamanian dictator Manuel Noriega. SOF secured even more plaudits from the conventional military during the first Gulf War in 1992. Displaying an attitude often found among conventional officers at the time, Central Command, commanded by General Norman Schwarzkopf, was at first reluctant to use SOF. Pressed to do so by authorities in Washington, Schwarzkopf ultimately employed SOF somewhat conservatively and later conceded that they had performed well in support of conventional force operations. As the 1990s progressed, SOF became involved in a series of contingency operations, from noncombatant evacuations in Africa to providing order in the interior of Haiti, that demonstrated their versatility. In the late 1990s, the Government Accounting Office found that the regional combatant commanders and their staffs considered special forces "an essential element for achieving U.S. national security objectives" and the "force of choice for many diverse combat and peacetime missions."[40] These operations called on the full array of SOF's skills, including civil affairs and psychological operations, and showed the utility of having forces who could work easily with indigenous military forces. The one setback in this string of operational successes was in Somalia, which we discuss in detail in the next chapter.

SOF also picked up a new mission in the 1990s, counterproliferation. The Clinton administration came to office convinced that addressing the problem of the spread of weapons of mass destruction (WMD) was important. Military analysts also thought this problem significant, as the increased prevalence of WMD would complicate fighting regional wars. Yet, the military generally was reluctant to accord more importance to proliferation. Facing significant cuts in funding and personnel, the military was reluctant to take on a new mission. SOF was not. As the Cold War ended, SOF, like the rest of the military, was searching for relevance. This problem was more acute for SOF than for conventional or general purpose forces because, in a way, SOF could be seen as a luxury. SOF could not do what conventional forces do but, when necessary, conventional forces could be pressed into service to do most of what SOF did. Not being specially trained and equipped, general-purpose forces would not do special operations as well as SOF, but in an austere budget environment "not as well" might be thought well enough. SOF were acutely aware of this possibility, as were their supporters, some of whom tried to establish the relevance of SOF to a budget-conscious Congress and peace-minded public by suggesting that, among other things, SOF might teach languages in inner city schools. Always aware of the need to show its relevance, SOF responded to the Clinton administration's lead and embraced countering the proliferation of WMD as a new mission. SOF's part in this mission fell to the special mission units, which developed techniques for dealing with "loose nukes" and other devices that the United States might need to seize and render safe. As the 1990s progressed and the threat from terrorism receded, counterproliferation became the principal mission of these special units. As they continued to take the most important missions assigned to SOF, and unconventional warfare—SOF working by, through, and with indigenous people—faded in importance because of its association with counterinsurgency and the Cold War, the special missions units came to dominate the special operations community. For example, the officers who achieved highest rank in SOF tended to come from the special mission units and the Rangers.

In the 1990s, the special units also continued the practice of training and consulting with law enforcement Special Weapons and Tactics Teams. This practice came under review following the siege of the Branch Davidian compound in Waco, Texas. The fiery demolition of the compound in April 1993 by the Federal Bureau of Investigation and the Bureau of Alcohol, Tobacco and Firearms led to accusations of excessive and inappropriate use of force. The report that some members of SOF units had reviewed the assault plan led SOCOM to restrict consultation and training with law enforcement. These restrictions, however, did not prevent SF from participating in counterdrug operations in the United States later in the 1990s. In these operations, SOF conducted the kind of long-term surveillance that was part of their strategic reconnaissance mission. SOF also provided another kind of support to law enforcement. In December 1999, the arrest of Ahmed Ressam in Seattle, Washington led authorities to believe that they had come across a plot to carry out terrorist attacks in the United States to coincide with the millennium celebrations. Short of Arabic speakers, the FBI requested the assistance of SF. Several soldiers who spoke Arabic assisted the FBI with its investigation of Ressam and the larger plot.[41]

As the 1990s drew to a close, SOF had become more integrated into and accepted by the American military establishment than ever before. This was the result of a deliberate effort by SOF, in response to institutional and bureaucratic pressures from within the military. At the activation ceremony for SOCOM in 1987, Admiral William Crowe, then the JCS chairman, who had been an opponent of the new command, offered the following advice to the command and its new commander, General Lindsay

> First, break down the wall that has more or less come between special operations forces and the other parts of our military, the wall that some people will try to build higher. Second, educate the rest of the military— spread a recognition and understanding of what you do, why you do it, and how important it is that you do it. Last, integrate your efforts into the full spectrum of our military capabilities.[42]

Without suggesting whether SOF or conventional forces were responsible, Crowe's comments indicated the problem that existed between SOF and the rest of the military. The conventional military saw SOF as outsiders whose capabilities and even reason for existence were largely unknown. In a 1992 interview, SOCOM's commander in effect paraphrased Crowe's remarks, distancing SOF from the idea of "unconventional warfare" because it suggested that SF "were outside the mainstream Army." Instead, the commander wanted to send the message that the United States had "very capable special operations forces that are partners— work together—with other elements of the armed forces to accomplish the mission."[43] Ironically, even as they were being deemphasized, it was

SOF's unconventional warfare capabilities that made them so useful, such good partners, in operations in the Balkans, Haiti, Colombia, Liberia, and elsewhere, whereas its direct-action capabilities, for example in Somalia, sometimes generated controversy and less than the hoped for results.

In fairness to those who conduct and favor SOF's direct-action missions, especially when they are undertaken independent of other forces, one must acknowledge that such missions often occur when other options have been foreclosed and operational and political risk is high. This was clearly so in the case of the Iranian hostage rescue. We discuss in detail another example, Somalia, in chapter 4. In such circumstances, failure is not unlikely and carries a big penalty. This is an important respect in which these missions differ from the typical unconventional warfare mission. It also explains why, as the threat from Islamic extremism rose in the later 1990s, SOF were not called on to carry out direct-action missions against al-Qaeda in Afghanistan. Civilian and military leaders with the ultimate responsibility to approve such missions simply did not think that the potential gain from such operations justified the risks involved. This assessment rested in part on an assessment of the threat posed by this extremism.[44]

The terrorist attack on September 11, 2001, changed that assessment and brought greater prominence to SOF than they had enjoyed since the early 1960s. The Bush administration turned to the CIA and SF because a conventional attack against the Taliban and al-Qaeda in Afghanistan would have taken too long to mount. The agency facilitated contact between SF units and members of the Northern Alliance, a movement resisting Taliban dominance of Afghanistan. Operating in some cases on horseback and always in difficult conditions, SF supplied, directed, and fought alongside the Northern Alliance forces against the Taliban. Using laser designators, SF and Air Force combat controllers directed Navy and Air Force bombing runs that shattered Taliban resistance. Throughout the campaign, Air Force special operations aircraft supported SF and their indigenous allies. As we saw in one of the interviews in chapter 1, the operation that destroyed the Taliban was a textbook case of SF working with local forces to achieve U.S. objectives. In doing so, SF combined traditional infantry skills, high technology, political guile, and a sensitivity to the preferences and beliefs of their indigenous allies.

Following the rout of the Taliban, SF teams continued to work with indigenous forces and the local population to capture or kill what was left of the Taliban and al-Qaeda. The teams trained and led Afghan military forces, providing security to the local population and using the medical and other skills resident on the teams to win the confidence and support of local populations. From this confidence and support, which came to teams even when they were operating in tribal areas supportive of the Taliban, came the information that allowed the teams to identify those they needed to kill or capture. In operating in this way, SF was conducting unconventional warfare. In this type of warfare, military operations do not aim directly or even primarily at killing or capturing the enemy but, rather, at building influence among the population by providing it security and other assistance. As these military operations produce influence with the local population, they also produce as a byproduct the intelligence that allows U.S. forces to kill and capture key enemy leaders and organizers. The unconventional warfare effort that followed the collapse of the Taliban was not part of a larger plan, however, which became clear as the numbers of conventional forces in Afghanistan grew and they came to dominate the U.S. military presence there.

A lieutenant general from a conventional Army unit took charge of ground operations in Afghanistan in November 2001, about a month after SF teams first set foot in the country. Conventional Army personnel were in Mazar-e-Sharif in early December. Large deployments of conventional Army units did not appear in Afghanistan, however, until later. Elements of the 101st Airborne Division, for example, arrived in January 2002. Conventional force deployments continued to grow in the spring and summer. As they did, conflicts with Special Forces came into the open. These received coverage in the media in September 2002 with reports, reminiscent of the First Air Commando's experience in World War II, that the Army leadership had told SF personnel in Afghanistan to shave their beards and dress in regular uniforms. One report explained the order as the result of complaints from relief agencies, whose work in Afghanistan was critical to the U.S. government's objective of getting the country functioning again. The relief workers feared, reportedly, that they might be mistaken for SF and thus be put at risk. While the objection from the relief agencies may have been part of the explanation for the order to SF to look more like regular soldiers, it was also clear that tensions existed between SF and the conventional military. SF felt that the conventional military units did not work enough with the local population and in fact used tactics that did not respect local customs and thus alienated the indigenous population and put at risk the collection of the intelligence necessary to kill or capture Taliban and al-Qaeda. Conventional commanders, for their part, expressed incomprehension at the tactics of the Special Forces. "I don't know what they are trying to achieve," one told a reporter. Behind such comments appeared to be the general sense that the SF were not acting as soldiers should. The chief spokesman for coalition forces in Afghanistan, an American Army colonel, told a reporter at one point that it was better to have larger conventional units operating in Afghanistan because this allows us "to get the use of them we're supposed to."[45]

The result of such attitudes was that post-conflict operations in Afghanistan came to be more and more conventional. Instead of working through, by, and with indigenous people to build the trust and influence that might lead to better intelligence and produce a social environment inhospitable to al-Qaeda and the Taliban, the principal objective of military operations became the direct pursuit of "high value targets," important enemy personnel. In this understanding, intelligence results from such operations through interrogations and the seizure of documents or by sweeps through villages where indigenous people are screened and questioned. Often in such operations, intelligence comes from paid informants or agents, who can use their role as agents to settle personal or clan scores. By late summer 2002, SF dress and appearance had changed while getting approval for operations had become more difficult. Initially, SF teams had authority to conduct operations in their areas of responsibility, but this was slowly curtailed as conventional forces and approaches became more dominant. In late September, the same colonel who had spoken in favor of larger numbers of conventional forces operating in Afghanistan told reporters that the military focus was not humanitarian operations. "Currently the main mission of the force is to close with and destroy the enemy."[46]

The difficulty with this approach is that it is unlikely to work well if the enemy is not in fact an organized military force that can be closed with. Although the Taliban and al-Qaeda were the military force of the de facto governing power in most of Afghanistan, neither was an organized military force in the conventional sense. The Taliban could put fighters in the field and to some degree control their movements, but this military force had only a minimal existence as a separate institution. It was more a tribal militia than a professional military force.[47] The numbers in the field and their discipline derived more from tribal connections and traditions than from the rules and incentives of a separate military institution. When American armed force made it impossible for the Taliban to operate militarily in large numbers, this did not reduce members of the Taliban's militia to isolated individuals or small groups. They remained members of the tribe or, in the case of at least some of al-Qaeda's members, under the protection of the tribe with the added protection of a religious sanction that transcended tribe. In defeat as in victory, the Taliban was principally not a military or even a political organization. It relied on preexisting and deeply rooted tribal connections, which, in a tribal society such as Afghanistan, made it a prefabricated political movement. In chapter 7, we will return to this issue and consider some ways that the U.S. government might improve its ability to operate against such traditional social structures. For the time being, the point to note is that having thought of the Taliban and al-Qaeda as a military force to be destroyed as it invaded Afghanistan, the U.S. military continued to think of them that way once it had disorganized them. Hence, post-conventional conflict operations retained a conventional character.

If SF experience in Afghanistan showed the limitations of SOF integration into the American military establishment, the role of SOF in the Iraq war (April 2003) showed how far SOF had come in this regard. In the first Gulf War, General Schwarzkopf had used SOF reluctantly and conservatively. In the second war, SOF was part of the plan from the beginning and given responsibility for the western desert of Iraq, where, operating in small groups on specially designed desert vehicles, they performed reconnaissance missions, hunted for SCUD rockets, the launching of which could have seriously threatened U.S. and allied forces, and took control of an air base. In northern Iraq, SOF directed, supported, and fought with Kurdish forces that drove out the Iraqis and took control of Mosul, the most important city in the north. They also attacked and destroyed the base of Ansar-al-Islam, a terrorist group associated with al-Qaeda. Because Turkey would not allow the Fourth Infantry Division to enter Iraq through Turkish territory, SOF's ability to lead the fight in the North became the decisive element in victory in that area of operations. In a tacit acknowledgment of the importance of SOF in the fight in northern Iraq, for the first time in American military history, conventional brigades were placed under the command of a SOF Colonel.

Although there was tension between SOF and the conventional forces in both Afghanistan, and, as we saw in the account of civil affairs in chapter 1, in Iraq, overall the war on terrorism has shown that SOF is better integrated into the nation's military strategy and operations than it has ever been. It has also highlighted SOF's versatility. SOF were able to work with conventional forces and indigenous personnel in a variety of conflict environments around the world, from Iraq to the Philippines. As the war on terrorism continued, SOF also carried out their more normal activities, such as training foreign forces involved in interdicting drug trafficking. As the war on terrorism showed SOF's utility, it also created new opportunities and questions for these forces. The Bush administration's focus on capturing and killing terrorists through direct action has reinforced the preeminence within SOF of the units that carry out those missions and led even its unconventional warfare forces to put greater emphasis on "warrior skills."[48] As a result, the administration pushed to have the Marines take more responsibility for the training of foreign forces, a traditional SOF mission that the administration no longer values highly, in hopes that this will allow SOF to focus on direct action. Similarly, at one time, the administration was apparently thinking of moving responsibility for civil affairs from SOCOM to conventional forces, at least in part to allow SOCOM to better concentrate on direct action. (CA and PSYOP reserve forces were moved from SOCOM to another command.) The administration has also ordered SOF to develop intelligence and other operational capabilities that were once held to be solely the responsibility of the CIA. Finally, the administration has given SOCOM new responsibilities for planning and directing operations in the war on terrorism. This means that SOCOM must change from a command that largely supported other commands by providing combat ready special operators to one that is in charge of operations and that other commands support.

Are these changes right for SOF and the national defense? What missions should SOF concentrate on? How should they be organized and what are the best command and control arrangements for these forces? How is the changing character of war and conflict affecting SOF? We address these questions in the chapters that follow. Before doing so, however, we examine in detail SOF operations in Somalia in 1993. This case shows that questions about appropriate missions, organization, and command and control arise not just from current operational concerns but are inherent in SOF.

SOMALIA

LITTLE MORE THAN A YEAR after SOF had shown in the Gulf War that it could operate effectively in support of a major military operation, it had a chance to prove that it could perform just as well independently, as the lead force charged with resolving a significant problem, when President Bush decided to intervene in Somalia. Fractious warlords were preventing the rapid distribution of aid to the needy, and the president decided to try to prevent the mass starvation of millions of Somalis. Initially, SOF accompanied the Marines to Somalia and performed admirably in their support. Eventually U.S. forces passed the mission to a United Nations command. When the situation deteriorated, SOF were sent back to Somalia to take the lead in dealing with the most troublesome warlord, Mohammed Farah Aideed. The assumption was that if SOF could capture or eliminate Aideed, the other warlords would fall in line and negotiate a new government with the United Nations.

Unfortunately, as mentioned in the previous chapter, the SOF mission was not successful. On October 3, 1993, SOF forces were forced into a protracted engagement with Aideed's forces after one of their helicopters was shot down by a rifle-propelled grenade. After inflicting close to a thousand casualties on the enemy and losing eighteen soldiers, the Rangers and special mission unit members were extracted by tardy UN conventional forces. The United States negotiated for the release of the lone special operator that Aideed had captured and then left Somalia to its fate. The proposition that Aideed was the singular problem preventing national reconciliation was not tested until years later when Aideed died in Somalia's continuing orgy of factional fighting. As it turned out, the internecine conflict continued despite his

death, but some would say that was because the steadying hand of the
United Nations and its forces had long since departed in the wake of
the October 3 disaster.

Somalia is a worthy case study because it perfectly illustrates how
SOF can be misused and why it can be difficult to use them to accomplish policymaker objectives. However, it is not possible to extract the
lessons of Somalia for SOF without first having a solid understanding
of what happened and why. The immediate tactical situation as it developed in Somalia is important, but so is the decision-making in Washington and at the United Nations. Ultimately, the use of SOF in Somalia
cannot be evaluated without understanding the way national objectives
evolved and were (or were not) communicated to SOF commanders in
the field.

DEBATE OVER THE SCOPE OF THE SOMALI
INTERVENTION OBJECTIVES

In 1992, the United States was providing airlift and relief supplies in
support of the United Nations assistance effort in Somalia. About two
thousand C-130 sorties were made in support of humanitarian relief efforts. The United States also airlifted Pakistani peacekeepers to Somalia,
but they were soon pinned down in Mogadishu and unable to ensure safe
delivery of humanitarian assistance to those parts of the country most in
need. Aid officials estimated that as many as two million Somalis were
at risk of starvation. The third week of November 1992, President Bush
decided to use U.S. military forces to lead a multinational force to ensure
that the aid was delivered. Operation Restore Hope began on December
7, pursuant to United Nations Security Council Resolution 794 adopted
on December 5, 1992.

President Bush's decision to intervene in Somalia came at an awk-
ward time. Following the president's defeat in the November election,
the government was in the midst of one of its quadrennial turnovers.
No one in the Office of the Secretary of Defense knew precisely why
President Bush made the decision to intervene in Somalia, although the
dominant motive appeared to be genuine humanitarian concern. He did
so after consulting with top advisers at a National Security Council meeting, selecting the most muscular option from an earlier Deputies Com-

mittee Meeting. Most accounts indicate there was very little thinking about or analysis of the longer-term implications of intervention. The president's principal military adviser, the Chairman of the Joint Chiefs of Staff, General Colin Powell, expressed concerns about whether conditions in Somalia would permit a smooth handoff to a UN peacekeeping force after a relatively brief deployment of U.S. troops. Nevertheless, this was precisely the U.S. plan. At a press conference on December 4, 1992, Secretary of Defense Dick Cheney said: "We believe it necessary to send in U.S. forces to provide U.S. leadership to get the situation stabilized and return it to a state where the normal UN peacekeeping forces can deal with the circumstances."[1] U.S. Marines arrived in Somalia on December 7, preceded by Special Operations Forces and followed by U.S. Army and coalition forces. The total U.S. force reached 29,000, plus some 10,000 coalition forces and was called The United Task Force or UNITAF. President Bush named Ambassador Robert Oakley, who had previously served as Ambassador to Somalia, as special envoy. He arrived in December to take charge of the political and diplomatic dimensions of the mission.

While the Marines were told to prevent the mass starvation of Somalis through a brief and limited intervention that would quickly transition to UN forces, it was apparent early on that the UN defined the problem and the mission more broadly. The United Nations wanted to establish conditions that would preclude another famine in the future and resolve the underlying problems that had led to the civil war. In particular, the UN pushed hard for more aggressive disarmament of all Somalis. As early as November, the U.S. diplomatic mission to the United Nations in New York was agreeing with the UN position, arguing that the United States had a stake in strengthening UN peacekeeping operations, and that it was in the U.S. interest that the UN should succeed in bringing peace to Somalia. In Washington, D.C., other officials in the Department of State also agreed with the United Nations about intervention objectives in general and disarmament in particular. The point repeatedly made by the Department of State was that ignoring the larger security problem meant that the delivery of aid would only temporarily solve the humanitarian crisis. Officials in the Department of State argued that the United States should address the disarmament issue quickly, decisively, and comprehensively, and that failure to do so could seriously complicate the follow-on UNOSOM II peacekeeping operation, which in turn would jeopardize long-term prospects for Somali peace and reconciliation. Ultimately, the Department of State believed that the United States would be held to account for undertaking an operation that addressed only the symptoms and not the causes of the Somali disaster.

Other parts of the Bush administration resisted the broader mission proposed by the United Nations and Department of State. The Department of Defense succeeded in convincing National Security Council officials that the human tragedy in Somalia did not affect U.S. national security interests. The leadership left in the Department of Defense at the time argued that the U.S. mission was famine relief. Resolving broader problems was not a prerequisite for taking immediate steps to ensure food distribution. Thus, it was argued that U.S. forces should be used to establish security at ports, airfields, and on convoys, but not to establish countrywide security. The limited goal was to provide enough local security to permit the distribution of aid at a level that staved off immediate mass starvation. Defense officials worried that if U.S. and coalition forces attempted to involuntarily disarm the warlords there would be protracted resistance, which simply was not in the interests of the United States. From Mogadishu, Ambassador Oakley also weighed in against forcible disarmament as unrealistic and idealistic. The National Security Council in November and December of 1992 sided with the Defense Department in favor of limited disarmament just to ensure a safe environment for U.S. military forces, and not as a more general objective. Thus, in mid-December the president as well as the Departments of State and Defense made it clear publicly that the United States did not view disarmament as an objective in and of itself, but rather as a limited means to accomplish the humanitarian mission.

The United Nations remained unhappy with this policy and continued to press the United States to do more. The prerequisite conditions for the UN accepting a mission turnover from U.S. forces, identified in a report from the Secretary General that was required by UN Security Council Resolution 794, amounted to general disarmament of the warlords throughout Somalia, and not just in key famine areas. While disarmament was the key UN requirement, the more ambitious goals of UN leadership included seizing large weapons stocked around Galcaio in the north of Somalia, building a police force, and rehabilitating infrastructure. In general, the United Nations wanted to leave behind a new and functioning Somali government. Toward that end, UN leaders resisted creating a follow-on force to take over from the United States until U.S. forces had established nation-wide security. UNITAF forces and Ambassador Oakley's staff worked out a voluntary disarmament plan with the Somali factions and offered it in late February 1993 to the UN for implementation, but the UN preferred instead to continue to pressure the United States to disarm the Somalis.

During this time of transition, Congress was confirming Clinton administration officials, who were finding their way to their new positions in the national security bureaucracy. Many were more sympathetic to the UN and Department of State positions on Somalia, including some in the Department of Defense, and policy evolved accordingly. They agreed that Somalia was a test case of whether a multilateral institution in the post–Cold War world could use armed force effectively to bring governance to a wartorn country. The initial Clinton administration national security policy stressed the importance of "aggressive multilateralism," so it was consistent to argue that it was in the United States' interest to help ensure that the first attempt at forceful peacemaking by the United Nations was a success. If it was not, the United States would continue to be called upon to shoulder the majority of the burden whenever such problems of general import to the international community arose.

Many Clinton appointees supported the broader mandate for the UN intervention in Somalia.[2] For example, Ambassador Frank Wisner, a career State Department officer and the Under Secretary of Defense for Policy, the principal policymaker in defense matters beside the secretary of defense, was sympathetic to the Department of State's arguments. Other Pentagon officials looked askance at the nation-building mission of resurrecting Somali political, economic, and security institutions before U.S. forces departed. General Powell testified later that he was not informed of and disagreed with the mission to disarm. General Joseph Hoar, the regional commander responsible for Somalia, himself a Marine, was particularly alert to attempts to saddle the Marines with a general disarmament mission, but he had support from the Joint Staff and some career officials in the Defense Department as well.[3]

It took time for the Clinton administration to sort out its conflicting views, overcome bureaucratic resistance, and establish its policy. In the meantime, U.S. and coalition forces aggressively enforced their day-to-day rules about Somalis bearing arms and placing heavy weapons in controlled areas, but they did not go out of their way to track down weapons being hidden by Aideed (or others). As Ambassador Oakley argued, "given the limited ... mandate, which deliberately excluded general disarmament, there was no perceived need to confront Aideed over the disappearance of weapons as long as they posed no threat to UNITAF forces or humanitarian operations."[4]

Despite internal bureaucratic debate and UN foot dragging, the limited mission viewpoint prevailed. U.S. forces went ahead and prepared to withdraw in the spring of 1993 without having secured a general disarmament of the Somali factions, and this course of action finally prompted the UN to pull together a follow-on force. The United States did agree, however, in keeping with the Clinton administration emphasis on UN success, to remain engaged with the follow-on UN forces and to facilitate their efforts by providing six thousand personnel for logistics assistance and a small quick reaction force in case UN forces ran into trouble they could not handle. In addition, Ambassador Oakley, who had coordinated his political efforts so closely with Marine military operations, was replaced by another senior American official. Admiral Jonathan Howe was chosen to lead the follow-on UN force (called UNOSOM II, "United Nations Operation in Somalia," and the successor to UNOSOM I, which ran from April 1992 to March 1993) as the Special Representative of the Secretary General of the United Nations.

POLICY, STRATEGY, AND THE TRANSITION TO UN COMMAND

In the first week of February, not long after the new president took office, the Clinton national security team reviewed policy on Somalia, after which they decided to focus on what could be done to prevent Somalia from falling back into anarchy and famine. By March the new administration had established a policy of helping ensure the success of the Somali "testbed" for UN peacekeeping, but acknowledged that the Somali people had to seize the historic opportunity offered by the U.S. and UN interventions. If not, more modest goals might be in order, but the minimum goal would be to ensure that Somalia did not return to the anarchy that precluded relief assistance from being distributed. These goals required assisting the UNOSOM II mission.

If the UN force was to be successful, it clearly had to be at least as potent a force as the one the Marines had assembled. In testimony to Congress on January 29, the senior Pentagon military official in charge of operations promised that the follow-on UNOSOM II mission would, in fact, be structured to have essentially the same capability as the U.S. intervention force it was relieving. Many doubted that the UN force would be effective, however. Even if total planned numbers were similar, its combat capability was seriously doubted, which is why the U.S.-led quick reaction force was left behind. In addition, an internal Pentagon field assessment in late spring noted other critical shortfalls, including the woefully inadequate special operations and particularly psychological operations capability. Under UNITAF, Army Special Forces monitored and influenced various warlords around the country, and Psychological Operations forces constantly communicated coalition perspectives to the host population during operations. Both had received high marks from Ambassador Oakley and Lieutenant General Robert Johnson, the military commander of UNITAF, and many thought their absence in the follow-on UN forces was a crippling defect.[5]

Robust UN force capabilities were even more important because the UNOSOM II mission mandate was significantly broadened in keeping with long-standing UN and Department of State preferences. With enthusiastic U.S. support, the Security Council gave UNOSOM II a much broader mission than UNITAF. UNOSOM II was to establish security, political reconciliation, and economic reconstruction. Emblematic of the Clinton administration position at this juncture was U.S. Ambassador to the UN Madeleine Albright's March 1993 statement that "we will embark on an unprecedented enterprise aimed at nothing less than the restoration of an entire country as a proud, functioning and viable member of the community of nations."[6]

Albright's enthusiasm may have reflected the predominant attitude among senior administration officials, but many in the Department of Defense remained unconvinced. As decisions about how much to assist the UNOSOM II efforts were debated, it remained clear that the fundamental schism over interpretations of U.S. national interest remained. Those who believed that the United States had no national interests that would justify a nation-building effort in Somalia, which they judged to be an enormous undertaking, were unenthusiastic about helping the UN. They further argued that it was not in the UN's interests either, pointing

out that scarce UN peacekeeping assets were stretched thin and that Somalia was one of the few peacekeeping challenges in the world that did
not threaten to blow up into a larger regional conflict.

Those arguing the United States and United Nations had a lot at
stake—prestige, credibility, precedent for future crises—wanted both to
stay the course and prevail. They pointed out that the Somalia intervention was a Chapter VII peace enforcement precedent,[7] and that it was
in the interest of the United States that the effort be seen as a success,
both for what it said about U.S. leadership and because the United States
needed a strong UN as a partner in conflict resolution.

Clinton administration policy statements attempted to resolve this
tension by insisting the Somali people must be responsible for their future, and simultaneously noting that they needed help to make the transition to national self-governance. The UN was to bear the burden, but
the United States would help initially, and gradually wind down even that
modest support. The upshot was that a large proficient U.S. force (essentially the Marines, Army, and SOF, with numerous small international
contributing forces, in the form of UNITAF I) completed a limited and
manageable mission, and then passed on a vastly increased and more
difficult set of responsibilities to a much less proficient force (UNOSOM
II) in May 1993. In short, insufficient means were employed to secure
greatly expanded objectives. American policy and strategy for Somalia
was long on hope and short on a sober calculation of requirements.

UNOSOM II IS CHALLENGED

With few casualties (eight servicemen through mid-May), the Marines
had been relatively successful in adopting a posture of impartiality and
responding forcefully but fairly to any challenge to their authority and
mission. UNOSOM II would not be nearly as successful on any of these
counts. Aideed perceived the UNOSOM II mission as hostile to his interests. Before the UN intervention, Aideed was clearly the strongest
warlord, controlling most of Mogadishu and much of southern and central Somalia. Aideed increasingly felt threatened militarily not only by
UNOSOM II but also by rival warlords. For example, in late February,
Aideed suffered a military setback in Kismayo, a city in southern Somalia. Omar Jess, a local warlord allied with Aideed, was forced out of

Kismayo by Hersi Morgan's forces in a surprise attack under the nose of Belgian and U.S. Army soldiers who were charged with keeping the peace there. An angry Aideed held UNITAF responsible and encouraged large-scale anti-UN demonstrations in Mogadishu that rocked the city for days. Politically, Aideed was threatened by UNOSOM II as well, since it seemed inclined to abandon the top-down political reconstruction begun at a January conference in Addis Ababa, where the power of the warlords was recognized, in favor of bottom-up political reconstruction through elected regional and district councils that would limit the power of the warlords. Ali Mahdi, Aideed's toughest political competitor, had formed a political alliance of eleven factions that managed to consistently outvote Aideed's Somali National Army (SNA) faction at UN-sponsored conferences.

In response, Aideed mounted an increasingly hostile public relations campaign against the UNOSOM II forces and mission. The United States encouraged a more aggressive public relations campaign to counter Aideed's propaganda, but the UN was unable to respond effectively. Over the course of May it was clear to all concerned that the UN was failing to make its case to the Somali people. Whereas the Marines and SOF's 4th Psychological Operations Group had over 150 personnel working on information dissemination with a Somali-language radio station and daily newspaper, UNOSOM II had less than five persons working on information full-time. In addition, and in contrast with UNOSOM II—which gradually decided to ignore Aideed—UNITAF leadership had maintained a constant high-level dialogue with Somali leaders of all factions, including Aideed. In light of the propaganda beating the UN was taking, some felt that Aideed's radio station had to be silenced one way or another. And, of course, there was the general disarmament mission to attend to as well. Both the need to silence Aideed, since the UN could not compete with his rhetoric, and the need to disarm Aideed, in keeping with the broader UN mission, put the UN on a collision course with Aideed's forces.

The collision was not a surprise; indeed it was fully expected and even welcomed by both sides. In mid-May it was rumored that Aideed might be looking for opportunities to assassinate Americans as a way of expressing his displeasure with political and military trends. At the time, American officials were sanguine about the threats, noting privately "that if Aideed was resorting to threats, their strategy of trying to 'marginalize' him was paying off." One American civilian working for the United Nations concluded, "it shows we're doing something right."[8] In fact, the United States was suffering from strategic confusion of the first order.

Whereas the United States government declined comprehensive disarmament because it would require fighting the warlords, which was deemed inconsistent with U.S. national interests, it approved the comprehensive disarmament mission for far less capable UN forces. UNOSOM II was too weak to complete the mission of general disarmament, a mission that would have required fighting Aideed. The United States did not want its forces to battle Aideed's, and the terms of reference for the Quick Reaction Force stated that it would not be used for routine patrolling and other activities required for comprehensive disarmament. However, the Quick Reaction Force was used for these activities anyway, since it was the most (some would say only) capable force available. By extension, it was predictable that the U.S. Quick Reaction Force would end up fighting Aideed as well because other UNOSOM II forces were unable to do so effectively.

Thus, on both the broader question of how to define the mission and what forces would be necessary to accomplish it, as well as on the narrower question of how the U.S.-manned Quick Reaction Force was to be employed, U.S. policy was inconsistent with operational realities. The United States government inconsistently adopted a policy of preventing U.S. forces from doing comprehensive disarmament when they were most capable of it, and obliging them to do it under UN auspices when they were least capable of it. The use of the Quick Reaction Force for disarmament activities contrary to its terms of reference was an early indicator that U.S. policy was not well aligned with operational reality, one that did not register with authorities in Washington. Aideed, however, quickly sent a signal that could not be ignored.

THE JUNE 5 INSPECTION, AMBUSH, AND AFTERMATH

Although the collision course between the UN and Aideed was predetermined by their conflicting goals, the UN took the initial action that precipitated a confrontation. In keeping with its mandate to achieve general disarmament, the UN decided to conduct its first weapon storage area inspection and audit on June 5 with a list of weapon sites that belonged exclusively to Aideed and his faction.[9] One of those sites was also the site of Aideed's Radio Mogadishu, which Aideed had captured after a bitter struggle with Ali Mahdi's militia and which was tormenting the UN with heavy-handed propaganda. UNOSOM II was determined to enter and search all designated sites to establish its authority to do so, an authority the Marines possessed but exercised only with advance approval by Aideed. The June 5 UNOSOM II inspection of five Aideed weapon depots was a break from the recent practice of the Marines. The last UNITAF site visit had been four months earlier, in February. In addition, the UNOSOM II inspection also was conducted on short notice (less than 24 hours), and without Aideed's agreement.

The Aideed representative notified of the inspection was surprised, shaken and refused to approve the inspection. Perhaps he knew that the site-inspection would reveal an Aideed arms build-up, which it reportedly did, showing "three times the number of arms officially listed."[10] In any case, he recommended against the snap inspection and candidly warned the UN personnel "you are starting this war tomorrow." The UN representatives simply responded that he should contact appropriate SNA personnel (i.e., Aideed's clan) to ensure compliance. The UN knew that Aideed had told his supporters that he was prepared to fire on UNOSOM II forces if they "invaded" his weapons storage areas, and thus the Pakistanis assigned the inspection mission were told they might encounter resistance and were instructed to force their entry if necessary. The Quick Reaction Force was notified to be ready to support the Pakistanis. In short, all concerned were prepared for a showdown, and no one at the UN or U.S. headquarters in Mogadishu was surprised when it came. Washington and New York, however, were surprised at the result.

After the Pakistanis secured the radio compound, several Aideed supporters arrived and began to incite the crowd. They also appeared to be giving direction to the crowd's feeling that the Pakistanis were fellow Muslims collaborating in the seizure of the radio station. The situation then deteriorated rapidly. After killing one Somali, the Pakistanis disengaged from the radio station location but quickly came under ferocious attack as they passed other sites, particularly feeding station 20. The fighting quickly escalated, and when the Pakistanis finally reached safety, they had sustained twenty-four dead and fifty-seven injured, with six captured.

The events of June 5 were important because they revealed the extent to which Aideed could resist the UN. The UN knew Aideed might resist the inspection, but miscalculated his ability to orchestrate a violent response. Aideed's response thus invited the UN and United States to rethink their strategy. They had three options. They could back off and negotiate the best agreement possible with the warlords, Aideed in particular. They could hit back at Aideed to punish him for his provocation, but keep open channels of communication for further negotiation. Finally, they could attempt to make an example out of Aideed and eliminate him from the political landscape. The U.S. government and UN chose this latter option. In Washington, a hastily arranged interagency meeting approved a quick and forceful UN response. It came less than forty-eight hours after the event in the form of a new Security Council Resolution (837), strongly supported by the United States, that authorized punitive action against the SNA. UN forces quickly arranged for military action against SNA sites, destroying known weapon caches, and a little later Howe put a $25,000 reward on Aideed, which was too little to have much effect but enough to infuriate Aideed and solidify the state of conflict between him and the UN. Thus began a series of small raids and ambushes by both sides over the course of the summer that inflicted a growing number of casualties. The significance of Aideed's violent actions and the UN response was that it locked both parties into a struggle from which it was difficult to retreat.

For the UN, the events of June 5 irrevocably marked Aideed as an outlaw. The UNOSOM II warrant for Aideed's arrest specified three categories of crimes: conspiracy to conduct premeditated attacks against UN forces, endangering civilians and UN personnel through organized incitement of violence, and crimes against humanity. Admiral Howe and the American diplomatic representative in Mogadishu, Ambassador Robert Gosende, used the terrorist/terrorism epithet to characterize Aideed and his activities, perhaps to facilitate their increasingly frequent requests that Washington dispatch SOF to deal with him. The views of Howe and Gosende on Aideed and the need to deal with him expeditiously understandably hardened, as did their commitment to their mission, as more of their personnel died. In a September 6 cable entitled "Taking the Offensive," Gosende wrote that "any plan for negotiating a 'truce' with Aideed's henchmen should be shelved. We should refuse to deal with perpetrators of terrorist acts."[11] Jonathon Howe insisted on June 12 that he still had plans to extend disarmament to the rest of the country. While he was coy about whether force would be used against other warlords, Turkish General Bir, the Commander of UNOSOM II, noted that he "would not lose any sleep if another warlord gave us reason to bend his cannons."[12]

Officials back in Washington, such as Defense Secretary Les Aspin, fully supported the disarmament mission that had brought UNOSOM II into conflict with Aideed, but they were less inclined to brand Aideed a terrorist. Officials in both Washington and New York preferred to simply label Aideed a criminal and fugitive from UN justice. By treating Aideed not as a belligerent but as a criminal, the UN hoped to undermine his legitimacy with Somalis. The problem with this approach was that it precluded negotiations; criminals are apprehended rather than invited to the negotiating table. The problem with refusing to negotiate was that the UN did not have the power to eliminate or apprehend Aideed. Whereas the earlier refusal to aggressively disarm was a decisive limitation on U.S. support to the UN, the decision to get Aideed following the events of June 5 was the opposite: a major escalation of U.S. commitment to the UN effort. It led to an increasingly active role for the American Quick Reaction Force and eventually to the SOF mission to capture Aideed.

As for Aideed and the SNA clan, simultaneously fighting and talking were standard operating procedure. Aideed kept his lines of communication open. He communicated with major political leaders in the international community. For example, in a letter to German Chancellor Helmut Kohl, Aideed pleaded his case with a mix of fact and fiction, arguing that "the crisis started in Mogadishu on June 5, 1993 when a contingent of American and Pakistani troops seized Radio Mogadishu. Upon hearing the seizure of the Radio studio, thousands of Somali citizens demonstrated peacefully around the station. The troops opened fire on the crowd killing 3." While making every attempt to characterize himself as the injured party, Aideed succeeded through intermediaries in making his positions known to the UN. Aideed made sure that U.S. and UN observers in Mogadishu concluded, based on contacts with his closest advisers, that he wanted to be accommodated. Aideed believed UNOSOM II would back down. Instead, U.S. and UNOSOM II leadership concluded that the UN must not give in to Aideed, for if it failed to enforce order in Somalia the credibility of UN Peacekeeping operations in general would diminish significantly.

Almost a month after the June 5 firefight, and after numerous small engagements, SNA clan leaders were having second thoughts about the protracted conflict with the UN and United States. They gathered on July 12 at a site known as the Abdi House to reconsider the SNA's path of confrontation. Having received intelligence on the meeting, U.S. helicopter gunships from the Quick Reaction Force—with White House and UN approval—attacked the house with no warning killing over thirty senior SNA leaders and wounding perhaps another fifty. Four international journalists who arrived to cover the carnage instead became part of it when a frenzied crowd beat them to death. The attack hardened SNA clan attitudes as much as the June 5 attack on the Pakistanis had hardened the resolve of the UN. Until that time many SNA had believed that the United Nations, and its Egyptian Secretary General, Boutros Boutros-Ghali in particular, had been manipulating the naïve United States into supporting an Egyptian agenda under cover of a humanitarian mission. Years earlier Boutos Boutros-Ghali had been an Egyptian diplomat promoting assistance to former Somali President Siad Barre in his clan-based civil war (a war Aideed and his clan largely won). The SNA just tended to assume the naïve Americans did not understand Boutros-Ghali's ulterior motives. However, the July 12 Abdi House ambush wiped away any residual sympathy for American simplicity, and the SNA rallied behind Aideed with greater purpose, fully united in pressing the attack on U.S. forces directly rather than as an incidental result of engaging UN forces.

SOF AND THE SWING BACK TOWARD THE POLITICAL TRACK

Admiral Howe began requesting SOF the day after the June 5 attacks. Believing Aideed to be the main roadblock to progress, it was natural to request forces that were most capable of tracking and capturing or eliminating him. A failed attempt by Marine forces to apprehend Aideed on June 23 both alerted Aideed to the threat posed by U.S. forces and seemed to underscore the need for more capable forces. By early July, Ambassador Gosende was also making explicit requests for SOF to capture Aideed and his senior officials. Yet decisionmakers at higher echelons of command and officials advising them in the bureaucracy remained highly skeptical of such a mission. The Deputy Assistant Secretary of Defense for Special Operations and Low-Intensity Conflict put his objection in writing, noting the intelligence on Aideed was insufficient, but more fundamentally that it was not in the U.S. interests to get involved in a counterinsurgency campaign against Aideed. In remarks tied to a June 23 supplemental appropriation of $750 million for the Somalia operation, two senators criticized the hunt for Aideed and went on record against it. General Hoar, the commander of Central Command, famously recommended against it to those in the Office of the Under Secretary of Defense for Policy, who were inclined to support the SOF mission against Aideed. General Hoar said there was only a 50 percent chance they would get the necessary intelligence, and then only a 50 percent chance they would get Aideed. In sum, he considered it a 25 percent chance of success and a high-risk mission in any case. General Powell concurred.

Meanwhile, Aideed's hit-and-run attacks were having some political effect. On July 2, Aideed's forces killed four Italians in an ambush, ending Italian support for UNOSOM II combat operations. The Italians announced they would be taking orders only from Rome after that event. However, when on August 8, Aideed's forces killed four U.S. soldiers with a command-detonated landmine, the U.S. response was to escalate. On August 10, UN Ambassador Albright promised that U.S. forces would "stay as long as needed to lift the country and its people from the category of a failed state into that of an emerging democracy." Meanwhile, inside the Defense Department, Under Secretary of Defense for Policy Frank Wisner now personally made the case that more casualties would occur until Aideed was dealt with, and that SOF was the best chance for dealing with him. Wisner made this recommendation despite the position adopted by his staff responsible for SOF policy and mission oversight, who argued against the expanded mission or deployment of special mission units.[13] But even within this staff element there were conflicting views. Many with a Special Forces background looked askance at the mission, while those with more special mission unit experience tended to support aggressive intervention. In any case, with casualties mounting, Wisner decided to recommend unequivocally more emphasis on military options at this juncture, and SOF in particular. Thus he broke from the positions advocated by career Department of Defense officials and sided with the views of the Department of State and those in the field. Secretary Aspin agreed, and

General Powell came on board after consulting with the commander of the Quick Reaction Force and the SOF forces that were to be deployed. A mid-August senior interagency meeting on Somalia concluded with a four-part plan: continuing efforts to apprehend Aideed; pursuing the possibility of forced exile for Aideed; assisting the UN in arresting key Aideed deputies; and pressing the UN for detailed plans for detention and trial of Aideed if captured. With the Department of Defense now on board, all that was required was a presidential decision. When a landmine injured six soldiers on August 22, President Clinton ordered Task Force Ranger to Somalia.

The task force, consisting of Rangers and special mission unit personnel, arrived on August 26. Aideed welcomed the task force with a mortar attack that wounded several of their personnel. Within days the task force struck back, but due to poor intelligence, they descended on a UN location and detained UN personnel in a case of mistaken identity. This event only deepened the concern of critics like General Hoar, who continued to lobby against the Task Force Ranger mission to get Aideed. His view seemed to be that the Aideed problem could be handled only by a major infusion of ground forces, and that level of commitment exceeded U.S. interests in Somalia.[14]

The day after Task Force Ranger arrived in Somalia, Secretary Aspin gave a major speech on policy in Somalia. It was designed to finally clarify U.S. objectives, but it only succeeded in demonstrating that policy had not yet come to grips with the cost of continued support for the expanded UN mission. Aspin noted that the current crisis was the result of UNOSOM II's mandate and activities, which undermined Aideed's position politically and militarily and, like earlier UN officials in Mogadishu, concluded that the fighting was therefore evidence of success. He went on to identify the real threat to U.S. interests: "The danger now is that unless we return security to south Mogadishu, political chaos will follow the UN withdrawal.... The danger is that the situation will return to what existed before the United States sent in the troops." Meanwhile, CIA and senior military observers were concluding that precisely because the United States and UN were threatening Aideed's power base, he would fight, and that contending with him would be a drawn-out affair requiring years of patient effort and the continued employment of sizeable military forces. For precisely this reason, and because the deployment of Task Force Ranger constituted further U.S. military escalation,

General Hoar sent a message in the first week of September warning that the UN mandate in Somalia was too ambitious. He bluntly stated that the current strategy was inconsistent with the available resources, and he urged Washington to convince the UN to scale back its objectives in Somalia. The message was sobering, but did not have an immediate impact on policy.

Following the initial Task Force Ranger raid that went awry, the task force trained but otherwise did not launch any operations for the next six days or so. The intelligence community recognized that real-time intelligence on Aideed's whereabouts was degrading precipitously. For one thing, their agents were suddenly disappearing. Perhaps in recognition of this fact, Ambassador Gosende, the senior U.S. diplomatic representative in Somalia, began having some second thoughts, which he shared with Washington. He argued that it might just be better to negotiate a solution with Aideed, perhaps convincing him to accept a golden parachute into exile. This was the first crack in the united front from Mogadishu that favored pressing the attack on Aideed, and it suggested the political tide was already turning against the SOF mission. The very next day (September 7), Major General William Garrison, the commander of the task force, launched an attack against less important SNA targets and succeeded in capturing seventeen suspects, but it was not enough to impress Gosende. A week or so later, he sent a pointed high-priority cable from Mogadishu underscoring again his transition from a passionate advocacy of arresting Aideed to an equally heartfelt recommendation to enter into a cease-fire and negotiate with him.[15]

Meanwhile, Aideed was busy on the political front as well, having launched an appeal to former President Jimmy Carter requesting help in preventing an impending disaster. Aideed claimed the U.S. government and UN were trying to handpick leaders for Somalia against the wishes of the vast majority of the Somali people, and this was the root cause of the conflict between the SNA and the U.S.-led mission in Somalia. On September 13, Carter met with Clinton to discuss Somalia. Carter advised Clinton to abandon the military confrontation in favor of a political solution. Carter had the impression that President Clinton agreed with him. On September 20, Secretary of State Warren Christopher gave UN Secretary General Boutros-Ghali an informal memo recommending that the UN shift to a political track and negotiate with Aideed. Boutros-Ghali rejected the recommendation and said it was necessary to continue to hunt Aideed.

Whatever his private reservations, President Clinton made it clear that he was not ready to break with the UN publicly. When he spoke to the UN General Assembly on September 27, President Clinton expressed concern about Somalia but indicated no change of course was in the offing. However, a *New York Times* article on September 29 provided details on the difference of opinion between Boutros-Ghali and the United States. Boutros-Ghali continued to insist that the Security Council resolution obliged him to try to bring Aideed to justice, despite the new American strategy, not yet announced publicly, to move away from the goal of capturing him.

In summary, as September drew to a close, U.S. policy and strategy were seriously conflicted. On the one hand, Task Force Ranger had been dispatched and was actively hunting Aideed. On the other hand, as the costs of the UN mission climbed and the likelihood of quickly capturing Aideed waned, U.S. commitment to the overall mission appeared to be declining. A September 14 request from General Montgomery, commander of the Quick Reaction Force, for armor to help deal with Aideed's roadblocks was denied. Montgomery worried that UN troops with armor would not respond if called upon. General Powell and Secretary Aspin denied the request as incompatible with the desire to gradually reduce the overall U.S. military presence in Somalia.[16] According to one account of Aspin's conversation with Powell about the request for armor, "the secretary told Powell that in terms of overall strategy in Somalia 'the trend is all going the other way' and that Congress would be all over the administration if it raised the visibility of its presence there." General Hoar agreed with Montgomery's request for additional armor but "added there was a political downside to the proposal. Sending armor would expand the 'U.S. footprint in Somali,' elevate 'Aideed's stature,' and increase 'collateral damage in Somalia due to the increased firepower.'" As this decision indicated, there was no interest in increasing the number of U.S. forces in Somalia. As General Hoar noted at the time, given these circumstances, it was incumbent upon the United States to either persuade the UN to scale back its mission and activities in keeping with the effects its military forces could deliver, or the United States had to significantly increase its commitment and underwrite the UN mission for an indefinite period of time.

Other tactical and political factors argued for a policy reassessment as well. Aideed's forces began to demonstrate competence in shooting down helicopters. In fact, Task Force Ranger began training for how it would react to a downed helicopter around the third week of September.

A bit later, on September 25, Aideed's forces succeeded in shooting down a helicopter with a rocket propelled grenade, killing three Americans. While some considered it a "one in a million shot," Task Force Ranger's training for the possibility of a downed helicopter suggested the Task Force Ranger leadership had a better understanding of such risk. On the political front, Congress was increasingly alarmed about the course of events in Somalia, where humanitarian assistance had become what appeared to be an open-ended nation-building mission. Congress passed a nonbinding resolution requiring the president to seek specific Congressional approval by November 15 to keep any troops in Somalia. Public support was flagging as well. In the last week of September, polls indicated public support for U.S. troops in Somalia was down from 79 to 46 percent, with only 22 percent in favor of trying to disarm warlords.

In fact, a policy reassessment of sorts was under way by late September. Increasingly, there was talk of finding a political solution. Even the Department of State was acknowledging that the military track was proving ineffective. Department of State position papers at the end of September observed that as the political track built up, the military track should build down. It was suggested that the withdrawal of Task Force Ranger could best be covered as a logical part of the first phase of a new political strategy, even though the real reason would be the task force's lack of effectiveness. Internal Department of Defense strategy papers concurred that it was unlikely that Aideed would be captured, and advised a transition to the political track while keeping up military pressure. The explicit assumption was that in order for Aideed to be pressured into accepting a political solution, the military efforts needed to continue for the time being. The implicit assumption in this dual track strategy was that the military operations of Task Force Ranger were not particularly high risk, at least politically. No one in Washington seemed to have any appreciation for the likelihood that a major firefight was about to take place that would change the course of the U.S. intervention in Somalia.

THE OCTOBER 3 FIREFIGHT:
SOF DEFEATED IN VICTORY

While officials in Washington were aware that capturing Aideed was increasingly less likely, they seemed unaware of the growing risks to Task

Force Ranger operations. In the field, however, the troops were better aware of the situation. On September 30, several days before the October 3 battle with Aideed's forces, the Boston Globe reported that, according to a CIA report and official sources in Mogadishu, UN troops were isolated and facing the risk of a major assault by Aideed forces. In addition to quoting an official who said on September 29 that "the efficiency of the U.S. Army Ranger ... teams sent in to track Aideed [was] decreasing by the day," the article noted that analysts knew Aideed was consolidating his position, able to move with increasing ease, and capable of hitting U.S. helicopters. More to the point for a discussion of special operations, the commander of Task Force Ranger, General Garrison, understood not only his tactical but also his political situation well, both of which were turning against his Ranger and special mission unit operations.

Garrison knew Aideed and his forces were concentrated in the Bakara market area, and that going in there would be a high-risk enterprise. Reportedly, he noted that going into the Bakara market might be a "win the gunfight, but lose the war" scenario, a concern that turned out to be prophetic. Prior to October 3, when Garrison ordered a daylight raid into the Bakara market, Task Force Ranger had conducted six live missions (three of which were conducted in daylight), while another thirty-five or forty were aborted because of insufficient intelligence. Much time had elapsed since the last "go," and Garrison knew that the political winds were blowing against the military option and in favor of negotiations. As he later said, he knew General Hoar was expressing reservations, as was Ambassador Gosende. Garrison and Hoar had discussed the risk of going near the Bakara market, and Hoar had told Garrison in certain circumstances not to do so. Garrison also knew the intelligence was not getting any better. On the October 3 mission, Garrison did something he had not done for any of those previous missions. He ordered that the helicopters carrying and supporting the troops on their raids be armed with rockets. He then went to salute personally each helicopter crew and its other SOF occupants before takeoff. In another first, he ordered the task force to shoot any threatening Somalis rather than giving them a chance to surrender.[17] SOF participants later told senior diplomatic leaders on the scene that they knew they were operating "at the edge of the envelope"; i.e., that the operational risks they ran were high and that operating in the vicinity of the Bakara market was particularly dangerous.

So by all indications, General Garrison knew the risks he was running. However, his superiors in Washington did not. As the *New York Times* reported at the time, "...administration officials were at a loss to explain why a military raid...was conducted at the same time that Mr. Christopher was waging a campaign to persuade a reluctant Mr. Boutros-Ghali to pursue a political track aggressively.... At the State Department, some senior officials said they were surprised by news of the military operations."[18] The *Washington Post* reported that "internally, the President complained that without a full debate and without him understanding the implications, the United States signed on to a UN agenda that turned out to be a fatal error: pursuing the factional leader Mohammed Farah Aideed. Clinton told lawmakers that changed what he signed on to and was a mistake. He said this even though the United States approved the UN resolution authorizing the hunt for Aideed, which has been conducted almost exclusively with U.S. forces."[19] When the father of one of the slain Rangers met with President Clinton, he asked why the raid had taken place if the U.S. government was pursuing a political solution. The president agreed that the raid was incomprehensible. He would later say it was the low point of his presidency. When the president met on May 12, 1994, with families of the soldiers slain in the October 3 fight, he offered as explanation for the debacle his reluctance to micromanage the military. He told the families that he intentionally remained disengaged from military matters in Somalia. He accepted Secretary Aspin's resignation, but it was not clear that the Secretary of Defense was uniquely responsible. Lower ranking officials soon admitted that even when the Administration began to rethink its approach in September, it did not tell the U.S. forces in Somalia under Pentagon control to abandon their hunt for General Aideed. Orders to try to capture Aideed were not rescinded, "one senior official said, because Washington had not yet given up the idea of capturing him."[20] In short, Clinton's senior foreign policy advisors were still pursuing a two-track military and political strategy when the October 3 raid took place.

While some expressions of shock and ignorance about ongoing military operations in Mogadishu may have been exaggerated, the surest sign that Washington was genuinely surprised by the scale and intensity of combat on October 3 was the inept public affairs response to the battle. For months senior administration officials had argued against abandoning the UN in Somalia because it was in U.S. interests to ensure the success of the first Chapter VII peace enforcement operation. Yet when President Clinton spoke to the American people, appalled and outraged by photos of desecrated American dead on October 6, he could only observe "it curdles the stomach of every American to see that, because we went there for no purpose other than to keep those people alive. We had no other purpose than a humanitarian mission."[21] With the President of the United States only able to articulate a humanitarian purpose for the mission, there seemed no point in remaining in Somalia and shooting people. At an October 6 NSC meeting, Clinton decided to shift completely to a political track. He gave orders that U.S. forces would no longer pursue Aideed and dispatched Ambassador Oakley and U.S. Marine Corps General Anthony Zinni to Somalia to be sure that Aideed and U.S. and UN forces got the new policy guidance. Aideed's faction agreed to release warrant officer Durant, the one American captured on October 3, with no compensation or conditions as part of the new political approach. In an October 7 meeting with Congressional leadership the president encountered total opposition to the United States staying in Somalia, but was able to negotiate a five-month delay in the pullout, during which the Administration would try to strengthen UNOSOM II. A week later, in a letter to Congress, President Clinton offered only an inadequate rationale for hanging on in Somalia, noting that "having been brutally attacked, were American forces to leave now we would send a message to terrorists and other potential adversaries around the world that they can change our policies by killing our people. It would be open season on Americans."[22]

With the administration unable to articulate a better strategic rationale, Congress pulled the plug on the operation. With eerie parallels to the Tet offensive in Vietnam, Aideed had secured a strategic political victory with a huge tactical defeat of his forces. Task Force Ranger had inflicted almost a thousand casualties on the SNA on October 3, and by some accounts, Aideed's blood-soaked clan was traumatized at the scale of death and destruction they had suffered without being able to overrun the small American contingent. Some intelligence later suggested that SNA support for Aideed's policy of confrontation was dealt a lethal blow on October 3. If so, Aideed masked the dissension well by continuing to inflict casualties with mortar attacks three days later and on through the month until the UN declared a ceasefire. Finally, in November Aideed complied with the ceasefire so the United States could organize its withdrawal without the SNA sustaining further casualties. The United States sent a large joint military task force to ensure that U.S. forces could withdraw safely, but it was not authorized to undertake offensive actions or even to enter the city of Mogadishu for fear of casualties.

LESSONS FOR TODAY: SOMALIA AS A POLITICAL, STRATEGIC, OPERATIONAL, AND TACTICAL FAILURE

Somalia is an intrinsically interesting and worthy case study for SOF. Like several previous smaller conflicts, it produced deep policy divisions in Washington and poor results in the field that shook up presidential cabinets and marked a high or low point of a presidential administration.[23] Somalia effectively ended the Clinton administration's policy of "aggressive multilateralism," terminated Secretary Les Aspin's short career as secretary of defense, and increased tensions between senior civilian and military leaders. Somalia also arguably encouraged America's enemies to challenge American interests. Just as Aideed bluntly told Ambassador Oakley that American failures in Vietnam and Beirut proved the United States did not have staying power, Osama Bin Laden and others would similarly but erroneously conclude from Somalia and other events that the United States lacked the will to protect its interests. When the United States performs poorly in smaller conflicts where less than vital interests are at stake, it nevertheless pays a price for failure, inviting miscalculations on the part of its enemies and higher overall costs for ensuring its security.

Since the failure in Somalia had significant repercussions for the nation, understanding what went wrong and how to prevent it is valuable. Learning from Somalia is also important for the SOF community for two reasons. First, Somalia hurt the reputation of SOF in addition to that of America and the Clinton administration. The credibility SOF built up in the first Gulf War was set back in Somalia, and the positive SOF achievements in Somalia during UNITAF were all but forgotten. Some thought Somalia lent credence to the old saw that SOF can get you into, but not out of, trouble. SOF skeptics have long argued that SOF cannot secure important national objectives at disproportionately low costs as their proponents advertise, and accordingly should not be trusted with independent national-level missions. Rather, SOF should be assigned the more limited role of supporting conventional force operations. To counter such critics, SOF has a significant institutional stake in learning from Somalia.

More broadly, since SOF is often assigned missions in stability operations and low-intensity conflicts like Somalia, and indeed are generally seen as uniquely capable of contributing to such endeavors, it is important that SOF understand the requirements for success and how to avoid the mistakes that undermined efforts in Somalia. Just as the failure to rescue American hostages in Iran galvanized reform of America's SOF capability, Somalia should have prompted a similar reassessment of both SOF and America's approach to special operations. Unfortunately, it is not clear that either the nation or the SOF community have learned much from the failure in Somalia.

The Wrong Lessons

The Somalia experience was a notable failure for the United States in two respects. First, to paraphrase what Henry Kissinger once said in the aftermath of an inept handling of a crisis, there is evidence that the poor performance dismayed our friends and emboldened our adversaries (for example, Osama bin Laden as mentioned above). In fact, there is evidence that we dismayed our own leadership about SOF and in effect deterred ourselves from using SOF (e.g. against al-Qaeda) when arguably they were the appropriate option.[24] Second, we did not actually learn the right lessons from Somalia, either in the SOF community or in the broader national security community. In fact, many of the more popular lessons learned about Somalia have been the wrong ones. Before reviewing the correct political, strategic, operational, and tactical lessons from Somalia, it will be helpful to debunk of few of the better known erroneous lessons, of which the following are a sample:

The most immediate, and to some extent persistent, lesson attributed to Somalia was that it demonstrated how casualty-adverse the American public is. Americans are, comparatively speaking, loath to suffer or to some extent inflict casualties needlessly. However, as the account provided here demonstrates, the Clinton administration was not obliged to abandon Somalia simply because U.S. forces suffered casualties. If the American public understands the rationale for a military operation, it typically supports an operation until success is secured,[25] in part to minimize unnecessary casualties by making the military contest as short as possible. This proved to be the case in Somalia, as evidenced by the decisions to authorize increasingly lethal action against Aideed. The public and Congress demanded a withdrawal only when no good strategic rationale could be offered that would justify such sacrifices.

Beyond the fallacious observation about a dramatically low tolerance for casualties, the most popular explanation for failure was lack of commitment. Those who thought UN success was an important U.S. security objective wanted comprehensive disarmament. They lamented the fact that those who argued UN success in Somalia was not a critical U.S. interest ended up thwarting a comprehensive disarmament when the Marines had a chance to enforce it. They argued that the United States should have disarmed Aideed and the other warlords when it would have been easy to do so. Two objections may be raised to this speculative defense of the broader mission mandate. First, the country was awash in arms and would have required a much larger force than the Marines fielded to enforce comprehensive disarmament, something military leaders unanimously agreed upon. Second, it ignores the basic fact that Aideed (and perhaps other warlords) was prepared to fight to protect his perceived interests. The job could have been done, but at what cost? For many, the costs were easily assessed as too high from the beginning, and in this regard history proved right those who wanted to avoid disarming the Somalis. Whether the costs would have been politically bearable had the Clinton administration made the case for "aggressive multilateralism" more systematically to the Congress and the public is impossible to say.

Another popular lesson from Somalia draws a contrary conclusion about commitment. It asserts that the United States was overly committed and lacked an "exit strategy." This lesson suggests that the United States got mired in Somalia and simply could not extricate itself before disaster struck. This lesson does not accord with the facts. The Marines had an exit strategy. They left; and it did not matter that the UN threatened not to send a replacement force. The point is that discussion of exit strategies just obscures the central issue: U.S. interests and the costs they justify. Since the costs cannot be perfectly known before the operation, they must be assessed as the operation unfolds and resistance and force performance become evident. It is always possible to find a way to minimize damage to prestige or, more happily, to pass a successful operation on to others with greater interests in the outcome. In fact, the State Department was planning its face-saving rationale for a return to negotiations with Aideed when the October 3 fight occurred.

A more extreme version of the lesson on the value of an exit strategy is the observation that stability operations are not appropriate for military forces, but if the military is assigned to conduct them, it should be allowed to use overwhelming force in order to terminate the problem quickly and allow a successful withdrawal on our own terms. This lesson is internally inconsistent. If nonmilitary forces could accomplish the mission, there would be no need for any force, much less overwhelming force. As always, the point is to match the forces and their rules of engagement to the mission. In low-intensity conflict, excessive force is usually counterproductive because it alienates the population that is assisting the adversary and that must be wooed away from providing that assistance.

Another popular lesson learned about Somalia—related to the previously mentioned argument for overwhelming force—is that the failure was due to civilian meddling in operational military affairs. Some argue that political leaders interfered and precluded the deployment of AC-130s, armor, and other military weapons that would have made it possible to save the day when SOF were pinned down in extended urban combat in Mogadishu on October 3, 1993. The task force arrived in Somalia without AC-130 gunships, which can provide highly precise close air support for ground forces. Task Force Ranger did not have them because they require a lot of support personnel and decisionmakers wanted to limit the numbers of U.S. personnel in Somalia. A later request for armor was also turned down. However, General Garrison, who claimed he had all the firepower he needed, discounts the significance of the decisions not to send the AC-130s and armor. By some assessments, one man, who bled to death, might have been saved had the armored relief force arrived earlier, which helps substantiate Garrison's belief that lack of more readily available firepower was not a key factor in the firefight.

While mostly moot in terms of the battle's outcome, the decisions to limit the means available to SOF raise broader questions about the right of senior leaders to impose such limits when approving special operations. In this respect it should be noted that gunships and armor were not the only additional forces requested by commanders in the field. Admiral Howe wanted virtually everything in the U.S. arsenal, including aircraft carriers and field artillery, to throw at Aideed. Both military and civilian officials in the chain of command thought his requests were ridiculous. General Hoar and others argued that such firepower was inappropriate to a counterinsurgency campaign. More ground forces were needed if such a determined effort was judged to be in the nation's interests. President Clinton, for his part, used the popular prejudice that elected authorities should stay out of operational military matters when he later wanted to obscure his administration's responsibility for events in Somalia. As noted earlier, he explained to the families of the deceased soldiers that his inability to explain his administration's policy inconsistencies in Somalia was due to his personal preference not to meddle in military matters. But of course, such management is necessary. Sensitive special operations require close oversight from national leadership, just as a Senate investigation correctly concluded two years after the event.

Another erroneous lesson, albeit one that has diminished with time, is the allegation that U.S. forces failed in Somalia because they were under UN command. This charge has been debunked by a number of sources. As the account here makes clear as well, at no time did the UN control U.S. military forces and employ them in a manner inconsistent with U.S. policy. In fact, France pulled its forces out of the UN chain of command when it discovered that the American Quick Reaction Force would take orders only from American commanders. There may be some truth in the suspicion that some of America's allies were trading intelligence with Aideed to secure his agreement not to target their forces. If so, it helped Aideed secure his tremendous intelligence advantage, but this kind of treachery was simply part of the operational milieu and not a characteristic of UN command and control, nor a major determinant of the success or failure of the mission.

Yet another popular but ultimately mistaken observation about Somalia is that the command and control of such difficult operations ultimately is a question of leadership. General Johnson and Ambassador Oakley were effective in a complex and shifting environment; Admiral Howe, Ambassador Gosende, General Bir (and other military leaders) were not. While Oakley and Johnson were extraordinary in their rapport and practical wisdom, this explanation for success and failure in Somalia is unfair and misleading. It is unfair because it ignores the fundamental policy and strategy failures that Howe, Gosende, and others in the field had to contend with after Johnson and Oakley left: a U.S. government divided and promoting contradictory policy positions that assigned them a vast mission and insufficient resources for its accomplishment. The broader UN mission would not allow those responsible for its completion the luxury of remaining nonpartisan. To accomplish their broad mandate of comprehensive disarmament and bottom-up political reconstruction, they inevitably had to challenge the warlords. This was so much the case that they interpreted Aideed's wrath as evidence that they were doing their job right. Thus, the problem was fundamentally one of policy choices, not personalities. Moreover, the emphasis on individual leaders is misleading. It suggests nothing can be learned or done to improve performance in stability operations other than to stumble upon effective leaders.

Despite the number and popularity of these false lessons, there are real lessons that can be learned from Somalia about SOF and one of its most important missions: combating irregular warriors. This kind of warfare requires patience, persistence, discriminate force, popular support, and unity of effort in all levels of both political and military action. SOF should be at the forefront of efforts to identify, retain, and apply lessons on irregular warfare, but in the spring and summer of 1993, Aideed understood low-intensity conflict imperatives better than those he was fighting.

The Right Lessons

First, Somalia was primarily a policy failure, not because the policy was wrong, though it was, but because it was not clarified, communicated, and defended. Oddly, a Republican administration decided to intervene while claiming no national security interests that would justify risks to servicemen who swear allegiance to the defense of the Constitution rather than a president's moral sensibilities. The Democratic administration, on the other hand, argued that U.S. interests actually were at stake. However, the new administration, just getting situated, tried to please all major parties—the United Nations, Departments of State and Defense, and other nations—without reconciling competing policies or being clear-headed about their implications. The administration's representatives waxed eloquent at the UN about a new unprecedented undertaking in nation-building but did not acknowledge the costs of such an undertaking. The administration promulgated confused policy guidance, simultaneously insisting that the United States draw down its support and that it not let the UN fail. In essence policy was torn between those who thought American interests were tied up in the UN's success in Somalia and those who did not, and the inconsistency was resolved with confused and wishful thinking. Despite every expectation that Aideed would fight for his perceived interests, the Clinton Administration hoped he would be less recalcitrant, and then that he would be easily thwarted, and finally that SOF would deal with him quickly. Worst of all, when SOF was not able to capture Aideed and paid a heavy price for trying to do so, the Administration could not articulate to the American people a rationale to justify the blood that was shed.

Thus the lesson in this policy failure for SOF is that even the United States, temperamentally inclined to persist rather than retreat, must nevertheless balance rising costs against limited objectives. Evaluating policy objectives in light of uncertain but growing costs is difficult and requires a hardheaded assessment of risks and likely chances of success. Only General Hoar was providing such assessments and calls for reevaluation as costs increased and intelligence on Aideed's whereabouts degraded. General Garrison, the SOF commander, focused more narrowly on the possibility of tactical success, which he knew was declining, irrespective of risks, which he knew were increasing. Garrison's decision to enter the Bakara market did not violate his guidance, but neither did he make an effort to share his knowledge of risks with political authorities. Independent SOF operations require close supervision by senior leaders in Washington, as the Senate investigation prompted by the events of October 3 concluded.

> U.S. foreign policy was and will be affected for years as a result of the raid of October 3–4. It is clear that both civilian officials and military leaders should have been carefully and continually re-evaluating the Task Force Ranger mission and tactics after each raid, with an eye toward recommending that the operation be terminated if the risks were deemed to have risen too high.[26]

This kind of policy and operational coordination in national-level special operations used to be axiomatic in SOF doctrine but was not honored in

Somalia. Special mission units originally complained that the creation of SOCOM would distance them from national leadership with an intervening level of command. Since the creation of SOCOM, however, SOF has evolved to the point where SOF commanders are more likely to avoid than demand a tight coordination of their operations with policy objectives. In the case of Somalia, it is notable that SOCOM and the office of the Assistant Secretary of Defense for Special Operations and Low-Intensity Conflict, the policy office in the Pentagon responsible for SOF, recommended opposite courses of action. SOCOM wanted the mission while staff in the office of the Assistant Secretary of Defense for Special Operations and Low-Intensity Conflict recommended against the mission.[27] Relations between the two organizations were so poor that a reasoned debate between them over such courses of action and their merits was not possible.

Admittedly, it is hard to say in retrospect whether a frank assessment of the tactical situation from the on-scene SOF commander would have galvanized policymakers to a sober assessment of their chosen course of action, or better prepared them to defend it after the October 3 battle. Certainly General Hoar's remonstrations were not successful in that regard. However, the broader point is that SOF commanders (and policymakers) should have made the effort. To minimize the chances that a typically heroic tactical effort by SOF will end in a strategic setback, all national-level SOF missions must be closely coordinated with national policy on an iterative basis.

A related point is that SOF operations must be supported with active information campaigns. This is another area where SOF leadership must accept some responsibility for the policy failure. In the end, the greatest error was simply failure to comprehend the political importance of a major firefight and be well prepared to defend the results to the public in Somalia, the United States, and elsewhere. Such an information contingency plan might have salvaged the devastating blow SOF inflicted on the SNA forces; its absence relegated SOF's tactical excellence to a poignant afterthought. SOF leadership not only failed to apprise civilian leadership of the risks SOF were running in Mogadishu, but also had no information campaign ready to exploit successes or limit damage as events dictated. Recognizing that tactical operations and their outcome can have political and strategic significance is conventional wisdom among those who study small and irregular wars, and used to be orthodox thinking in SOF. It also used to be standard thinking in SOF that special operations are defined in part by their psychological impact, which would underscore the requirement to have a PSYOP and public relations plan ready to cover likely outcomes. None of these historic SOF perspectives were on display in the oversight and leadership of Task Force Ranger, and the consequences of the policy failure were magnified as a result.

Somalia was also a strategy failure, one which contains key lessons for SOF. First, and most broadly, insufficient means were employed to secure objectives that were dramatically expanded. As noted above, the United States wholeheartedly endorsed, and some would say engineered, the broader UN mandate, which if anything would require an even more potent force than the Marines had on hand. Yet, as one confidential assessment after another concluded, UNOSOM II forces were not up to the task. Second, and more specifically, as it became apparent that snatching Aideed was a long shot, the United States increasingly pursued political options while keeping up military pressure on Aideed. Aideed was pursuing the same strategy of talking while fighting, and the Marines had similarly combined a judicious use of force with constant communication. In theory Gosende and Garrison should have been able to execute such a strategy, but they were handicapped by two critical limitations of their own making.

First, having essentially declared Aideed a criminal if not a terrorist, no one in Mogadishu (or Washington or New York) was inclined to try to negotiate with him. The use of lethal force against an adversary while trying to negotiate is always a complicated and delicate enterprise. It is an impossible one if either side is unwilling to communicate, which essentially describes the U.S. and UN post-June 5 position. Second, even when Gosende changed his mind in the fall and concluded that negotiations might be necessary, he did not have the relationship with Garrison that Ambassador Oakley had with his military counterpart, General Johnson. Hence Garrison went his own way and Gosende sent his missives to Washington, which was even further removed from a tactical understanding of the situation and still not of one mind on how to proceed. The Senate report correctly concluded "the decision to continue the raids should have been better coordinated within the Administration with the concurrent U.S. effort to revitalize the political process to produce a two-track approach."[28]

Again, the lesson for SOF is that they must work with and not around political authorities, participating fully in the development and evolution of plans for strategic special operations. Since good strategy is a product of good analysis of ways, ends, and means, SOF must know its strengths and limitations and communicate them effectively. Special-mission units, in particular, are not inclined to recognize any limitations, which in part is what makes them such formidable forces. Again, the Senate investigation of the events of October 3 makes a keen observation in this regard:

> One of the weaknesses of a unit like Task Force Ranger, whose combat capabilities are unparalleled, is the belief by the unit members and its commanders that they can accomplish any mission. Because of the supreme confidence of special operations forces, the chain of command must provide more oversight to this type of unit than to conventional forces.[29]

The Senate's conclusion was a blow to SOF's reputation. However, the rare public rebuke of a subordinate SOF commander recorded in the Senate report from the Commander of SOCOM, General Wayne Downing, was even more so. "I kept telling General Garrison not to do anything crazy. I told him to wait Aideed out, be careful, this is a tough mission, but we can do it; be patient, be careful, eventually you will get a shot at Aideed."[30] A Pentagon saying has it that we dispatch special mission units "when we care enough to send the very best." The real issue is which type of unit, in the wide range of SOF forces available, is best prepared to conduct a mission. It may not always be the special mission unit. Other SOF forces, such as Army Special Forces, may be more inclined toward creative assessment of alternative ways and means and more willing to work in ambiguous situations requiring patience. A current example from the war on terrorism is the tendency of special mission units to argue that their direct action operations will create their own enabling intelligence. Closer to the truth is the Army Special Forces' belief that intelligence necessary for operations against specific individuals is best derived from the time-consuming work of establishing relationships with indigenous personnel.

Somalia was also an operational failure insomuch as the United States did not adopt the type of systematic counterinsurgency campaign that would have been required to root Aideed out of Mogadishu and eliminate him as a force in Somali politics. SOF should have been the lead planners for the concept of operations in Somalia insofar as they are the nation's premier experts on irregular warfare. When national authorities opted instead to snatch Aideed, SOF should have been the first in line to explain the importance of tactical surprise. Instead, the United States abandoned the element of surprise, normally a key prerequisite for success in this kind of special operations. SOCOM said shortly after the June 5 attack on the Pakistanis that SOF could nab Aideed. It would have been easier then, certainly, but the United States took a series of steps that substantially increased the operational difficulties for SOF. First the United States declared Aideed a criminal and put a reward on his head, effectively putting him on his guard. Then the Marines tried to capture him and failed, further increasing his alert status. Finally, the United States sent SOF, but not before publicly announcing that it was doing so; in effect, this further warned Aideed that he would have to take extraordinary security precautions. He did so, ruthlessly eliminating or turning agents reporting to American intelligence officers. After ceding so much to Aideed, it might have been better to allow SOF the latitude of taking him dead or alive. Apparently SOF had several opportunities to eliminate Aideed at a distance, but there was concern that doing so would make him a martyr and hero (a notion which runs contrary to the assumption that Aideed was the particular problem and not the SNA more generally). As it was, policy and strategy were so confused that the Administration never figured out what it would do with Aideed even if SOF succeeded in capturing him.

With operational surprise gone and lethal fire not an option, SOF could only hope for an immediate and short-lived tactical element of surprise. But after Aideed's forces struck Task Force Ranger with mortars, General Garrison, with General Hoar's approval, adopted an operational approach that had the effect of further reducing even these fleeting elements of surprise. Garrison argued that going after Aideed's lieutenants would somehow pressure Aideed. While no doubt it would have increased his anxiety, eliminating many of Aideed's senior advisers in the missile attack on the Abdi House did not pressure Aideed; it simply had the effect of reaffirming the SNA's political loyalty to Aideed and increasing their willingness to attack American targets. In truth, as Garrison later said in testimony, he really just wanted to go on the offensive after the mortar attack so his men would not adopt a "bunker mentality." The Senate investigation report condemned this rationale, being particularly critical of the first raid conducted by Task Force Ranger. "The lack of a valid rationale for launching the raid should have alerted superiors in the chain of command to the need to carefully reevaluate the Task Force's mission after each operation."[31] In other words, SOF's concept of operations needed to be reassessed. Ostensibly attacking Aideed's lieutenants to pressure him into the open while actually just satisfying a broader desire to take and sustain the offensive was a flawed approach given Aideed's intelligence advantages and the uncertain willingness of political authorities to support a more general offensive against the SNA clan. The special mission unit's desire for action irrespective of the primary goal, and its inability to patiently wait for an opportune moment to achieve the main goal, made an already difficult mission much harder.

The extent to which Somalia represented a tactical failure—that is, a failure of the means used to execute the operational concept—for SOF is debatable. Certainly it is true that SOF repeatedly displayed their tactics, techniques, and procedures while pursing less important targets than Aideed, and in so doing slowly sacrificed the element of tactical surprise and increased the vulnerability of the operations. The Senate concluded that it should have been obvious that the risk of failure was increasing each time SOF displayed their tactics in daylight. JCS Powell testified that the "first raid was an embarrassment" and after it he laid down the rule that Task Force Ranger had to have good intelligence before conducing a raid. Secretary Aspin, who did not follow events in Somalia all that closely, was coached in preparation for his testimony on Somalia. He was told that the Task Force Ranger missions followed too much of a "cookie cutter" approach. In retrospect, repeatedly displaying such tactics does seem ill advised since the real target was Aideed.

However, the questionable practice of repeatedly demonstrating SOF tactics is an observation that may benefit too much from hindsight. Momentary tactical surprise is possible to achieve even when conducting multiple raids. Neither Aspin, Powell, nor even General Hoar—a noted skeptic on the likelihood of success—ever told Garrison to stop the raids. Hoar later testified quite candidly when he noted that he did not give much consideration to high U.S. casualties, and that he "didn't think in terms of shutting the operation down," although he later wished he had.[32]

Aideed had demonstrated his ability to launch and carefully orchestrate larger operations against the Pakistanis, but he had been careful over the course of the summer to target Americans in small attacks, hitting and running quickly. On October 3, Aideed surprised most observers—ironically with the possible exception of General Garrison—when he was able to marshal a determined and large-scale effort to overrun SOF forces in such a short time. It is not clear whether Aideed's command of intelligence sources and the situation was such that he actually set the trap for SOF, but even if he did, SOF's tactical excellence in turn surprised him as his forces proved incapable of overrunning the small SOF forces despite taking grievous losses.

The United States was hurt by the failure in Somalia in numerous ways, and so was SOF. SOF were sent to Somalia to obviate the need for a huge conventional force deployment to deal with Aideed. The value of neutralizing Aideed was not absolute but rather relative to the interests that the United States had in Somalia. It was therefore incumbent upon those responsible for SOF command and control to ensure that the risks SOF were running in their operations were commensurate with the objectives of senior leaders. As it was, SOF pursued a course of action with much higher risks than senior military and civilian leaders were willing to pay. Leaders in Washington did not understand the risks that the world's best forces were running in their repeated attacks on poorly equipped and trained third world forces, and the SOF commander in the field viewed his objective as an absolute requirement to be achieved regardless of costs. Thus, instead of reducing political pressure for terminating U.S. support for UN operations, SOF operations in Somalia ended up forcing the withdrawal of U.S. forces and encouraging U.S. adversaries to underestimate U.S. resolve.

This turn of events led some to question whether SOF should undertake independent missions of strategic import, such as the attempt to capture Aideed, or whether they should work only in support of conventional forces, as they did in Desert Storm. Indeed, according to one account, the firefight in Mogadishu "confirmed the Joint Chiefs in the view that SOF should never be entrusted with independent operations."[33] Consistently, the Joint Chiefs recommended against such operations numerous times thereafter. As much as the events of October 3, 1993, damaged the reputation of SOF, the events of September 11, 2001, and subsequent SOF endeavors returned SOF to the forefront of national attention in a much more positive manner. In fact, some argue that taking the strategic lead in irregular warfare is the principal strategic role SOF ought to perform for the nation's defense. If this point of view suffered a setback in Somalia, it has returned forcefully in debate over the war on terrorism, as we will discuss in the next chapter on SOF roles and missions.

SOF ROLES AND MISSIONS

THE DEBACLE IN SOMALIA caused military and civilian leaders to question the strategic value of Special Operations Forces (SOF). As the historical review of SOF in chapter 3 illustrated, such debate about how best to employ SOF is a recurring theme that predates Somalia. It remains a point of contention today. It was recently raised, for example, in the context of the war on terrorism. The RAND Corporation, a major think tank supporting the Pentagon, recommended to the secretary of defense that SOF put greater emphasis on training and advising indigenous forces to combat terrorists as opposed to attacking them directly. In Pentagon parlance, this debate over the purpose and scope of SOF activities is a "roles and missions" issue.

The Department of Defense defines military roles in legal terms as the broad and enduring purposes for which Congress established the services and the Special Operations Command (SOCOM), and missions as the more specific tasks assigned to the combatant commanders, which would include the commander of SOCOM.[1] There is no clear-cut agreement on a more substantive definition of roles and missions. For our purposes, however, we may think of a military role as a broad strategic purpose, and a military mission as the application of that role in specific circumstances. For example, preserving freedom of navigation is a strategic role for the U.S. Navy, and undersea warfare is a mission that supports that role. In the case of SOF, one might argue they have a strategic role to attack adversaries and targets not vulnerable to conventional forces, and that unconventional warfare is a mission that supports that role.

Military forces need clearly defined roles and missions in order to determine how they should be trained and equipped. In turn, roles and missions must be derived from well-defined strategic concepts:

> The fundamental element of a military service is its purpose or role in implementing national policy. The statement of this role may be called the strategic concept of the service. Basically, this concept is a description of how, when, and where the military service expects to protect the nation against some threat to its security. If a military service does not possess such a concept, it becomes purposeless, it wallows about amid a variety of conflicting and confusing goals, and ultimately it suffers both moral and physical degeneration.[2]

If, like the military services, SOF aspire to strategic significance, they also need a strategic concept that explains their value to the nation in terms of roles and missions they are prepared to conduct. Without such a strategic concept and clearly derivative roles and missions, SOF is more likely to be ill-prepared and used ineffectively. Moreover, without clearly defined roles and missions, SOF is more likely to have problems justifying the political and material resources they need to function well. Political leaders allocate resources to military forces in part based on their understanding of their strategic value. For example, in the 1960s the United States adopted a mutual assured destruction strategy that diminished the value of air and missile defenses, and resources for those forces were severely cut. Similarly, SOF's bureaucratic fortunes waned after Vietnam, when the perceived value of their missions declined, but recently increased with their growing role in the war on terrorism.

Defining the strategic value of military forces is difficult. It requires understanding three factors that interact and change over time: the intrinsic and distinguishing capabilities of the forces; the nature of the most important security challenges facing the nation; and the military requirements that emanate from the nation's strategy for dealing with those challenges. Articulating a strategic concept for SOF is even more difficult. SOF and their operations are so captivating that they tend to overshadow discussion of SOF's strategic value. Volumes are devoted to chronicling SOF operations, but very few to examining their strategic value.[3] When SOF's strategic value is discussed, it often is without much discrimination. Because SOF and their missions vary in ways that defy easy summary, there is a tendency to describe SOF's strategic value simply in terms of their diversity and flexibility, which is not very useful. For these reasons, SOF's core strategic purpose is often construed too broadly or overlooked altogether, which is unfortunate for SOF and its ability to serve the strategic purposes of the United States.

In this chapter we demonstrate that a strategic concept for SOF requires an assessment of how SOF attributes can best support national strategy for dealing with the most pressing current and future security challenges. Different security strategies place more emphasis on some SOF attributes and missions than others. Different strategy choices also may dictate whether SOF are employed directly or indirectly, and as support to conventional-force operations or as the leading effort. Once these choices for employing SOF are clear, we will review how SOCOM has defined SOF's strategic value to date in light of U.S. defense strategy and the demands of the security environment. We will see how SOCOM's strategic concept for SOF has guided the evolution of SOF missions over the past two decades, and identify the two major shifts in the strategic environment that now argue for a reconsideration of SOF's strategic concept.

WHAT MAKES SOF SPECIAL?

It is impossible to articulate a strategic concept for SOF and derive associated roles and missions without considering the distinguishing characteristics that make SOF valuable. Although SOF characteristics can and should evolve somewhat over time, there are core attributes of American SOF that are enduring and that shape the ways SOF can be employed to address security threats. The most basic distinguishing characteristic of SOF is that they are special rather than just elite. This distinction requires explanation. As we described in chapter 2, selection in to most SOF units is quite rigorous. Not every volunteer makes it. In this regard, SOF are elite. But careful selection is also true for those who wish to join elite ceremonial units, so being elite is not the same as being special. The distinction between elite and special units depends upon the purpose for which the units are created, prepared, and employed. Elite units are used for the same purpose as general-purpose forces, but receive special designation, training, and resources so that they may perform at a higher level. Thus the distinguishing characteristic of elite units is that they perform traditional tasks with greater proficiency. Some air squadrons have developed reputations as elite units because of their competence. Another common example of such forces is shock troops, which storm a particularly challenging defensive position as a prelude to assault by less capable forces. Such units are elite but not "special."

SOF are not only elite but special because they conduct missions that conventional forces cannot perform, or at least not at acceptable levels of risk and costs. Thus special units have special purposes and special capabilities that transcend conventional-force operations. It is not always easy to distinguish special from elite units. They may differ by degrees rather than with a sharp qualitative distinction. For example, in World War II, Lt. Col. Jimmy Doolittle led a bombing raid on Japan that damaged oil stores, factory areas, and military installations. His B-25s took off from the aircraft carrier *Hornet*, hit Japan, and then attempted to reach Chinese airfields; although many had to ditch at sea, or crash-land for lack of fuel. The raid boosted American morale after the shock of Pearl Harbor and caused the Japanese to transfer some fighter units back to the home islands. Was the Doolittle raid a bombing mission like any other albeit with a higher degree of difficulty, a bombing raid to support broader military operations by forcing Japan to provide air cover for the home islands, or an independent mission designed to signal political resolve and bolster the morale of the American body politic? To answer the question historians might examine the degree to which the operation required special training and equipment, and the true purposes motivating the operation (as opposed to the effects after the fact). The Doolittle crews did receive special training; their planes were modified for carrier and long-range operations; and there were political motives for the risky operation. It seems to qualify as a special operation, but the categorization is not immediately self-evident and may be debated.

Also complicating the distinction between elite and special units is that over time elite and special units can be used for multiple purposes that demand different skills. As noted in chapter 3, Army Rangers on occasion were used as elite shock troops in World War II to support specific general-purpose force operations; for example to secure high value targets in support of the D-Day landings in World War II. In the French and Indian wars, however, Rangers launched independent missions such as the raid that succeeded in destroying the Abenaki Indians as a threat to the colonies, and more recently in 1993, Rangers were used to assist with an independent operation to capture a warlord in Somalia. Rangers, as a military unit, have been used for both elite and special operations. Today the Rangers are part of SOCOM, but there is still debate over whether their inclusion in SOCOM is appropriate.

The fact that it can be hard to distinguish special from elite units and their operations in particular circumstances does not negate the value of doing so in general. It remains true that the more a unit's purpose deviates from traditional military missions, the more appropriate it is to designate the unit and its activities as special. Failure to distinguish units and their missions as special increases the risk that they will be used inappropriately on elite but not special operations, as many would argue is the case when SOF are used to carry out recovery operations of downed pilots. Making the distinction between special and elite forces correctly increases the chances that the requirements for special missions will be well understood and that SOF will be well prepared for them.

What are the mission characteristics and force attributes that distinguish SOF as special? Pentagon policy notes that all SOF missions take place in "hostile, denied, and politically sensitive areas," and that "a simple way to remember the difference between SOF and conventional forces is that SOF's unique training, capabilities, and skills" allow them to operate successfully in such an environment.[4] These SOF attributes can be illustrated with historical examples. One of the most notable cases is the Dutch-origin Boer "commandos" who fought against British rule in South Africa. Commando is a Dutch term meaning, "a command." The Boers used unconventional strike tactics that took advantage of their scouting and tracking skills to achieve surprise, and of new technology (e.g. smokeless powder, and the greater range of their Mauser rifles). When the British responded to early defeats by pouring in half a million troops, the Boers improvised with guerrilla tactics made possible by their knowledge of the land and popular support (including from a substantial number of black Africans). They were only ground down when the British responded with blockhouses to protect railroads, concentration camps to separate the fighters from their popular support, and mounted rapid response units to counteract Boer mobility.[5] The Boer special operations were conceptually and physically removed from large conventional-force operations (i.e., they took place in hostile, denied, and politically sensitive areas), and they benefited from and were distinguished by both excellent unconventional small unit capabilities and local political, cultural and linguistic skills (i.e., those that allowed them to operate successfully in their difficult environment).

Thus SOF, like the military services, are distinguished by their operating environment's unique characteristics and the capabilities required for successfully operating in such environments. However, the services are distinguished from one another primarily by the nature of their physical environment (land, air, sea, amphibious, or littoral environments), whereas SOF are distinguished from the services by their conceptual and sometimes physical distance from conventional forces and/or their proximity to indigenous forces and populations. When SOF operate behind enemy lines, in close contact with indigenous forces and populations, or under special political constraints, such as the desire to eliminate any collateral casualties in a close-quarters combat, they are physically and/or conceptually removed from conventional-force operations and their organic mass and firepower. Because they operate in these unique environments, SOF have five special requirements.

First, SOF must possess political sophistication. Special operations are often conducted in a politically sensitive context that constrains virtually every aspect of the operation. Local mores may dictate methods, and political considerations may require clandestine, covert, or low-visibility techniques, as well as oversight at the national level. As the previous chapter on Somalia and other historical research demonstrates, SOF must be prepared to work closely with political authorities and capable of using good judgment in a fast-evolving and politically sensitive environment.[6]

Second, SOF must have an uncommon will to succeed. Special operations often are conducted under extreme duress that requires a rare commitment to persevere. Accordingly, SOCOM emphasizes that it takes special individuals to succeed in special operations—individuals who are determined to persist in the face of adversity and without support. Thus the argument that some SOF (e.g. the British) stress the human element of SOF while the United States stresses technology is not convincing, and certainly not consistent with SOCOM's emphasis on the priority of the human element of special operations. SOCOM has often stressed that its philosophical approach is to "equip the warrior, not man the equipment." [7]

Third, SOF must use unorthodox approaches. SOCOM also stresses creativity as a core value because special operations require creative approaches to problem-solving that sometimes defy American norms and military doctrine without violating fundamental American values. For example, in contrast to conventional-force operations, surprise achieved by innovative approaches that utilize speed, stealth, audacity, and deception is far more important than mass in special operations. Similarly, creative approaches to working with indigenous populations and forces are a norm for some SOF units, whereas conventional forces generally try to minimize such contact. Some concepts pioneered by SOF may be passed along to conventional forces once they are perfected, but others require so much training or costly technology that they can never be employed efficiently or effectively by larger conventional forces.

Fourth, unorthodox approaches require unconventional equipment and training. What is defined as "unconventional" changes. Night-vision devices and deep-precision strike capabilities pioneered by SOF are no longer considered unconventional and now are practiced by general-purpose forces. However, SOF continue to develop capabilities that are unconventional in comparison to existing conventional capabilities in order to help achieve surprise or overcome unanticipated obstacles in rapidly evolving circumstances. Thus, constant improvements in equipment and training help SOF transcend conventional operations.

Fifth, SOF have special intelligence requirements. There are two reasons for this: Special operations either take advantage of indigenous forces or else they exploit enemy weaknesses that are not readily apparent. SOF need current information on foreign political relationships to work effectively through indigenous forces and populations, and fine-grained intelligence to attack a difficult target with precision..

All SOF missions—whether civil affairs, hostage rescue, counterinsurgency training, unconventional warfare, or some other primary SOF mission—require forces with these attributes, which often are collapsed into two broad sets of unique characteristics:

> Special operations forces have a *dual heritage*. They are one of the nation's key *penetration and strike forces*, able to respond to specialized

contingencies across the conflict spectrum with stealth, speed, and pre-
cision. They are also warrior-diplomats capable of *influencing, advising,*
training, and conducting operations with foreign forces, officials, and popu-
lations. (Italics added.)[8]

For easy reference, SOF's superlative small-unit penetration and strike
skills are frequently summarized and referred to as SOF's commando
skills, and SOF's political, cultural and linguistic skills are often referred
to as SOF's "warrior-diplomat," or "cross-cultural" skills.[9] Sometimes one
or both of these sets of SOF attributes is undervalued or denied to be
special. For example, in 1962 President Kennedy fired Army Chief of
Staff General George Decker for asserting "any good soldier can handle
guerrillas," a comment that seemed to deny the importance of SOF's
cross-cultural skills. Others have insisted that any good infantry soldier
can assault a difficult objective, an assertion that denies the need for
special commando skills.[10] Today, however, both SOF's commando and
warrior-diplomat skills are generally recognized as distinguishing attributes of SOF.

How these distinguishing attributes are applied to defeat a threat depends upon the nature of the threat and the strategy used against it.
To better illustrate both the general value of SOF's attributes and why
their application must be considered in the context of specific threats
and strategies, we can place special operations on a theoretical spectrum
of warfare. At one end of the spectrum is war by attrition, where the
objective is simply to grind down enemy forces until they collapse; at
the other end is war by relational maneuver, where the objective is to
use some element of superiority to exploit a perceived enemy weakness,
whether it be physical, psychological, technical, or organizational. Attrition warfare is high cost and low risk, especially for the side with greater
resources. War by relational maneuver is relatively low cost but high risk.
It offers the possibility of obtaining disproportionate results for the resources committed, and thus the possibility of victory for the materially
weaker side; but it also includes the possibility of complete and rapid
failure. Edward Luttwak categorizes special operations (i.e., commando
operations) at the extreme end of the relational maneuver spectrum since
they are conducted by small forces who seek to exploit specific enemy
weaknesses at risk of catastrophic failure. He also notes they require "accuracy in identifying enemy weaknesses, as well as speed and precision

in acting against them..."[11] The warrior-diplomat dimension of SOF also requires accurate assessments of enemy weaknesses, but sometimes patience and perseverance rather than speed and precision in acting against those weaknesses.[12]

Thinking of special operations in contrast to "attrition" warfare and as an attempt to exploit enemy weaknesses with highly specialized strengths is helpful. It illuminates their strategic value but also their high risk. "High risk" should not be interpreted exclusively as physical danger. SOF "commando" operations that are time-sensitive and rely on surprise, security, and audacity to achieve success fit this characterization of risk. However, SOF training missions, civil affairs, and psychological operations that take advantage of SOF warrior-diplomat skills can take place in a relatively benign environment, such as a foreign government's ministry or training site. These missions nevertheless can have substantial political costs if mishandled. Thus SOF missions are better understood as "high risk" in the sense that tactical mission failure can have strategic consequences.

SOF missions may be high risk in general, but they are lower risk when conducted by SOF instead of conventional forces. What kind of missions most require SOF's generic attributes? SOF's commando skills make them an attractive option for targets that must be neutralized using human judgment at the scene (for example, a booby-trapped weapon of mass destruction), or which must be neutralized without collateral damage to adjacent noncombatants (as is typically the case when fighting terrorists and insurgents). In certain circumstances, this discriminating capability makes all the difference. SOF also can use nonlethal force to track and capture human targets, or to retrieve vital information or resources that would simply be missed or destroyed by long-range weapons or conventional forces. SOF use human judgment and persistent surveillance at the scene to discover what is hidden in plain sight; that is to discriminate between real targets and fake ones that deceive nonhuman sensors.

Threats that require SOF collaboration with indigenous forces and/or psychological and political isolation of the enemy, sometimes as a prelude to and sometimes as a substitute for physical attack, also play to SOF's strengths. For example, a small number of U.S. SOF helped Colombian authorities eliminate drug lord Pablo Escobar. The cost of leading and advising foreign forces is relatively small. More important, working through indigenous forces may be the only means of solving a problem such as insurgency or terrorism. SOF can obtain intelligence about insurgents, terrorists or other adversaries by steeping themselves in local knowledge provided and shared by indigenous forces that have come to trust and respect them.

When SOF succeed, they often produce strategic effects at low political cost, which is always useful and sometimes imperative, as is generally the case in irregular warfare. Experts also argue that SOF's strategic value includes the ability to boost public morale, or reassure the public that action is being taken, which can reduce political pressure to take less prudent courses of action.[13] SOF can also display military competence in a way that humiliates the enemy and emboldens one's own forces, and their low profile and tactics can minimize chances of unwanted escalation of a conflict. In other words, SOF theoretically can provide disproportionate value by controlling military and political costs, both domestic and international, through small-unit activities that produce discriminate effects in ways that conventional forces cannot.

Yet, as Luttwak argues is the case with relational maneuver in general, special operations can also fail catastrophically if the enemy's weaknesses are assessed incorrectly. Commando raids that do not achieve surprise, psychological operations that inflame rather than win over public opinion, and training missions that appear to sanction repugnant behavior on the part of the indigenous forces who have been trained are all examples of possible SOF failures. The potential for such failure explains why those who prefer the lower risk inherent in attrition warfare dislike SOF as a matter of principle, and why any leaders employing SOF must carefully assess the threat they are dealing with and the best means of employing SOF in a strategy to counter that threat.

The Boers can be used again to illustrate this point that SOF's strategic value is not just a function of their distinguishing skill sets, but also a question of the strategic problem and the strategy employed against it. The Boers knew they could not hope to match British conventional forces, so they used small-unit strike operations that initially defied the advantages of British conventional forces. When the British brought in overwhelming conventional force the Boers relied more on guerrilla operations that leveraged their support in the local population. The strategic value of special operations for the Boers was not just a function of their intrinsic attributes; it evolved along with their security challenge and chosen strategy. In considering the role of SOF within a preferred strategy, one must understand not only SOF skill sets, but also the advantages and disadvantages of employing SOF directly and indirectly, and as the leading effort rather than a supporting effort.

SOF'S DIRECT AND INDIRECT MISSIONS

SOF can operate directly against enemy targets themselves, and indirectly through their influence on indigenous forces and populations; for example, by training or advising foreign forces on how to do the mission. While most SOF missions may be conducted directly to neutralize enemy targets or indirectly to achieve broader political-military objectives, some missions tend to align better with the direct or indirect approaches because of the nature of the threats they address and preferred U.S. strategies. For example, SOF can train a foreign force to conduct direct action to build host government support for U.S. counterterror policy. Yet when terrorists strike directly at U.S. interests the tendency is to desire more control over the outcome by conducting counterterrorism missions directly. On the other hand, while SOF can conduct foreign internal defense directly against insurgents, the political value of allowing local forces to conduct the mission usually argues in favor of an indirect approach for SOF. Generalizing in this manner it is possible to categorize currently recognized SOF missions as more direct or indirect in the manner shown in Table 5.1:

TABLE 5.1

SOF CAN OPERATE DIRECTLY OR INDIRECTLY

Direct	Indirect
Counterterrorism	Unconventional Warfare
Counterproliferation	Psychological Operations
Direct Action	Foreign Internal Defense
Strategic Reconnaissance	Civil Affairs
Information Operations	

This general categorization of SOF missions as direct or indirect is not perfect; it is merely useful. SOCOM acknowledges, for example, that unconventional warfare is *"predominantly* conducted by, with, or through indigenous or surrogate forces" (emphasis ours), a tacit acknowledgement that U.S. forces might themselves carry out guerrilla warfare. Similarly, some would observe that SOF can pursue counter-terrorism indirectly by training and supervising foreign forces. Even so, the categorization of SOF missions as direct and indirect is useful since it underscores the diverse commando and warrior-diplomat skills that SOF must have in order to perform well, and the fact that SOF must specialize between the two to some extent. Both points can be illustrated with the German use of SOF in World War II.

The Germans emphasized SOF unconventional small unit strike capabilities and in-depth political, cultural and linguistic skills differently depending on the missions their SOF had to carry out. Brandenburger units (so called because they trained south of Berlin in the state of Brandenburg) were formed in 1939 as part of the German military intelligence branch under the command of Admiral Canaris. They were an all-volunteer force of men whose salient, indispensable skill was the ability to speak a foreign language fluently. Most of these men had lived abroad for extended periods. With these foundational skills they were then taught to operate in enemy territory for extended periods. They learned how to move quietly through forests, survive without supplies, produce explosives, and kill silently. The most important part of their training, however, prepared them to pose as soldiers of the enemy army, to capture bridges and other important infrastructure, and to confuse the enemy.

Germany also had units that conducted special operations of short duration that emphasized speed and surprise without reliance on linguistic and cultural knowledge. The German air force had paratroopers who from time to time were trained for a specific operation, such as the well-known raid on the Belgian fortress of Eben Emael in 1940. The Germans also used a special air unit (the Kampfgeschwader 200) to recover agents behind enemy lines, support encircled German units and anti-Soviet insurgents in the Ukraine, and bomb high-value bridges and other installations with guided planes filled with explosives. The German navy developed special "K units" in 1943 that used small submarines and boats to attack the Allied fleet in places like

Normandy and Italy. These forces received training in close combat, survival, naval engineering, foreign languages, and navigation.[14] Like the Germans, the British and French used special units during their post–World War II colonial wars that excelled in both direct and indirect approaches.

Thus, SOF missions tend to align with the direct and indirect approach, and each approach requires some degree of specialization with SOF's commando and warrior-diplomat skill sets. When SOF operate directly against enemy targets they tend to use their commando capabilities more, and when they operate indirectly through their influence on indigenous forces and populations they tend to rely more heavily on their political, cultural, and linguistic skills. In short, for SOF to be well prepared for indirect and direct missions, some SOF units must weight their training and equipment toward either the commando or warrior-diplomat skill sets.

When should SOF's direct or indirect approaches be used? Again, it depends on the nature of the security problem and the strategy devised in response, but some general observations are possible. The direct approach provides more control over outcomes. If split-second timing and complex collaboration with other U.S. forces is required, commanders may not want to rely on SOF's ability to work with foreign forces who are less familiar with U.S. tactics and techniques, but instead will want U.S. SOF to accomplish the mission directly. When SOF directly undertake a mission it is more likely that it will be well coordinated with other U.S. military operations and activities, carried out with high competence and full commitment, and completed consistent with U.S. objectives and values. In fact, some SOF missions cannot be worked through foreign forces with an acceptable chance of success. For example, even highly competent foreign special operations forces may fail when the plan is compromised because other host government officials do not support their objectives. Employing SOF directly also means that the success or failure of the effort will redound primarily to the credit or discredit of the United States. Whether this is advantageous or not depends on the political situation. Sometimes it is preferable to give others credit for the effort even when U.S. SOF conduct the mission themselves.

There are also advantages and disadvantages to SOF acting indirectly. The obvious advantage to working through foreign forces and populations is that it reduces the resource and political commitment of the United States. Sometimes the scale of the problem precludes a direct approach. When there are not enough SOF or other U.S. forces to meet mission requirements, then SOF must work at least to some extent indirectly through advice and training to foreign forces. For example, Special Forces working in conjunction with the Kurdish Peshmerga and a good deal of U.S. airpower were able to tie down and rout Iraqi forces in the northern regions of Iraq in Operation Iraqi Freedom. The mission was originally assigned to the 20,000-man Fourth Infantry Division, but they were unable to get to the fight in time. The indirect approach also has the advantage of a lower profile, such as when a handful of U.S. SOF advised government forces in El Salvador on how to defeat Farabundo Martí National Liberation Front guerrillas. In some cases, a government will only allow the United States to take an indirect approach, as was the case in the Philippines described in chapter 1. Sometimes, it is better to work through foreign forces and populations simply because this is the best or only way to accomplish U.S. objectives, especially in the cases of insurgency or terrorism. SOF can obtain intelligence about insurgents, terrorists, or other adversaries by steeping themselves in local knowledge provided and shared by indigenous forces that have come to trust and respect them. By contrast, trying to solve the problem directly with larger U.S. forces can engender disproportionate resentment and resistance from foreign populations that is counterproductive for overall objectives.

Solving a problem indirectly often means objectives are achieved more slowly, with less certainty, and sometimes with questionable methods. Some forces trained by SOF have been accused of torture or other behavior at odds with U.S. values and objectives. Working through other forces invariably means ceding a degree of control over behavior. In the case of the Kurdish Peshmerga in northern Iraq, Special Forces and other U.S. government representatives had to work hard to keep the Peshmerga from irritating the government of Turkey by pursuing their objective of an independent Kurdistan. SOF can use persuasion to guide indigenous forces, making it clear that continued U.S. support requires limits on their behavior, but working through third parties invariably is tricky business, and SOF must often settle for less than optimum outcomes and iron control over tactics in exchange for lower overall costs to the United States.

SOF INDEPENDENT AND SUPPORTING ROLES

SOF commando and/or warrior-diplomat skills, applied directly or indirectly in SOF missions, may supplement other means of defeating a threat, or they may constitute the main effort. Different circumstances and strategy choices determine whether SOF are employed in a supporting role to facilitate conventional-force operations, or whether they are asked to generate the strategic effects themselves. When Congress created SOCOM, it wanted standing special operations forces that were prepared to conduct independent missions (terrorism, nation-building and training friendly foreign forces):

> The Congress finds that ... the special operations forces of the Armed Forces provide the United States with immediate and primary capability to respond to terrorism; and the special operations forces are the military mainstay of the United States for the purposes of nation-building and training friendly foreign forces in order to preclude deployment or combat involving the conventional or strategic forces of the United States.[15]

Congress also explicitly allowed the Commander of SOCOM to exercise command of a selected special operations mission if directed to do so by the president or secretary of defense, which at the time ran contrary to the normal practice of having regional combatant commanders direct any forces operating within their geographic spheres of responsibility. Allowing the Commander of SOCOM to command a special operation is tantamount to saying the operation is a strategic event that transcends geographic considerations and/or one that requires deep special-operations expertise; points that underscore congressional intent that SOF should be able to take the lead in countering some threats.

Missions where SOF take the lead as the primary force, we refer to as *independent* SOF operations. Independent SOF operations may receive some support from conventional forces, but the entire effort is organized according to SOF principles and preferences. Well-known examples would be rescuing hostages from terrorists or executing a raid for political effect. In contrast, when SOF are in a supporting role to conventional forces, their special missions are executed so as to facilitate the achievement of conventional force objectives. For example, in World War II Navy

TABLE 5.2

INDEPENDENT AND SUPPORTING ROLES: HISTORICAL EXAMPLES

	Independent Role	Supporting Role
Direct Missions	Attempted capture of Aideed in Somalia	Attack on Iraqi border radar to open first Gulf War
Indirect Missions	Training El Salvador's forces in counterinsurgency	Leading Kurdish tribesmen in Operation Iraqi Freedom

underwater demolition teams surveyed beaches and mined underwater obstacles. These special missions were undertaken explicitly to assist the assault on the beach by general-purpose forces. Some SOF missions assigned by Congress, including Civil Affairs and Psychological Operations, support conventional military operations quite prominently. This fact, along with historical accounts of congressional motivations, indicate that Congress was not trying to limit SOF to independent operations of strategic significance and that it understood that SOF would be asked to support conventional forces.[16]

Thus, in the United States at least, both congressional intent and historical precedents illustrate that special operations may be conducted directly or indirectly, and in support of conventional forces or as part of an independent strategic effort. Table 5.2 illustrates the point with historical examples.

The effort to capture Aideed was a direct action mission that SOF undertook independently of, but with support from, other military forces to achieve a strategic objective. The attack on the Iraqi radar at the beginning of the Gulf War was a direct action mission that supported a conventional military operation. Training Salvadoran forces to improve their ability at counterinsurgency was an indirect way of getting at our enemies and was done independently of other U.S. military forces. SOF worked through, by, and with Kurdish forces in support of the broader conventional military effort in Iraq.

THE STRATEGIC VALUE OF SOF'S SUPPORTING ROLE

In general, when SOF perform in an independent role they provide greater strategic value since they provide the primary effort. In a supporting role, SOF make a strategic contribution only to the extent that the conventional force operations depend upon SOF for success. If the overall conventional force campaign plan is critically dependent upon SOF's contribution, then SOF's strategic value would be almost as high as when they perform independently, but this is almost never the case. Seldom does it make sense for a world power like the United States, whose conventional military forces are currently unrivaled, to build a war strategy around higher risk special operations. Not surprisingly, military leaders prefer strategies built around lower risk conventional force strategies. They also generally prefer that SOF support conventional force operations with their direct action skills, which seem more immediately relevant to conventional warfare since they involve destroying priority targets. Yet, precisely because SOF direct action has more in common with conventional force operations, it provides less strategic value when used for their support.

SOF direct action that only augments the conventional force plan of attack rather then critically enabling it makes a tactical rather than strategic contribution. For example, SOF might be asked to help improve the odds of success against a difficult command and control site by infiltrating behind enemy lines and using laser designators to illuminate the target for pinpoint bombing by aircraft. Since aircraft could attack the target without SOF, SOF merely improve but do not critically enable the conventional force scheme of attack. It is easy to envision plans of attack that are critically dependent upon a SOF contribution (think "the Trojan Horse,") but they are not the norm for superior conventional forces that need not accept the higher risks inherent in SOF-centric conventional warfighting strategies. SOF direct action missions in support of larger conventional force operations only hasten victory or retard defeat, which is pretty much the historical norm in the modern era for all special operations.

Moreover, what SOF direct action can accomplish better than conventional forces is changing as conventional forces expand their ability to identify and destroy targets quickly, accurately, and at ever-greater distances. As the ability of conventional forces to see targets and strike quickly, deeply, and with precision increases, the number of instances where commanders would otherwise need SOF direct action missions decreases. It does not make sense to risk SOF when a missile can accomplish the same task unless the situation requires human on-the-scene judgment to obtain the desired effect, which is something other than the mere destruction of the target. It is either a different effect altogether, such as the propagation or retrieval of information, or an extremely discriminate effect that larger munitions cannot produce, such as the targeting of specific individuals or information nodes critical to command and control of the enemy's forces.

The strategic value of SOF direct action missions in support of conventional force operations also must be assessed in light of their costs, which have increased over the past decade. Since the end of the Cold War, both conventional force commanders and SOF leaders increasingly default to special operation plans with large elements of conventional force support to reduce SOF risks as much as possible.[17] For example, SOF-led force packages in Operation Iraqi Freedom were often large, especially if including forces that were put on standby to rescue SOF should they need assistance. While allocating large supporting-force packages to SOF may make sense in light of the commander's overall objectives, it inescapably diminishes the strategic value of SOF direct action contributions by raising their costs relative to the value of their contributions.

SOF direct action missions take on relatively greater strategic significance in small contingencies or irregular warfare. First of all, SOF are the force of choice when the requirements for on-scene human judgment and exceedingly discriminate firepower are manifest, as is the case when operating against terrorists and other irregular enemies hidden among the general population. SOF direct action also offers the possibility of eliminating a charismatic or powerful leader, which sometimes seems to be a key factor in defeating irregular warfare threats. An example would be the use of SOF in attempts to neutralize Noriega in Panama and Aideed in Somalia. It is difficult to deal a decisive blow even against such lesser opponents, and much more difficult to do so against more formidable opponents. A world power such as the United States certainly would not want to rely exclusively on SOF's ability to decapitate enemy leadership in any case. Generally it would be preferable to take a shot at a leader when possible and continue with the main military effort regardless, as happened at the opening of the recent war in Iraq.

SOF's indirect action missions, which rely on cultural and political skills, arguably can make comparatively greater contributions to the success of conventional force operations than SOF direct action skills. Conventional forces need SOF cultural and political skills and cannot easily substitute for their absence. These skills take years to develop, and conventional forces, which must commit ever more training time to mastering their own increasingly complex operations, do not have time to acquire such skills. Nor are their personnel selected with such skills in mind. Thus, all other factors weighed equally, SOF indirect action missions make a comparatively larger strategic contribution in SOF's supporting role to conventional-force operations because they differ the most from conventional force operations and are more difficult to substitute for if not provided by SOF.

It also is true that some SOF indirect missions make sense only when they are conducted in support of conventional force operations. Unconventional warfare against highly authoritarian regimes is a case in point. For example, it is often observed that OSS Jedburgh teams accomplished the most at the least cost with missions conducted immediately in advance of the D-Day operations. In fact, some military scholars disparage allied unconventional warfare in World War II. John Keegan argues it had little effect in France and that it did positive harm in the Balkans at terrible cost.[18] He notes Churchill's desire to "set Europe ablaze" with SOF was based on a misapplication of lessons from the Boer War in South Africa. The Boers employed special operations tactics against the British, but both sides retained a civilized ethos, which included a refusal to directly harm prisoners or civilians. In contrast, the Nazis' ruthless tactics allowed them to use no more than a single division in France for counterinsurgency work. In the Balkans, Keegan argues that the Cetnik leader Draza Mihailovic actually had the correct strategy. Mihailovic wanted to lay the groundwork for a general uprising but conserve his strength until allied conventional forces were in close proximity. Churchill, however, supported Tito's communist guerrillas because they were willing to initiate hostilities that produced little other than horrendous civilian casualties. Similarly, unconventional warfare in the Korean War accomplished little, but wasted a lot of precious manpower[19] after the conventional conflict ground down to a rough geographic stalemate and North Korean internal security forces could concentrate on eliminating infiltrators.

Some would point to the Special Forces experience in Afghanistan as a successful independent case of unconventional warfare. Special

Forces leading and advising Afghan tribesmen did successfully depose the Taliban regime in Afghanistan, but it is difficult to argue their effort amounted to traditional, behind-the-lines unconventional warfare. They worked superbly, but with standing forces in the field who were not vanquished or reduced to guerrilla operations, and against adversaries who did not control the theater of operations or the terrain from which SOF operated. History illustrates that unconventional warfare against established and ruthless regimes works best in close cooperation with large conventional forces that can keep the enemy's security forces too busy to track down the unconventional units.

The limited utility of unconventional warfare absent a complementary conventional force effort reflects some hard political realities that inform U.S. strategy. No U.S. forces, including SOF, will employ or allow those they work with to kill innocents wantonly to generate terror, while the governments we employ unconventional war against are often the types that will terrorize their own citizens in order to eliminate a small SOF-backed group of insurgents. For this reason, SOF generally conduct unconventional warfare at a disadvantage. The unconventional warfare mission can take the strategic lead against incompetent adversaries, or those restrained from brutal and indiscriminate behavior, or from a protected sanctuary, but otherwise it ought to be conducted as support for larger conventional force operations.

THE STRATEGIC VALUE OF SOF'S INDEPENDENT ROLE

When do independent SOF operations make strategic sense? Some notable examinations of strategic special operations argue that political leaders are too easily beguiled by the opportunity independent special operations offer to solve a strategic problem at low cost. One such study even concludes that strategic special operations should be considered a "last resort ... when no other option is at hand."[20] These studies, which actually look only at direct rather than indirect special operations, correctly note that such special operations are relatively high risk. Moreover, it is true that political leaders can underestimate their potential risks (as was the case in Somalia). It is easy to overstate this point, however. Frequently senior leaders understand perfectly well that such operations are high risk but approve them as the best among a poor set of alternatives.

Rather than concluding independent SOF direct action missions should be considered a last resort, it makes more sense to simply observe that their risks should be soberly assessed in light of other alternatives and the interests at stake.

This is particularly true now that senior leaders must consider the incalculably high threat represented by small groups of terrorists employing weapons of mass destruction. Independent SOF direct action missions that allow on-scene human judgment to be applied on how best to neutralize such threats often will compare favorably with other military alternatives. If some sort of military action seems unavoidable because the cost of taking no such action is prohibitively high, then the risk of independent special operations simply must be deemed less than that of larger conventional force operations. In addition, it should be noted that even a failed direct action mission may convey some political advantages, as occurred when SOF attempted to rescue prisoners in Vietnam and diplomats held hostage in Iran, or when they tried to locate Iraqi missiles in the first Gulf War. The failed special operation to free prisoners in North Vietnam signaled U.S. capabilities to the enemy, and by some accounts led to improvements in the prisoners' conditions. The failed effort to rescue hostages in Iran ultimately lent credibility to the newly elected President Reagan's threats to end the ordeal by force if necessary. And the failed attempt to locate missiles that could strike Israel helped reassure that country that all necessary action was being taken to protect their interests, which served the strategic purpose of keeping Israel out of the war.

Independent SOF missions that take an indirect approach typically have a lower profile and represent a lesser commitment of prestige and political support. They particularly make strategic sense in limited contingencies against irregular forces. SOF have the skills necessary to discriminate between combatants and noncombatants and to mobilize the indigenous support that is essential for isolating the irregular forces politically and tactically. In contrast, conventional forces typically prefer to focus on directly eliminating the insurgents or terrorists rather than indirectly gaining long-term political support from the population. Such a direct approach cannot produce the necessary intelligence to enable attacks on the insurgents or terrorists, and it cannot by itself reduce the number of irregular force supporters. If an insurgency has grown to the point where SOF working with local forces cannot contain it, then they may require supplementation by and close collaboration with conventional forces. The French discovered as much in their counterinsurgency efforts in Algeria in the late 1950s and early 1960s, as did the United States with respect to its experience in Vietnam.

To summarize the argument so far, SOF's strategic value is in part a function of their intrinsic attributes, which are grounded in their commando and warrior-diplomat skills, which they may employ directly or indirectly, independently, or in support of conventional-force operations. When SOF should be assigned independent or supporting roles, and whether they should use their direct or indirect approaches, depends on the nature of the security problem and our strategy for dealing with it. For the United States, we can say that the relative strategic value of direct action in support of conventional force operations has declined as conventional force strike capabilities have improved, while the value of SOF indirect action missions in support of conventional force operations persists and perhaps has grown when the threat is irregular warfare. The strategic value of independent SOF operations remains highly situation-dependent, but generally has increased along with the stakes involved in combating terrorism and irregular warfare.

These observations suggest that over the past decade SOCOM's strategic concept for SOF should have put relatively more emphasis on independent SOF missions rather than support to conventional-force operations, and at least as much if not more emphasis on indirect missions as direct. However, this is not quite what happened, as a review of the evolution of SOF missions since the creation of SOCOM demonstrates.

THE EVOLUTION OF SOF MISSIONS

SOF missions have not changed dramatically since they were defined by Congress. SOCOM made some minor terminological adjustments to the list of congressionally assigned missions. What Congress called Strategic Reconnaissance, SOCOM christened Special Reconnaissance to distinguish the way SOF collects information from the use of strategic assets such as satellites. SOCOM redefined Theater Search and Rescue as Combat Search and Rescue to limit SOF's responsibility for personnel recovery to selected high-risk combat situations, and it uses a category called "special activities" as a euphemism for SOF loaned to the Central Intelligence Agency in support of covert operations. SOCOM also designated Humanitarian Assistance and Combat Search and Rescue as collateral missions to deemphasize their importance. Other so-called "collateral missions," such as humanitarian demining and security assistance have been added and dropped by SOCOM over the years, but always considered peripheral to SOF's core missions. In fact, stretched thin by the war on terrorism and needing to jettison less critical missions to other forces, SOF leaders eventually stopped making reference to any SOF collateral missions (anti-terrorism, peacekeeping, search and rescue) in 2003 and chose to emphasize SOF's "core tasks." We summarize these changes in Table 5.3.

These trends illustrate the powerful influence of supply and demand in how military roles and missions are articulated. When demand for forces is high, military leaders are more selective about how they define roles and missions. When demand for forces declines, roles and missions are defined more broadly. As an example, when U.S. military force structure was being cut in the early 1990s in response to the demise of the Soviet Union, arguments were made for an expanded definition of national security. Many commentators redefined "threats" as any untoward event, including disease and natural disasters, rather than the purposeful actions of an adversary. Threatened with the prospect of dollars migrating to those who could address such nontraditional problems, all sorts of creative arguments about the use of U.S. military forces suddenly were given a respectful hearing. For example, noting with approval the organizational and administrative triumph of the first Gulf War, many commentators opined that the military could use its vast logistics capabilities to provide relief in the aftermath of hurricanes or other natural disasters.[21]

SOF were not immune from such reasoning. On the contrary, the cutting-edge and diverse skills inherent in SOF led to a wide variety of proposed missions, some of which would significantly alter the definition of SOF's strategic role for the Department of Defense. For example, some thought SOF should take on a larger role in support of domestic authorities—aiding local law enforcement, disaster-relief and development programs. Considering well-publicized law enforcement disasters such as the botched operation against the Branch Davidian compound in Waco,

TABLE 5.3

Evolution of Primary and Collateral SOF Missions

Core Missions

Primary Missions	92	93	94	95	96	97	98	99	00	01	02	03	04	05	06
Foreign Internal Defense	▲	▲	▲	▲	▲	▲	▲		▲			▲	▲		▲
Special Reconnaissance	▲	▲	▲	▲	▲	▲	▲		▲			▲	▲		▲
Direct Action	▲	▲	▲	▲	▲	▲	▲		▲			▲	▲		▲
Counterterrorism	▲	▲	▲	▲	▲	▲	▲		▲			▲	▲		▲
Unconventional Warfare	▲	▲	▲	▲	▲	▲	▲		▲			▲	▲		▲
Psychological Operations	▲	▲	▲	▲	▲	▲	▲		▲			▲	▲		▲
Civil Affairs	▲	▲	▲	▲	▲	▲	▲		▲			▲	▲		▲
Collateral Special Ops	▲			▲											
Counter Proliferation			▲		▲	▲	▲		▲			▲	▲		
Information Warfare					▲	▲	▲		▲						
Information Operations							▲		▲			▲	▲		
Collateral Missions															
Coalition Support				▲	▲	▲	▲		▲						
Combat Search & Rescue	▲		▲	▲	▲	▲	▲		▲						
Counter Drugs	▲		▲	▲	▲	▲	▲		▲						
Humanitarian Demining			▲	▲	▲	▲	▲		▲						
Humanitarian Assistance	▲		▲	▲	▲	▲	▲		▲						
Security Assistance	▲		▲	▲	▲	▲	▲		▲						
Special Activities				▲	▲	▲	▲		▲						
Peacekeeping			▲	▲	▲										
Coalition Warfare					▲										
Antiterrorism	▲		▲												
Ecology & Biodiversity			▲												

Data is taken from two Department of Defense sources; SOF Posture Statements for the years 1992, 1993, 1994, 1996, 2000, 2003–4, and 2006, and from Annual Reports to the President and Congress for the years 1995, 1997, and 1998. No data was available for 1999, 2001, 2002, or 2005

Texas, some said SOF could assist, or even assume responsibility from, local and national law-enforcement agencies in dealing with hostage or barricade situations. Others thought SOF skills that proved so useful to the humanitarian mission to the Kurds in northern Iraq could be used to similar effect during domestic emergencies like the catastrophic damage to south Florida caused by Hurricane Andrew. There were even suggestions that SOF use their training and language skills to good effect by teaching foreign languages in inner cities.

Although these suggestions seem unreasonable now that SOF is consumed with the far more important global war on terror, they are worth mentioning for two reasons. First, SOF traditionally argue they benefit from training in a wide variety of environments, usually foreign, but not exclusively so. SOF train with U.S. domestic law enforcement authorities and for other purposes in domestic settings.[22] Therefore, asking SOF to take up domestic responsibilities might not seem to some like a great distraction from their principal duties. Second, and more importantly, with the rising value of homeland security, calls for SOF to become more involved in domestic missions are again on the upswing. Even before the terrorist attacks of September 11, arrangements were being made to permit SOF to support domestic law enforcement on a case-by-case basis; e.g., in support of security for the 2002 Winter Olympics in Salt Lake City.

SOF are particularly valued in a domestic context because of the skills they have developed to deal with neutralizing weapons of mass destruction. Provisions in several federal statutes, including the Fiscal Year 2000 Defense Department Authorization Act, Public Law 106–65, permit the secretary of defense to authorize military forces to support civilian agencies, including the FBI, in the event of a national emergency, especially any involving nuclear, chemical or biological weapons.[23] Now press accounts[24] indicate that SOF also support the mission of protecting U.S. leadership and perhaps key infrastructure sites that previously were the sole preserve of domestic agencies. To meet the requirement for a standing SOF capability to act immediately in the event of a domestic crisis, SOF will have to familiarize themselves with presidential (and other key leader) practices and with the operational challenge of securing key sites like nuclear installations. SOF even have been assigned recently to perform bodyguard functions for senior foreign leaders. Both missions stretch the bounds of historically understood SOF roles and missions. They tie down SOF's direct action skills in the service of defensive instead of offensive operations.

Another proposal for expanding SOF roles and missions has been debated more publicly, and its implications are more significant than SOF domestic duties. There is increasing support for reconsidering the division of labor between the CIA and the Department of Defense in ways that directly affect SOF in two respects. First, some want SOF to assume more responsibility for generating human intelligence to support combating terrorism, and second, some want SOF to assume all responsibility for paramilitary operations. Both these issues have been debated back and forth between the CIA and the Department of Defense for decades. The Pentagon has long been interested in doing more to obtain its own intelligence. After the Carter Administration diminished CIA human intelligence capabilities in the 1970s, the Department of Defense felt the need to take up some of the slack. It also suspected that intelligence of military import was a lower priority for the CIA than intelligence on political developments; and this is especially true for SOF, with their highly detailed tactical intelligence requirements. Of course, the CIA resists such encroachment as meddling by amateurs. On the other hand, the CIA has tried multiple times to give responsibility for all paramilitary operations to the Pentagon, and the Pentagon has always rejected the mission expansion.[25]

Both of these issues recently assumed a higher profile due to congressional interest in the way the executive branch is managing the war on terrorism. The congressionally mandated commission to investigate the September 11 terrorist attacks recommended that CIA paramilitary clandestine and covert operations should become the responsibility of the U.S. Special Operations Command. "Clandestine" typically means the operation itself is hidden in order to increase its chances of success, and "covert" means the identity of those carrying out the operation and the nation they represent are hidden, or at least plausibly deniable. Operations can be both clandestine and covert, and often are. Paramilitary typically refers to covert military operations.

The commission felt that while the CIA was more nimble in responding to the events of September 11, the Department's paramilitary capabilities were more lethal. Combining the two seemed like a good idea. In addition to nudging the Bush administration to consider assigning SOF responsibility for covert paramilitary operations, Congress took remedial action to improve SOF's paramilitary capabilities. Congress passed legislation permitting SOF to pay and equip foreign forces or groups supporting the U.S. in combating terrorism.[26] In Afghanistan, SOF had to rely on the CIA to pay for such arms, ammunition, and supplies, and the CIA used this fact to persuade SOF to cooperate when there were differences of opinion between SOF and the CIA about courses of action. The legislation reduces SOF dependence on the CIA. It even allows SOF to pay for information, which strengthens SOF's ability to gather human intelligence and further blurs the line between SOF and the CIA. The CIA argued that this authority might encourage SOF to compete and interfere with CIA covert activities.

In response to the commission's recommendation to give SOCOM responsibility for all paramilitary actions, President Bush had the Pentagon and the CIA study the issue. Two powerful arguments for assigning all covert and clandestine paramilitary activities to SOCOM[27] needed to be considered. The first was that it would provide unity of command. CIA paramilitary operatives and DoD SOF operating in Afghanistan cooperated but reported up parallel chains of command. While the cooperation worked better than previously in Vietnam, Central America and other places, it still led to friction that on occasion detracted from the overall effort. The second argument was that giving SOCOM responsibility for all paramilitary actions would improve efficiency. In the 1970s, the CIA drastically reduced its paramilitary cadre when demand for them fell off after the withdrawal from Vietnam, and when it subsequently needed them against the Soviets in Afghanistan or to train contra rebels in Nicaragua, the CIA "borrowed" SOF from DoD or hired retired SOF to build them back up. Since 9/11, however, the CIA has expanded its paramilitary force to the point where, according to one source, "the CIA is practically creating its own army, navy and air force."[28] Arguably it would conserve resources if all such activities were brought under one organization in order to avoid duplicative capabilities. Despite these arguments, the current leadership of the CIA and the Department of Defense, like many before them, ultimately decided that it would be wise to leave their current division of labor for paramilitary operations in place. They felt it was better to allow the CIA a paramilitary capability that can be used in situations where SOCOM's political, cultural, and legal restrictions would not permit SOF to be as effective.

Concerning expanded SOF human intelligence activities, during the same period that the Department of Defense and CIA were reviewing paramilitary activities, press reports indicated that the Pentagon was unilaterally expanding Department of Defense capability to conduct human intelligence operations. The Department reportedly expanded intelligence training for Special Forces at several sites so that they could engage more effectively in operational "preparation of the environment," which includes surveying potential operating sites and in other ways preparing for future military operations. At least one retired senior officer from the Central Intelligence Agency believes these activities may encroach on the Agency's responsibilities.[29]

Senior Pentagon officials also confirmed that a new Strategic Support Branch in the Defense Intelligence Agency was created to provide SOF units with better battlefield intelligence.[30] The unit sends out teams of approximately ten civilian and uniformed personnel with case officers, linguists, interrogators, and other specialists from the Defense Human Intelligence Service who can scout potential targets and collect and integrate intelligence on the scene. The Department stressed that the new teams, which may operate in a clandestine manner, rather than competing with traditional CIA activities were enhancing the military's ability to gather intelligence to support its own operations. Although Congress was willing to give SOF limited funds for intelligence operations, and provided funds for the Strategic Support Branch teams in the 2005 budget, some were alarmed by press reports on the scope of the Strategic Support Branch team activities. Individual members of Congress reportedly questioned whether the secret missions carried out by the units might amount to covert actions, which would require a presidential directive and formal Congressional notification.[31]

Expanding SOF activities in human intelligence and paramilitary operations would not be an abrupt departure from SOF's current missions, which always have involved some of these types of activities. In particular, previous SOF unconventional warfare missions included limited human intelligence activities and paramilitary operations. For example, as described in chapter 1, PSYOP forces in Iraq carried out intelligence or information gathering missions in Iraq after the fall of Saddam. In Vietnam, SOF conducted human intelligence operations, although these had little success because of weak counter-intelligence capability. Adversaries penetrated the indigenous intelligence agencies

SOF worked with and compromised SOF's human agents. SOF partici-pation in paramilitary activities has a better record, but only because SOF personnel were loaned to the CIA, which was more supportive of their unconventional activities and better equipped to support them. In short, just as conventional forces cannot concentrate on SOF skills without reducing their competency in large-scale maneuver and fire op-erations, SOF cannot expand into covert intelligence tradecraft without risking a reduction in some of their special skills. Cost effectiveness is another issue. Infrastructure for covert activities is expensive. Can we afford to duplicate this expensive infrastructure? The better option, repeatedly arrived at by various commissions and panels, is to find a way to make SOF and the CIA collaborate well when circumstances demand it.

Thus a number of major expansions to SOF missions, and potentially to its strategic role, have been proposed and rejected since the creation of SOCOM—initially in response to a general decline in demand for military forces following the dissolution of the Soviet Union, and more recently in response to the rising demand on SOF in the war on terror-ism. SOF capability to act independently has increased with the addition of resources and new authorities, but a major expansion of SOF into do-mestic affairs, paramilitary, and human intelligence operations has been rejected for good reasons.

There have been two noteworthy changes to SOF missions since SOCOM's inception, however. First, a new commander of SOCOM, Wayne Downing, embraced counterproliferation as a mission in 1994. This mission is defined as actions taken to support DoD and other governmental agencies to prevent, limit, and/or minimize the develop-ment, possession, and employment of weapons of mass destruction, new advanced weapons, and advanced-weapon-capable technologies. Over the next few years, SOCOM elevated the new mission to the top of their special mission units' agendas. As a new mission that is gen-erally classified, historical examples are not readily available. A theo-retical example would be dispatching SOF to recover and neutralize a stolen weapon of mass destruction. Counterproliferation requires in-telligence on the location of weapons of mass destruction and on the intentions of those who possess such weapons. This mission also re-quires SOF personnel to obtain specialized knowledge of how to handle or render weapons of mass destruction safe without collateral damage.

The entire counterproliferation mission fits comfortably within the direct action tradition of SOF, and indeed, could just be considered an extension of SOF's direct action mission. It requires moving quickly and stealthily to an adversary's highest value target and neutralizing it or obtaining special intelligence on the target so that other forces can neutralize it if necessary. It is true that specialized training beyond what even SOF's direct action units regularly receive is required for neutralizing weapons of mass destruction, but that is true of many novel classes of targets.

Second, from 1996 on, SOCOM added information warfare (later changed to information operations) as a principal mission for SOF. Information operations are defined as actions taken to influence, affect, or defend information, information systems, and decision-making. They require a sophisticated exploitation of electronic warfare, computer network operations, psychological operations, military deception, and operations security. Like counterproliferation, and with the exception of psychological operations (a traditional SOF mission now considered part of information operations), SOF involvement in information operations is generally classified. A theoretical example would be inserting SOF behind enemy lines to insert false information into a computer network to deceive enemy commanders. In the context of support for conventional forces, information operations could provide SOF with numerous direct action targets, such as computer servers or communication links. The Department of Defense's stated purpose for information operations is to disrupt an adversary's unity of command, misdirect his plans, and ultimately control the adversary's communications and networks. A creative commander could think of numerous ways in which SOF could contribute to these objectives, and SOF could exploit information operations for its own purposes. At least some elements of SOF are inherently attuned to the importance of psychological operations, military deception, and operations security, and are familiar with some electronic warfare techniques as well. Therefore, the relatively new dimension of information operations for SOF is computer network operations. SOF must protect their computer network links for obvious reasons, including operations security, and they increasingly may use computer network attack to help conduct other SOF missions such as counterproliferation, combating terrorism, or unconventional warfare. Until SOF are used independently or by conventional force commanders to affect enemy information systems and decision-making decisively, SOF information operations are better considered a tactical improvement in SOF capabilities rather than a fundamentally new addition to SOF's list of missions.

In contrast to SOCOM action on counterproliferation and information operations, both of which fit best with SOF's direct action missions, the scope of SOF's indirect action missions has changed little despite some extensive debate on the matter. Within Special Forces, most of the debate has been about the value of unconventional warfare. After the fall of the Soviet Union, some thought there was little future to unconventional warfare. Others argued the mission should evolve.[32] For example, SOF could train small friendly governments with limited self-defense capabilities in the critical components of a successful popular defense movement, including preplanning activities to ensure unity of effort, popular support, will to resist, leadership, intelligence, propaganda, and outside assistance. The deterrence value of such planning and training for a small country with larger, more powerful neighbors is significant, as the Swiss experience attests.[33] All the bedrock unconventional warfare skills would be relevant for such a mission: training, language, cross-cultural communication, and guerrilla warfare tactics. Others argued that since unconventional warfare rarely works except in close proximity to large conventional force operations, SOF doctrine should be changed to reflect this fact. Finally, others argued that unconventional warfare is entirely situation dependent, and must be defined broadly so that it can be applied as circumstances warrant. This point of view eventually won out, and thus the status quo on SOF indirect missions was maintained.[34]

The same is true of psychological operations and civil affairs. Despite periodic debate about whether they really constitute special operations, the two missions remain assigned to SOCOM and little changed in scope or definition, with the exception that recently the Army's Forces Command took responsibility for Reserve CA and PSYOP forces. Within the psychological operations community, there is a desire to expand beyond tactical psychological operations to much more robust theater and even "strategic" psychological operations, but these aspirations have not materialized. Policymakers do not want psychological operations employed strategically, that is, against friendly and neutral populations. They prefer to leave that mission to public diplomacy and public affairs professionals. As for more robust theater psychological operations capable of disseminating themes and messages to large target audiences across a military theater of operations, SOCOM has not supported the reforms necessary to enable a major expansion of capabilities in this area.[35]

RECONSIDERING SOF'S STRATEGIC VALUE

The fact that SOCOM has increased emphasis on direct action missions such as counterproliferation and information operations is not surprising. SOF's commando skills, direct action missions, and role in support of conventional forces are all better accepted by senior Pentagon leaders who tend to favor short-term lethal operations against valued targets and give the bulk of available resources to the special units most dedicated to them. Some believe that SOCOM's leadership actually shares the conventional military preference for using SOF only in support of conventional forces and primarily with their direct action skills, and that as a result support to general purpose forces has eclipsed independent SOF missions as SOF's dominant strategic role.[36]

To the extent this is true it presents two general problems. First, overemphasis on support to conventional forces can easily lead to SOF being used for elite rather than really special operations. Arguably, the use of SOF to protect domestic facilities and foreign leaders is an example of such inefficiency, as would be their use for room clearing in urban fighting. These missions may require elite but not special forces. Second, using SOF predominately for direct action and in support of conventional forces may increase the chances that SOF will lose their unconventional mentality over time. A recent Special Forces officer's comment that "the most effective way to separate the insurgent from the populace is to kill him," seems indicative of such a problem.[37] Longer-term operations designed to influence political outcomes through use of indigenous populations and resources are less valued, and thus the SOF units that contribute most in this area, such as the Army's Special Forces, civil affairs, and psychological operations forces, are neglected by SOCOM leadership.[38] During the 1990s, SOCOM increasingly relegated Army Special Forces to nonlethal training of foreign forces, and their unconventional-warfare skills atrophied as a result. Civil affairs and psychological operations typically receive even less attention from SOCOM's leadership and its resource allocation processes.

Misconstruing SOF's primary strategic role as support to general purpose forces has a more immediate and pernicious effect. It reinforces the tendency to neglect SOF's indirect missions and the possibility that they should take the strategic lead in the war on terrorism. SOCOM and Pentagon leadership misunderstand what it takes to defeat insurgents and terrorists. In the current approach, special mission units have been married up with more robust intelligence support to help them obtain timely intelligence on high-value terrorist targets, which assisted in the apprehension of Saddam Hussein and the elimination of his two sons. Such direct action missions, when available intelligence and relations with allied governments permit them, are important. They keep terrorist leaders off-balance and eliminate their best trained personnel. Ultimately, however, killing terrorists alone is a losing proposition if terrorist leaders can replace those losses by raising up more leaders and foot-soldiers. To date, evidence suggests the ranks of the terrorists are being replenished. An October 16, 2003, memorandum from Secretary of Defense Rumsfeld to his top officials demonstrated that the secretary was sensitive to these issues.[39] In the memo he muses as to whether the billions being spent to defeat terrorist were having sufficient effect, and whether a new organization was needed. He expressed particular concern about whether the enemy was recruiting more to its ranks than we were capturing, dissuading or killing.

The secretary's concerns were well placed, which is why the broader objective of counterterrorism strategy must be a reduction in terrorism's mass appeal, a reduction in recruits, and growth in the willingness of those with knowledge of the terrorists to stop supporting them, or even better to betray them. This can be accomplished only by isolating the terrorists and their ideology within the broader span of Islamic communities, not by eliminating all the terrorists.

If SOCOM better appreciated the strategic value of applying SOF indirectly, it would prioritize its forces and their missions differently. Working through indigenous security forces and populations will produce broader and more enduring results over time by reducing the appeal of terrorism and producing better intelligence on terrorists' operations. Depending on context, civil affairs, psychological operations, and Special

Forces ultimately are more relevant for these purposes than special mission units. Forces expert in the indirect approach have the skills to use friendly indigenous forces for counterterrorism and counterinsurgency. They can help persuade local leaders and populations to support friendly governments and help provide for their security; and they can make and keep contacts with local populations and security forces to produce "actionable" intelligence for targeting terrorists. Resource and command decisions should reflect this fact, and there are some indications this is beginning to happen.

The Pentagon's 2006 Quadrennial Defense Review put more emphasis on the indirect approach, for example by stressing the need to undermine popular support for terrorists. It also included decisions to increase SOCOM's Civil Affairs and Psychological Operations forces by one-third (approximately 3,700 people), and Special Forces battalions by 33 percent. Recent reports also suggest they are receiving more funding from SOCOM.[40] The new forces will make less of a contribution, however, if they are not trained to appreciate the value of the indirect approach and resourced accordingly.[41] This was the point of the RAND Corporation's recommendations mentioned at the beginning of this chapter; SOF need to put greater emphasis on training and advising indigenous forces to combat terrorists and insurgents rather than doing so themselves. SOCOM must come to better appreciate SOF's role as an independent strategic option that can be applied indirectly in order to advise Pentagon leaders on the best means of employing SOF. If this had been done, more might have been accomplished against irregular forces in Afghanistan and Iraq. Instead, conventional force commanders are learning to approach the insurgencies more unconventionally, focusing less on attrition and control of territory and more on obtaining the support of the indigenous populations. This has been a slow and painful learning process with substantial and perhaps irreversible strategic costs to the United States.

CONCLUSION

Matching SOF's distinguishing attributes with the most important and appropriate security challenges is the key to identifying SOF's strategic value, and by extension their most appropriate roles and missions.

SOF's core commando and warrior-diplomat skills allow them to operate with discrimination in complex political-military environments that are inhospitable to conventional forces. The primary strategic value of these skills for the United States is their ability to counter unconventional threats (which includes but is not limited to undermining popular support for the enemy). Thus this should be SOF's primary strategic role. Whether SOF deal with unconventional threats directly or indirectly, they ought to take the strategic lead rather than supporting conventional forces. SOF skills provide a lesser strategic value by making conventional force operations more effective; directly by holding a wider set of enemy targets at risk, and indirectly by undermining popular support for the enemy. SOF support to conventional operations should therefore be considered a secondary strategic role that is only as important as SOF are critical to the conventional force plan of attack. We also have made a general case to the effect that when supporting conventional force operations SOF's indirect missions are comparatively more important than its direct action capabilities. Consequently, those SOF missions best categorized as indirect should receive priority from SOCOM.

Despite these conclusions, military leaders tend to prefer SOF support for conventional force operations, and SOF's direct action approach more than its indirect missions. This status quo on SOF roles and missions likely would prevail for the foreseeable future if it were not for a tectonic shift in the nature of the security environment that has pushed debate about SOF roles and missions to the forefront of military strategy. Over the past decade, the fundamental nature of military competition changed in two respects that cannot be ignored and that require adjustments to SOF roles, missions and oversight.

The two specific missions added by SOCOM—counterproliferation and information operations—reflect those seismic shifts in the security environment. Information operations are a reflection of the growing importance of information-age technologies in war, and counterproliferation is a response to adversary efforts to circumvent U.S. prowess in conventional war by acquiring unconventional means of attacking U.S. interests. Information operations may increase the strategic utility of SOF direct action against an important range of information targets that are not susceptible to precision bombing. Similarly, the concern that terrorists might acquire weapons of mass destruction accentuates the value of SOF when directed against unconventional threats. These two profound security trends, filtered through the strategic value of SOF's intrinsic attributes, are the key to how SOF should be raised, trained, equipped, and organized in the future. They are the subject of the next chapter.

6

SOF and the Future of Warfare

Preparing sof for the future requires an assessment of how changes in the security environment affect SOF. In the previous chapter we argued that SOF's ability to counter unconventional threats, hold a wider set of enemy targets at risk, and undermine popular support for the enemy provide enduring strategic value for the United States. While these SOF roles endure, their relative importance and supporting missions have changed along with the security environment. In particular, SOF's increasing attention to counterproliferation and information operations can be seen as part of a broader trend in security affairs that many argue will "transform" military affairs in our lifetime.

The profound change some defense planners argue is taking place in national security affairs is a function of vast improvements in information technology that are fundamentally altering social, economic, political, and military relationships, just as the agrarian and industrial revolutions did in previous ages. Many believe that these information-age technologies will generate sweeping changes across a range of human endeavors, including a revolution in military affairs. The nation that best exploits these new technologies and "transforms" its military capabilities will be rewarded with unprecedented military advantages.

To determine how and to what extent such a transformation of military affairs might affect SOF, a number of difficult questions must be answered. Will some or all of SOF's current missions be passed to or shared with transformed conventional military forces? If transformed military forces are able to perform some of SOF's current missions, will SOF's strategic role change? If some SOF missions or even SOF strategic roles change, how should SOF prepare for the future? Answering these questions requires sorting out elements of continuity and change in military affairs generally, and then applying those findings specifically to SOF in light of SOF's essential attributes. Doing so is the purpose of this chapter.

We begin by noting that information-age military transformation need not affect SOF to the same extent as conventional forces. The bold claim of transformation theorists is that smaller, information-dominant forces can readily defeat larger, less sophisticated forces. Why? Because information technology that enables highly precise targeting and a comprehensive view of the battlefield allows conventional forces to substitute information for larger forces or more firepower. But since SOF do not rely heavily on mass in the first place, they have less opportunity to substitute mass with information. In addition, terrorists and insurgents are resilient in the face of superior conventional forces precisely because they make targeting difficult by hiding in small numbers among the general population, so it is not immediately apparent that these traditional SOF target groups would be vulnerable to transformed forces.

Since SOF skills are especially well suited for combating terrorists and insurgents, it could be argued that the future for SOF is more attention to these familiar problems, irrespective of information-age transformation trends. In fact, that is what we argue in this chapter; that conventional forces are undergoing a fundamental transformation that will not affect SOF the same way or to the same extent.

TRANSFORMATION AND SOF

Assessing the impact of military transformation on SOF first requires a better understanding of transformation. The literature on the subject is extensive, but a brief overview will suffice for our current purpose.[1] The transformation concept in the United States evolved from debate among defense analysts on the military impact of revolutionary technologies and from studies on the implications of the American victory in the 1991 Gulf War. In 1993, Andrew Krepinevich suggested that the nature of the United States victory presaged a military revolution. He defined a military revolution as taking place "when the application of new technologies into a significant number of military systems combines with innovative operational concepts and organizational adaptation in a way that fundamentally alters the character and conduct of conflict." This results in "a dramatic increase—often an order of magnitude or greater—in combat potential and military effectiveness."[2]

Krepinevich asserted that since the fourteenth century the world has experienced possibly ten such revolutions, each of which wedded new technologies to new operational concepts and organizational structures. The relative balance between these three elements—new technology, concepts, and organizations—and whether each was directly manifest might vary. For example, the Napoleonic revolution featured mass mobilization of society for war, but arguably was made possible by industrial-age technologies that freed up large quantities of manpower for combat arms. Transformation in the twentieth century resulted in panzer divisions, naval airpower and carrier battle groups, long-range strategic bombers, nuclear-powered submarines, and intercontinental ballistic missiles. In the twenty-first century, Krepinevich speculated that information technologies would permit military organizations to detect, identify, track, and engage large numbers of targets with a higher degree of precision and lethality—over a far greater area, in a far shorter period of time—than was previously possible.[3] The first Gulf War provided early evidence of this emerging revolution, as U.S. forces proved able to blind Iraqi forces and then destroy them at will with highly precise fire.

Other transformation theorists noted, however, that the information-age revolution "will not render guerrilla tactics, terrorism, or weapons of mass destruction obsolete." Instead, the reverse might be true: "where unconventional bypasses to conventional military power exist, any country confronting the United States will seek them out."[4] In fact, some argued that U.S. conventional military advantages already were so significant that adversaries were developing weapons of mass destruction and irregular warfare as means to counter those advantages.[5] Security experts also worried about adversaries investing in inexpensive high and low technology options to exploit discrete U.S. conventional force vulnerabilities, such as cheap mines, missiles, and computer network attack capabilities. Collectively, these means of countering America's growing superiority in large-scale conventional warfare were called "asymmetric warfare." Asymmetric warfare captured the attention of defense reformers, who reasoned that transformed forces would have to be able to deal effectively with adversaries who employed asymmetric approaches.

Drawing on insights from transformation theorists and defense reformers, and pushed by Congress, the Pentagon increasingly embraced
transformation over the latter half of the 1990s. The services and SOF
initiated experimentation programs to devise new concepts that could
exploit emerging technologies, but they were not willing to embrace fundamental changes in their programs or operating concepts. During the
2000 presidential race, candidate George Bush made transformation a
major issue by arguing that the military was not changing fast enough.
He tied the diffusion of information-age technology across the globe to
asymmetric threats, arguing that nations such as Iraq and North Korea
were using such knowledge to develop biological, chemical, and nuclear
weapons of mass destruction as well as sophisticated delivery systems
as diverse as missiles and suitcases. Such technology also empowered
terrorists and posed "unconventional and invisible" threats the United
States could not ignore. In essence, the diffusion of knowledge was com-
pressing the traditional levels of war (strategic, operational, and tactical)
by allowing small irregular groups to conduct strategic operations directly against high-value targets virtually anywhere. America, the world's sole
superpower, was strangely more vulnerable than ever before. It could not
be adequately protected by a military still organized "more for Cold War
threats than the challenges of a new century—for industrial age operations, rather than for information-age battles." To reduce America's vulnerability, Bush promised to transform the military with new concepts
enabled by the "revolution in the technology of war."[6]

Thus transformation, which began with a focus on the opportunity for
conventional forces to exploit the information revolution, soon encom-
passed the goal of countering asymmetric warfare capabilities as well.[7]
Concerns that adversaries increasingly would use irregular warfare in
order to counter overwhelming post–Cold War American conventional
force superiority were spectacularly reinforced on September 11, 2001. If
there previously were any doubts, 9-11 made clear that some terrorists
would not be constrained by fear of provoking a devastating response
to mass casualty terrorist attacks. On the contrary, terrorists wanted
to provoke a massive U.S. response that previous attacks had failed to
stimulate, and even now are seeking weapons of mass destruction with
the hopes of using them to even greater effect than the 9-11 attacks. The
attacks also seemed to demonstrate that terrorists could use access to
global information sources to help plan and carry out their attacks. The

general diffusion of knowledge, enabled in part by global commerce and information flow, made it increasingly likely that terrorists could create their own weapons of mass destruction if they were unable to steal or buy them. Whereas terrorists and insurgents were a threat to U.S. citizens and policy objectives in the past, now their transnational nature, ability, and demonstrated intent to wield weapons of mass destruction made them a direct threat to the American way of life. Suddenly the price to be paid for a steep learning curve on irregular warfare—a price the United States has paid repeatedly over the course of its history—is prohibitively high.

The late Arthur Cebrowski, who was the leading transformation advocate and theorist in the Bush administration's Pentagon, captured this dimension of transformation succinctly and related it to new strategic principles that he argued should guide defense strategy and planning:

> In this age of strategic uncertainty, *risk is managed by increasing the breadth of capabilities,* no matter the imperfections, even at the expense of highly effective capabilities bought in quantity.... . The real issue is not how much is enough, but do we have the breath of capabilities necessary to address strategic gaps. The importance of this metric was dramatically demonstrated on September 11, 2001.[8]

The need to exploit information-age technology and simultaneously develop effective means of handling asymmetric threats was incorporated in the Pentagon's subsequent broad definition of transformation as a process that shapes the changing nature of military competition and cooperation through new combinations of concepts, capabilities, people, and organizations that exploit our nation's advantages and protect against our asymmetric vulnerabilities.[9] These two dimensions to transformation—the opportunity to exploit information-age technology and the need to counter asymmetric warfare—represent two primary issues for the future of SOF.

First, like all military forces, there is the question of how SOF can best exploit the information revolution (and other new technologies it enables), and whether doing so will open up new mission opportunities for SOF or merely improve their prospects for successfully conducting their historic missions. Second, given SOF's historic focus on unconventional warfare, there is the question of whether SOF already are optimized for asymmetric warfare, or whether there is room for improvement. As conventional force transformation stimulates adversaries to counter American superiority by asymmetric means, SOF's traditional focus on unconventional threats will grow in importance, but SOF must still consider how to respond. SOF could just expand the same forces and capabilities, or it might find it necessary to make changes that would significantly improve their capabilities against unconventional forces. We consider SOF's future in light of these two transformation issues—information-age warfare and asymmetric threats—beginning with the impact of information-age technology and concepts.

SOF AS A MODEL FOR INFORMATION-AGE FORCES

Advances in military technology can affect the scope and significance of special operations. For example, Colin Gray notes the impact that advances in mobility (aircraft) and the invention of plastic explosives by Britain had on strategic special operations in World War II. The mobility to operate deep behind enemy lines and cause considerable damage with lightweight high explosives opened up a much broader range of targets for special operators.[10] Mobility and explosives have advanced since World War II, and additional "breakthrough" technologies—especially in high explosives—are anticipated. Even now, stealthy, long-range means of inserting SOF into enemy territory and powerful lightweight explosives mean that today there are few targets beyond the range of SOF.

Even so, perusing transformation literature for insights on the impact of information-age technologies on SOF's future is not very fruitful. Typically, SOF are described as a model for information-age forces rather than as a major beneficiary of information-age technology. It is not hard to see why this is so. First, SOF already possess many of the characteristics that military forces should aim for according to transformation advocates. For example, three of the planning principles adopted by President Bush's Department of Defense in its pursuit of transformation already characterize SOF as models for transformation. Because nimble adversaries employing asymmetric means could achieve surprise, strike across national and regional boundaries, and adapt quickly to exploit opportunities and reduce vulnerabilities, Secretary of Defense Donald Rumsfeld focused defense planning on the need to manage uncertainty, respond globally, and adapt quickly.

To cope with uncertainty, transformed American forces would have to be flexible enough to contend with a greater degree of variability inherent in a more complex security environment. For example, since developing an international consensus on the nature of security threats is more difficult absent the unifying Soviet threat, allied support will have to be recruited on a case-by-case basis. Hence, U.S. forces must be prepared to work with "coalitions of the willing" as circumstances permit. And of course, given the more diverse set of security threats, military forces must be prepared for irregular threats, not just large-scale conventional force on force engagements. SOF are a good hedge against uncertainty because their skills allow them to work well with impromptu allies and counter unconventional threats.

Second, U.S. forces have to be globally responsive to threats. The ability of the United States to wield power is increasingly dependent on the ability of its military to control what often are referred to as the twenty-first century commons: space, air, sea, and cyberspace. U.S. forces need to overcome the historic tyranny of distance with increased speed and range. They have to plan and execute operations transregionally, on short notice over vast distances, and en route to their engagements, mixing diverse forces from regional and functional commands (e.g., for transportation, strategic forces, or SOF). Defense planners also argue that U.S. forces need a new global posture with a new and flexible set of valued partners, operating from main bases but also austere forward bases with little infrastructure. SOCOM already is able to rapidly undertake operations on a transregional basis, with a global perspective, and supported by very little established infrastructure, so SOF already possess many of the global force attributes that defense planners want for conventional forces.

Third, U.S. forces have to institutionalize adaptation. Since politico-military circumstances are evolving quickly, U.S. forces need to be capable of adaptive contingency planning that is nimble in the face of rapidly changing planning assumptions. They need to rapidly integrate improved intelligence from diverse classified and unclassified sources as planning evolves. U.S. forces also must plan on the diffusion of knowledge, assuming their technological advantages might be relatively fleeting. They need to overcome highly adaptive adversaries by constantly experimenting with new concepts, and by integrating commercially available technology on an iterative basis in order to field new capabilities more rapidly. SOCOM already has its own acquisition authority to permit rapid integration of technology, and SOF recruit and train personnel to think in a flexible and adaptive manner. So again, SOF is often considered a model rather than a target for these kinds of defense reforms. In short, many believe that SOF and SOF command structures are already optimized to make contributions to all the major transformation objectives established by Pentagon planners: working well with impromptu allies; developing flexible capabilities applicable to the full spectrum of security problems; rapidly planning and executing transregional operations en route from austere forward locations; rapid integration and adaptation of technology and concepts; and good integration of diverse intelligence sources.

Transformation theorists also highly value other intrinsic SOF attributes, for reasons well explained by this excerpt from a landmark Pentagon publication on transformation:

> In moving to the information age, the nation is entering an era where *advantages are conferred on the small, the fast and the many.* These capabilities in turn will be paid for by the ponderous and the massive. Size shrinks because of the "demassification" of warfare that comes about by substituting information for tonnage. The Air Force says that a target once requiring 1,000 bombs to destroy now requires only one. That magnitude of change is owed almost entirely to information technology and processes. A second key metric is increased speed, resulting not just from the decreased mass to be moved, but also from organizations streamlined to benefit from their superior information position. The result is a highly responsive, dispersed force with lower costs per unit of combat power. That is, increased combat power is vested in yet smaller units. One result of this is the need for new joint organizations and processes in small units, which were once considered the exclusive domain of the military services.[11]

Transformation theorists believe that small, agile, quickly deployable and networked forces will outperform the larger traditional military units that emphasize communicating up the chain of command at the expense of sharing information among distributed units. The possibility of rapidly sharing information about enemy and friendly activities, and the reality that fast, highly accurate, longer-range missiles can be launched from land, sea, or air—and hit targets in any of those domains—means that collaboration in both offense and defense among all tactical units, regardless of military service, is essential. Transformation advocates therefore argue that "jointness," or collaboration between the Army, Navy, Air Force, and Marines, is not only essential for managing the overall warfighting effort well, but also at the small-unit level. Since SOF pioneered new levels of joint integration at the small-unit level, this is another respect in which they are viewed as a model for conventional force transformation.

Indeed, there are so many SOF-like attributes associated with transformation that transformation theorists and other defense experts frequently explain transformation in part by noting that it means conventional forces will become more "SOF-like." In this regard, greater attention to SOF is seen as evidence that transformation is taking root in the U.S. military, so much so that SOF are regularly included in lists of transformational assets. For example, Eliot Cohen has argued that "the combination of precision weapons, Special Operations forces, and sophisticated intelligence-gathering systems indicates the beginning of a desperately needed "transformation" of the American military."[12] Numerous well-respected defense experts, and internal and external Pentagon studies, also use SOF as a model for transforming conventional forces. The prestigious Defense Science Board, for example, has recommended making more traditional Army units "SOF-like," with the 82nd and 101st airborne divisions among the most likely candidates.[13] The Marines are embracing a SOF-like emphasis on distributed operations, small-unit expertise and decision-making,[14] and, as noted in previous chapters, recently decided for the first time in history to send forces to join SOCOM.[15] The Marine decision to send units to SOCOM, apparently strongly supported by Secretary of Defense Rumsfeld and his transformation advocates, symbolizes the unprecedented support for collaboration between SOF and conventional forces.

Commingling SOF with transformation is so common that one distinguished Army War College analyst felt compelled to write a justification for the continued existence of conventional Army forces. Reacting in particular to commentary extolling SOF's excellent performance in routing the Taliban, he felt the need to make the point that "even if one posits a much larger role for SOF in future counter-terror warfare, this is still a long way from a sound case for a SOF-predominant military in 2020."[16]

If SOF are already "transformed," then they cannot exploit information-age reforms as much as conventional forces. There is another reason
why SOF are not likely to be affected as much by transformation as other
forces. The first SOF "truth" propounded by SOCOM is that humans are
more important than hardware. The "central defining quality of SOF has
always been its distinctive personnel."[17] Among those factors SOF can
control, the quality of SOF personnel—not technology—is a more critical prerequisite for success. So while SOF will exploit information-age
technology to improve their mobility and lethality, they will always derive
greater comparative advantage from their personnel and the methods
they can employ. This is all the more true as some SOF technology advantages over conventional forces are likely to decrease as conventional
forces absorb information-age technology and operating methods.

For example, consider SOF's direct-action mission. As the range, speed,
and accuracy of modern munitions increase, situations that require a SOF
direct-action solution decrease. All other factors being equal, the time and
risk involved in inserting SOF to destroy targets is far greater in most cases than using precision munitions. SOF can still improve the accuracy of
many munitions by using laser-designators to illuminate the targets, but
the need for such assistance is rapidly diminishing as the United States
builds up a formidable inventory of all-weather, satellite-guided munitions. The same point applies to strategic reconnaissance. As networks of
sensors increasingly are able to provide highly detailed, real-time surveillance of targets, the need to risk SOF personnel diminishes.

Currently SOF direct action still maintains some small but significant
comparative advantages over conventional munitions. Because of their
ability to tightly link reconnaissance of a target with the ability to strike
the target, and because of their small size and rapid decision-making
processes, SOF integrate intelligence and direct-action capabilities more
rapidly than conventional forces, which enables a faster response time to
fleeting targets. Even this advantage is diminishing, however. Some new
missiles can be reprogrammed in flight from satellites to acquire new
targets, and other missiles are launched directly from surveillance platforms. For these weapon systems the determining factors in response
time for a strike are the time it takes to integrate and confirm the intelligence that positively identifies the fleeting target, and the time it takes
to get authority to release the weapons. In some cases, SOF's ability to
distinguish targets rapidly with human judgment gives SOF an advan-

tage in rapid target confirmation, and SOF's distributed command and control arrangements may give SOF some advantage in weapon-release authority, depending on rules of engagement. However, conventional forces can be expected to close these gaps as network-centric warfare is further developed. Thus, over time, information-age transformation likely will further decrease the range of cases where SOF direct action makes sense to just those where the need to exercise human judgment in immediate proximity to the target is the paramount consideration. Examples would include deciding how to defeat automated defense systems, disarm a weapon of mass destruction, eliminate targets without unacceptable loss of innocent life, retrieve human targets for interrogation, discriminate between fake and real targets, and insert malicious code into computer systems.

Transformed conventional forces may constrain SOF operations in another respect as well. SOF's special attention to operational security means that their behind-the-lines activities are compartmentalized and not made known to conventional force commanders. SOF want to see the battlefield in a transparent and timely fashion, but they are reluctant to let other friendly forces see their activities in real time for fear that this information may be made known to the enemy. This may have to change. In some recent cases, surveillance assets have identified SOF units operating behind enemy lines. If SOF are not plugged into these information networks and identified as friendly forces, then they cannot be distinguished easily from the enemy and may be vulnerable to attack from increasingly lethal friendly units that do not recognize them as U.S. forces. For their safety, if not for greater effectiveness, SOF eventually will have to plug in to network-centric warfare when they support conventional force operations, or else develop new procedures to safeguard their activities from risk of friendly fire.

Of course SOF can exploit information technologies as well as conventional forces, but it is a mistake to think all advancing technology will contribute to SOF's comparative advantage over conventional forces, and thus its ability to provide the nation with strategic value. For example, it has been argued that advancing technology can enable "a small number of personnel, located far from the intended target and protected by a number of personal and collective systems ... to bring a disproportionately large amount of destruction to the battlefield."[18] It is assumed rather than demonstrated that this development would benefit SOF. More lethal, light-weight weapons are just as valuable for conventional forces since they now have the means of delivering them over great distances with precision. SOF must exploit technology that enables innovation in military competencies that cannot be provided by conventional forces, or they lose their comparative advantage.

For example, William McRaven notes in his excellent treatment of special operations theory that technology can help overcome obstacles that otherwise would reduce the simplicity and rapid execution of a direct action plan. He notes that past innovations in manned torpedoes, modified destroyers, shaped charges, and silenced weapons contributed to success in this regard.[19] Future technological developments will likely improve the mobility and lethality of SOF in ways that may facilitate innovative and elegant direct action solutions. Information networks can help SOF identify and navigate to targets, and computer network attack tools can permit SOF to enter and damage enemy information networks that are not susceptible to conventional weapons. SOCOM rightly is intent on exploiting global information networks to better locate and track individual targets, and also to improve SOF command and control. The range and resolution of modern surveillance systems is such that they now are capable of picking up individual human beings, and SOF must exploit this capability. SOF can look for emerging strategic demands that cannot be filled by conventional forces, but their surest guide for innovative use of technology is to focus on SOF's historic roles. They should seek the means to improve their ability to counter unconventional threats, hold targets at risk that are not vulnerable to conventional forces, and reduce popular support for enemies.

In order to make such innovation possible for special operations, Congress gave SOCOM broad budgeting and acquisition authority. Among other things, SOCOM uses that authority to field small advanced-technology systems in as little as seven days and most often in less than six months. SOF must use this authority to explore new and innovative ways to accomplish a mission so that their approaches are less easily countered. This is particularly true since some degradation in SOF comparative advantages over time is inevitable. As SOF pioneer new tactics and technology, some older SOF methods are absorbed by conventional forces. For example, SOF were instrumental in developing secure-burst and tactical satellite communications, night-vision equipment and tactics, extreme cold weather clothing and equipment, laser designator guidance equipment, and fast rope insertion techniques that are now standard practice for other military units. Once these techniques become standard practice even in conventional forces, the opportunity for SOF to use them to help surprise an adversary will be diminished. It is possible that some current SOF missions ought to pass to conventional forces in their entirety once conventional forces master the essential technologies and techniques that enable the mission. For example, the requirements for most combat search and rescue missions, or the close air support provided by SOF AC-130 gunships, arguably are already well within the capabilities of conventional forces. Improving conventional forces can slowly encroach on many SOF advantages over time, as we argue is currently the case with direct action missions in support of broader conventional force operations. In such circumstances, SOF's strategic value in comparison with conventional forces will decline if SOF are not able to consistently reinforce their core advantages through adaptation. Whether and to what extent this is true for SOF missions against unconventional threats is the subject of the next section.

ASYMMETRIC WARFARE AS A FOCUS FOR FUTURE SOF CAPABILITIES

One surprising development in the war on terror—the most compelling asymmetric threat of our times—is the willingness of SOF leadership to countenance the sharing of traditional SOF missions with conventional military forces. Current and former leaders in the SOF community agree that conventional forces can take on some SOF missions. General Peter Schoomaker, a former commander of SOCOM, testified to Congress that "there are a lot of tactics, techniques, procedures [and] technologies ... that will make the conventional force capable of doing many of the kinds of things SOF typically do."[20] The Assistant Secretary of Defense for Special Operations and Low-Intensity Conflict (himself a former special operator) recently noted that he and SOCOM's commander were looking at "ways to share certain SOF tasks with conventional forces that have similar capabilities." They both thought "core tasks such as direct action and special reconnaissance can be performed by regular units that have the specialized training."[21] While they apparently were focused on ways to pass some of SOF direct action missions to conventional forces, other sources, such as the Defense Science Board, seem more interested in having conventional forces take on some SOF indirect action missions; namely collaboration with indigenous forces.[22] All these men intimately familiar with special operations apparently agree that "U.S. conventional forces should continue to develop SOF-like capabilities, allowing SOF to hand off missions more seamlessly or yield missions completely to conventional forces."[23]

The relatively sudden interest in sharing SOF missions with conventional forces is surprising given SOF leadership's historic insistence on the special qualities of SOF that enable these missions. The willingness to share missions cannot be explained by forthcoming information-age improvements to the capabilities of conventional forces. Instead, the desire to share SOF missions with conventional forces coincides with and is best explained by the spike in demand for SOF following the terror attacks on September 11, 2001. SOF were quickly pressed into service around the globe at unprecedented levels of activity. At the same time, demand for people with SOF experience in private-sector security services soared, and SOCOM found it increasingly difficult to retain its personnel.[24] SOF, already accustomed to sudden and long deployments away from friends and family, were being used virtually nonstop in the war on terrorism. Since it takes time to grow new SOF force structure, it seemed wise to reduce pressure on current SOF forces by passing their missions to conventional forces wherever possible. In some cases, even SOF's willingness to experiment with new technologies such as unmanned aerial vehicles (UAV) seems induced by the demands of the war on terrorism. UAVs can provide surveillance without the fatigue associated with human operations.[25]

Sharing missions with conventional forces in the war on terror raises an obvious question for the future of SOF. If conventional forces can become more like SOF and conduct SOF missions against terrorists and insurgents, are SOF really that special, and do their missions really require their special background, training, and equipment? In other words, is SOF's strategic relevance in these mission areas gradually declining despite their heavy use in the war on terror? Are SOF destined to abandon unconventional warfare and concentrate on other niche missions like counterproliferation and information operations? First of all, the point must be made that the wholesale shuffling of SOF missions to conventional forces is not really what has happened so far. Counterproliferation and information operations were identified as SOF missions well before the current spate of interest in passing portions of SOF's portfolio to conventional forces. Instead of passing missions *in toto* to conventional forces, SOF is just discriminating qualitatively between missions on a case-by-case basis, trying to take those it considers most difficult and leaving the less demanding ones for conventional forces. Thus, neither new technology nor the immediate pressures of the war on terrorism have led to new apportionment of missions between SOF and conventional forces, but rather to a somewhat confusing case-by-case division of labor.

This arrangement, however pragmatic in the short term, is rather odd in the abstract. It contradicts the notion that special operations missions require "special" capabilities that cannot easily be provided with just an additional dollop of training for conventional forces. In sharing missions so willingly, SOCOM seems to be violating its four SOF "truths" ("Humans are more important than hardware; SOF cannot be massed produced; quality is better than quantity; and competent SOF cannot be created after emergencies occur"),[26] all of which underscore the fact that SOF characteristics and capabilities distinguish them from conventional forces in ways that cannot be quickly changed. These truths essentially assert that SOF missions cannot be passed to conventional forces without increased risks of failure. Either the missions being passed to conventional forces were not truly special operations, or else we do not really need special operators to combat terrorists and insurgents. In short, mixing the missions of SOF with those of conventional forces has introduced a degree of confusion about what distinguishes SOF from conventional forces—a problem both for the conduct of the war on terror and for the future of SOF.

Much of the confused division of labor between SOF and conventional forces in the war on terror originates in the mistaken assumption that SOF direct action makes the greatest contributions to the war effort. To reduce stress on overextended SOF, the Pentagon and SOCOM relieved Special Forces of their counterinsurgency and counterterrorist training missions in some key states contending with terrorism. Training of the Georgian military was passed from Special Forces to the Marine Corps, and conventional Army units replaced Special Forces in Afghanistan as soon as they could establish a physical presence on the ground. Even within SOF, there is an undue emphasis on direct action at the expense of indirect approaches. Allegedly SOCOM invariably assigns direct action missions to special-mission units even when other SOF units have a better chance of engaging the target. According to one source, Army Special Forces had an opportunity to catch or kill a key al-Qaeda leader but were told to wait until the special mission unit could be called up, by which time the fleeting target had escaped.[27] Other examples of insufficient appreciation of indirect missions are the late deployment of psychological operations forces to Operation Iraqi Freedom, and the historic lack of interest at SOCOM in improving the performance of civil affairs and psychological operations forces.

SOCOM confusion about how SOF can best combat terrorists and insurgents was also evident when Secretary Rumsfeld moved quickly after the terrorist attacks on September, 11 2001, to put SOCOM in the strategic lead on the global war on terrorism. SOCOM's leadership was slow to accept the new position of prominence. In fact, by some accounts then-Commander of SOCOM, General Charles Holland, did not want SOCOM to take the lead in the war on terror. The reluctance of SOF leadership to take the lead in forging an unconventional strategic approach to combating terrorism, along with their tendency to place emphasis on direct action operations (e.g., killing or capturing important personnel) arguably results in less effective prosecution of the war on terrorism. One internal Pentagon study by a former Special Forces officer makes the case that a strategic opportunity in Afghanistan to deal al-Qaeda and the Taliban a more devastating blow was missed because U.S. forces relied too long on the bombing campaign and did not follow up with an aggressive counterinsurgency campaign. When conventional forces arrived, their commanders' heavy-handed focus on attrition of enemy guerrillas squandered a lot of the good will built up by SOF. In a celebrated example of this conventional mindset, highlighted in chapter 3, new commanders forced Special Forces to shave the beards they had grown to facilitate their work with indigenous forces. These errors were compounded by the drawdown of Special Forces in Afghanistan. As the situation deteriorated, more emphasis was put on counterinsurgency beginning in 2004 but the insurgents are still far from defeated.[28]

A similar argument about undervaluing SOF's indirect approach can be made about the war in Iraq, the current center of gravity in the war on terror. Given that Saddam demonstrated he was prepared for unconventional warfare throughout the conflict, and in fact, that his irregular

forces were his most determined fighting units, it would have been prudent to be prepared for unconventional warfare after conventional force
operations wound down. SOF's approach would have been to screen local leaders and their followers, and then use indigenous forces to establish local security as soon as possible. In fact, the Army's Special Forces
took this approach.[29] They even managed to organize some indigenous
forces during the brief war, albeit with mixed results.[30] However, when
policymakers decided to disband civil servants and the Iraqi security
forces as a whole, they dumped a large number of intelligent, trained,
and disgruntled personnel into the ranks of the suddenly unemployed,
and the insurgency quickly became much more virulent. As the costs
of dealing with the insurgency rose sharply, Pentagon planners looked
for an alternative counterinsurgency approach, and considered the "El
Salvador" model; i.e. using small numbers of Special Forces to train and
advise the host nation's forces to defeat insurgents.[31] Since the bulk of
U.S. conventional forces have yet to withdraw from Iraq and turn over
counterinsurgency operations to SOF, the El Salvador model apparently
was found wanting.

SOF resource limitations may require SOF to collaborate with conventional forces in fighting insurgents and terrorists, but SOF should
retain the lead in the collaborative relationship because their intrinsic attributes make them the optimal forces for fighting irregular forces. If this
is the case, then preparing for SOF's future requires that every effort be
made to emphasize rather than obscure the attributes that make SOF so
valuable against asymmetric threats, and to improve SOF's performance
against asymmetric threats if that is possible. By some accounts, SOF do
not need improvement against asymmetric threats so much as they need
political support to do the job for which they are already well prepared.
All that is required is to let SOF "off the leash," liberating them from a set
of artificial political and leadership constraints that have unnecessarily
hindered their ability to take down terrorist organizations.[32]

For example, in retrospect it is easy to argue that SOF's highly discriminate and proportional use of force should have made SOF an attractive option for targeting Bin Laden in Afghanistan prior to the attacks
of September 11, 2001. The Clinton administration worried that cruise
missiles might hurt innocent civilians or miss altogether, thus humiliat-
ing the United States when the results could not be hidden or ignored. A
small SOF team on the ground to positively identify Bin Laden and then

guide in or actually deliver lethal strikes against him without collateral damage would appear to have been a perfect mission for SOF. However, concern about the large force package recommended by senior military leaders (in particular, by General Shelton, a former Commander of SO-COM) and their judgment that prospects of success for SOF would be poor swayed Clinton officials against putting men on the ground.[33] Similarly, in the case of combating insurgency in Afghanistan and Iraq, SOF again should have been an attractive option. By organizing, training, and leading indigenous forces against the insurgents, SOF could have kept the costs to the United States relatively low. In cases where more U.S. forces were obviously needed—and there were cases in both Afghanistan and Iraq—SOF would still have been a good choice for overall command of the counterinsurgency campaigns. Instead, conventional forces took the lead, and their learning curve was steep given their traditional focus on using fire and maneuver to defeat large enemy regular forces.[34]

The argument that already potent SOF goes unused because of political and military leadership concerns about the risk of independent SOF strikes has merit, but it does not account for strategic confusion in the SOF community itself about the value of SOF in the war on terror and SOF's appropriate division of labor with conventional forces. As noted, SOCOM leadership is too ready to support conventional forces even when the enemy is an unconventional one, and to use SOF direct approach when the indirect approach is more likely to yield better results. Thus to prepare SOF for a future that requires SOF strategic leadership in the war on terror requires reforms that address the internal SOCOM propensity to favor direct action and support to conventional forces over indirect action as an independent strategic contribution to the war on terror.

TRANSFORMING SOF FOR THE FUTURE OF
ASYMMETRIC WARFARE

Contrary to the view that SOF do not require reform, we believe that SOF, like all military forces, must transform consistent with the strategic environment and their strategic purposes, and broadly in ways that will affect their organization, concepts of employment, and tactical capabilities enabled by advanced technology. Conceptually, the point of departure for SOF transformation is the realization that, unlike conventional forces, the driving factor for SOF is not the availability of information-age technology so much as the nature of asymmetric threats facing the United States. Improving SOF's ability to counter unconventional threats requires attention to precisely those factors that are overlooked when people conclude conventional forces can conduct special operations; namely SOF's enduring strategic role and those attributes that most distinguish SOF from conventional forces. As argued in the previous chapter, SOF's primary strategic value is not their ability to support conventional forces in major combat operations but their ability to produce strategic effects through the highly discriminate and proportional use of force that avoids politically unacceptable collateral damage or escalation in ways that conventional forces cannot duplicate.

It is SOF's ability to use human judgment to render effects other than mere destruction that explain, for example, why SOF will always be called on for some types of direct action. SOCOM is adept at culling leading edge technology to hone the direct action capabilities of its special mission units, which is where SOCOM largely has focused its attention over the past decade. These investments are warranted so long as they reinforce SOF's enduring, distinct comparative advantages over conventional forces. In other words, one should ask whether the investments help SOF produce more discriminate and proportional effects. Do they improve their ability to make quick political and technically competent decisions at the scene, and to operate with lower visibility and political repercussions than missile strikes or airborne intelligence collection? To the extent the investments simply reinforce SOF's ability to acquire, get to, and destroy a target, the investments should be examined closely for their advantages over conventional options, since it is precisely these tasks where advanced information-age technology most likely will allow conventional forces to make inroads on SOF missions.

These observations underscore the need for SOF transformation and point to the area where transformation is most needed: leadership and organization, with organization defined broadly to include not only structure, but also the underlying theory of performance and its supporting culture. First, SOF must pay more attention to command and control, and in particular, to working closely with political leadership to minimize the perceived and actual risks of special operations. SOF leadership seems conflicted on this point. On the one hand, some SOF policy and doctrine publications stress the requirement for political sensitivity and accountability. Typically, Army SOF leaders and doctrine are more likely to stress the importance of recognizing the political and psychological implications of special operations, which is not surprising given the history of Special Forces and Psychological Operations.[35] In contrast, Navy SOF, almost exclusively focused on direct action, typically do not pay much attention to the issue of political accountability at all. Joint SOF leadership and those who produce joint SOF doctrine (i.e., SOCOM) is dominated by leaders from special mission units that emphasize direct action. SOCOM acknowledges the importance of political sensitivity,[36] but seems to act contrary to this principle on occasion.

Often the principle of political awareness is overridden by a stronger, more visceral conviction that the further SOF is distanced from political authority, the better it can accomplish its missions. In a widely acclaimed account of U.S. military activities in the war on terrorism that is popular in SOF circles, a journalist reached the conclusion that the "smaller the tactical unit, the more forward deployed it is, and the more autonomy it enjoys from the chain of command, the more that can be accomplished."[37] It is true that Washington bureaucracy is hidebound and incapable of rapid, well-informed decision-making, but SOF will not benefit by distancing itself from collaboration with political authorities. On the contrary, as the chapter on Somalia demonstrates, SOF's ability to perform a strategic role for the United States can be seriously diminished when special operations are not aligned with national objectives. The Army special mission unit that predated the creation of SOCOM objected to SOCOM on the grounds that the command would distance SOF strategic direct action forces from national decisionmakers, and that has been the case. For example, by one account the Pentagon has promoted a counterterrorism plan that would allow Special Operations forces to enter foreign countries without concurrence from U.S. ambassadors, a move resisted by the Department of State and CIA, who want to make sure that the operations do not conflict with other U.S. government programs and policy priorities.[38] SOCOM also intervened to make sure a small body of functional expertise in psychological operations designed to increase collaboration between policy officials in Washington and those developing themes, messages, and products for PSYOP forces would be located in Tampa rather than Washington. Located far from policy officials and other communication experts in the nation's capital whose advice is critical for crafting effective and acceptable psychological operations products, the group is not useful and instead simply duplicates work done by the 4th Psychological Operations Group at Ft. Bragg.[39]

Efforts to distance SOF from accountability to and close coordination with political authority will ultimately reduce the strategic value of SOF. If special operations are conducted in a manner inconsistent with the U.S. political system's demand for requisite levels of discrimination, proportionality, and propriety, they will gradually be reduced to less significant operational and tactical applications, not to mention calls for congressional intervention to ensure oversight and accountability.[40] SOF understand their strategic role in principle. They often observe that special operations require command and control different from other forces; that is, oversight at the national level and sharp sensitivity to political implications and local mores. However, in practice SOCOM has grown increasingly comfortable with detachment from Washington decisionmakers. This must change if SOF are to fulfill their strategic potential in the future and maximize SOF effectiveness against asymmetric threats.

If SOCOM wants greater connectivity with national decisionmakers and technical expertise otherwise not available, information-age technology can help overcome some impediments imposed by distance. Improvements in global communications increase the ability of SOF to reach back for both political and technical expertise, making the risk of certain special operations more manageable. Just as more reliable radios improved command and control of dispersed SOF in World War II, modern computer and satellite communications make it possible for SOF to call on expertise from forward locations. A common example is that SOF could tap into relevant experts on call to assist them in neutralizing a captured weapon of mass destruction. Improved communications also increase the value of SOF strategic reconnaissance as they allow SOF-generated intelligence (properly sanitized) to be immediately fed into the global network supporting senior decisionmakers.

Organizational reforms could improve SOF's ability to take advantage of such innovations by reinforcing a culture of innovation. In the past SOF innovation has come from both the senior leadership and from small-unit initiatives. For example, General Downing embraced the counterproliferation mission in the 1990s because he understood its relevance for national security. After his decision, the SOF community dropped its resistance to the mission and built a strong body of counterproliferation expertise. More frequently, creative thinking in the field stimulates SOF innovations.[41] SOF take pride in their reputation for innovation. As one member of the community notes:

> SOF, because of their adaptability, ingenuity, maturity, and organizational size (smaller organizations are more capable of rapid change), will remain the force of choice in a future environment characterized by a diffuse enemy, and ambiguous enemy command-and-control process, and an expanded array of enemy capabilities and methods of employment.[42]

While innovation is part of SOF history and ethos, there are some natural and artificial limitations on SOF innovation that need to be addressed. Innovation first requires an understanding of SOF's strategic value in order to identify areas where experimentation would be profitable. In this regard, confusion about the strategic relevance of SOF, and in particular SOCOM's predisposition to focus on marginal improvements in direct action capability, presents two possible problems for a robust and useful SOF experimentation program.

First, concentrating on marginal improvements in direct action could simply reinforce SOF strengths in areas of declining advantage compared to the growing capabilities of conventional forces. SOF are trying to innovate in ways that reduce risks of failure in direct action,[43] but they need to think broadly about the definition of success in direct action. To offer strategic value, SOF direct action must produce more discriminate and proportionate effects than possible for conventional forces. Surveillance innovations to increase confidence that SOF were tracking the right target would help, as would computer network attack options that could help secure the element of surprise and lower the visibility of U.S. special operations. By contrast, greater investments in lighter-weight munitions could probably be left for conventional forces to experiment with, as such munitions would do relatively little to improve SOF's comparative strategic utility.

Second, a SOF experimentation program concentrated almost exclusively on direct action missions could retard innovation in other areas. Although specifics are classified, there is a general recognition that special mission units dedicated to direct action receive a disproportionate slice of the SOCOM budget, leaving few resources for innovation by other members of the SOF community. The account of the warrant officer presented in chapter 1 supports this view. It is possible to envision experimentation and technologies that could improve SOF's indirect approach. Computer-assisted translation devices are mentioned frequently. Surreptitious means of tagging a target could be provided to indigenous personnel supporting SOF who have a better chance of getting access to the target. This would reduce risk to indigenous personnel and increase their willingness to cooperate with SOF. Secure cell phones, or even some forms of access to the Internet might be used for rapid, safe communication with indigenous forces. Self-organizing sensor nets could be deployed by SOF and monitored to limit the mobility of insurgents. Innumerable means are available to improve the performance of PSYOP should these forces be assigned a higher priority for SOCOM resources.[44]

Recently the alleged imbalance of resources available to different SOF units for research and experimentation has been aired publicly by SO-COM sources, and SOCOM leaders have said that non-special mission SOF are getting more resources.[45] Since these programs are classified, it is difficult to assess the extent to which the alleged imbalance remains a problem. This understandable penchant for secrecy points to another problem with SOF experimentation and innovation, however. To ensure innovative research and experimentation is not misdirected into areas of low marginal return, SOF requires not only a solid strategic concept to inform the design of the experiments, but also the willingness to solicit independent, empirical assessments of SOF performance tests and experiments. Without honest feedback on performance, it is not possible to identify problems or the value of postulated improvements.

Typically, the SOF community has not been open to such cost-benefit analysis, however. The secret world of special operations and the importance SOF place on operational security can engender an insular culture not readily amenable to empirical studies of performance. While understandable, this tendency must be overcome if SOF is to become more adaptive to rapidly evolving threats. Moreover, the problem extends beyond the classified SOF units and programs. Even parts of the SOF community dedicated to open communication such as psychological operations prove resistant to dispassionate debate about means to improve performance. Finally, another issue for SOF in this regard is a cultural bias toward action. While the relatively small size of the SOF community facilitates word-of-mouth transfer of knowledge, SOF's natural focus on action can lead the community to undervalue the importance of learning. Thus, not all of the laudable innovations pioneered at the small-team level are captured and extended more broadly through the SOF community.[46]

NEXT STEPS FOR TRANSFORMING SOF

As argued in the previous chapter, the value of a well-defined strategic role for a military force is that it keeps the organization focused on what is most important. The potential combination of terrorism and information-age technology, particularly in the form of weapons of mass destruction, is the seminal security challenge of our times. Thus SOF ought to focus on its historic strategic value as an independent means of combating such unconventional threats, and in particular, on the global Islamic extremism that is the most likely future source of terrorist use of weapons of mass destruction. There are still conventional military threats, but one might argue that the United States could better absorb the loss of democratic Taiwan or South Korea to their communist neighbors than it could absorb the loss of a major U.S. metropolitan area. More to the point, if South Korea, Taiwan, and other traditional allies are to be protected, it will be with overwhelming conventional military power and not because of the marginal contributions SOF could make in such large-scale conflicts. This argument will become even stronger as conventional forces improve in their ability to achieve effects with smaller, disaggregated forces, thus eroding the utility of SOF direct action support to conventional force operations.

Thus if SOF are to be transformed, priority should be given to making improvements in their ability to counter asymmetric threats, and particularly terrorism and weapons of mass destruction. Transforming SOF to realize its full potential as the primary strategic option for countering asymmetric warfare requires conceptual and organizational changes.[47] SOF need an organizational predisposition to emphasize independent SOF missions more than operations to support conventional forces, and to allocate resources and exercise command of missions with more appreciation for SOF's indirect approach through indigenous forces rather than through SOF direct action missions.

Transforming SOF for significantly better performance against asymmetric threats would help resolve a potential strategic problem for the United States. Following the terrorist attacks of September 11, 2001, many questioned whether the Bush administration's expensive transformation agenda could be sustained in addition to the costs of the war on terrorism. This concern echoes some long-standing concerns about whether a military force can be proficient in both conventional and unconventional warfare. Secretary Rumsfeld, however, squashed rumination about a Hobson's choice between transformation and success in the war on terrorism:

> Some believe that with the United States in the midst of a dangerous war on terrorism, now is not the time to transform our armed forces. I believe that the opposite is true. Now is precisely the time to make changes. The war on terrorism is a transformational event that cries out for us to rethink our activities, and to put that new thinking into action.[48]

The Secretary insisted that transformation was necessary for success in the war on terrorism, and he cited the creative use of SOF supported by high-tech standoff weapons in Afghanistan as evidence that the Administration's transformation strategy was applicable to the problem of terrorism.

Secretary Rumsfeld was correct to argue that it is not necessary to sacrifice transformation for success in the war on terrorism, but it is necessary to transform for conventional and unconventional threats in an efficient and effective manner. Confusion over the inherent differences between SOF and conventional forces, and the erroneous belief that conventional forces can perform SOF missions at minimal risk, can lead to an inappropriate division of labor between conventional forces and SOF and a misallocation of scarce resources. The Army can and should improve its ability to perform against asymmetric threats, but it needs to make the investments carefully in areas that allow light forces to support SOF in irregular warfare. Increasing the size of the Army's Foreign Area Officer cadre, improving light infantry training and doctrine, investing in greater force protection and social intelligence capabilities and other relatively inexpensive niche capabilities optimized for asymmetric warfare make sense for the Army. Trying to disseminate language training and cultural awareness or other SOF capabilities more broadly throughout the Army makes much less sense.[49] Competency in these areas requires a great deal of time, effort, and special personnel.[50] SOF-like language and cultural competency are beyond the reach of the conventional forces which must be expert in large conventional force-on-force engagements.

Clear choices about the division of labor between SOF and conventional forces are particularly important as high post–9-11 defense spending appears unsustainable.[51] A large, inefficient, and poorly focused attempt to improve the performance of conventional forces against asymmetric threats would reduce the resources available for conventional force transformation and increase the risk that such countries as China might more effectively exploit information-age technologies for their large conventional forces. More energy and resources would be available for transforming conventional U.S. military forces if SOF were transformed organizationally and conceptually to better fulfill their strategic purpose as the lead military forces capable of combating weapons of mass destruction, terrorism, and other forms of irregular warfare. The next chapter makes recommendations for how to accomplish such a transformation of SOF, and in particular for some changes in SOF command and control relationships meant to correct the shortcomings identified above.

RESTRUCTURING
SPECIAL OPERATIONS FORCES

THE PREVIOUS CHAPTER ARGUED that in transforming themselves Special Operations Forces (SOF) must do two things. They must remain true to their strategic purpose (producing strategic effects through the highly discriminate and proportional direct and indirect use of force) and they must take account of the changing security environment. In the future, that environment will undoubtedly contain conventional conflict—conflict between the organized and uniformed forces of states. SOF will be involved in these conflicts, as they have been in the past. But this environment also will contain unconventional conflict—conflict between forces that are not agents of states or are not uniformed agents of states. SOF can make its greatest strategic contributions in such unconventional conflict. In particular, we are likely to face two critical problems in unconventional conflict that SOF are particularly well-suited to deal with. One of these—the use by small groups of very lethal weapons—is relatively new, but we are already adapting to it. The other—violence supported by traditional social and communication networks—is longstanding, but we have largely ignored it because it is so foreign to our experience and ill-suited to our modern way of war. A close examination of these two problems will demonstrate the need to restructure SOF so that they are better able to deal with them.[1]

SMALL VERY LETHAL GROUPS

The proliferation of various lethal technologies is not a new problem. In the future, however, it may take a new form. As technology develops, it will put more and more power into the hands of individuals and small groups. To simplify but not falsify, we may divide such individuals and groups into three categories: criminals; those interested in gaining political power; and those interested in some apocalyptic change in the world as we know it. Criminals do not want to take over or change a political order but rather to live off it parasitically. For this reason, they pose a threat different from and less serious than political or apocalyptic groups. Historically, American military forces, including SOF, have not worked against domestic criminals (except in limited supporting roles), in large part because of American traditions of limited government. We believe that this restriction in scope of SOF's activities should remain in place in the future.

Those interested in political power fall into two categories: state and non-state actors. In the future, we should assume that we will continue to confront states that possess chemical, biological, and nuclear weapons. We have established over the years an array of responses to this situation, ranging from deterrent threats to regimes of cooperative control. As far as non-state actors are concerned, however, in the future we may see a change in their behavior. In the past, the political ambition of non-state actors seeking political power provided a limit to the violence they were willing to use. Political power came from having large numbers of supporters. Violent groups wishing to gain political power needed to increase their supporters through persuasion and intimidation. They thus had an incentive to moderate their use of violence lest they alienate potential supporters and stiffen the resistance of their opponents. If they did not moderate their violence, they were unlikely to win and risked creating a backlash that might destroy them. In the past, therefore, terrorist groups had a tendency to want to grow and become political movements and, for that reason, set limits to the amount of violence they used. This strategic logic characterizes even the al-Qaeda Jihadist movement, apparently. In a letter to Abu Musab al-Zarqawi, the head of the most violent insurgent group in Iraq, Ayman al-Zawahiri, al-Qaeda's second in command, warned Zarqawi that his extreme violence threatened to lose the Jihadists their popular support.[2]

The spread of increasingly lethal technologies, however, complicates the traditional analysis of terrorist violence. While it is not true, as often supposed, that terrorists are simply free to choose a level of violence or lethality based on their religious, ethnic, or idiosyncratic views,[3] extra-

ordinarily lethal technology is likely to lead, indeed has already led, some
terrorists to think that this technology is a short cut to power. If a group
possesses a chemical, biological, radiological, or nuclear (CBRN) weapon, its leadership may reason, it will have political power, without having to win more popular support. Thus, in the future, given advances in
technology and their diffusion, we are likely to see small groups, even
very small groups, that have no ambition to grow through political means
(and, hence, less motivation for moderation), but instead seek political
power through the possession of terrible weapons. In addition to such
groups, as in the past, we will also face from time to time apocalyptic
groups who will have an incentive to acquire and use such weapons because they see them as a way of ending the world as we know it. There
really is no solution to the emerging problem of small very lethal groups
other than taking all possible measures to prevent such people acquiring weapons of mass destruction, and directly eliminating the group or
its members before they can employ the weapons. The same holds for
small groups of state forces operating clandestinely, although if identified, these states may be subject to deterrence.

SOF's direct-action approach obviously is well-suited to combating
small, lethal organizations. While this problem is new, the Defense Department has already begun to sharpen its abilities in this area as it con-
centrates on hunting down the al-Qaeda leadership. More must be done,
but at least this new problem has received a lot of attention. In contrast,
the Department and the U.S. government have ignored a longstanding
problem of equal import: the way in which traditional social and communication networks may support terrorism and violent political movements. Since we have tended to pay little attention to this problem, it
requires some explanation. We will then turn to the issue of how we
might improve SOF's direct use of force.

TRADITIONAL NETWORKS AND POLITICAL VIOLENCE

The 9-11 plotters, like the Jihadist movement generally, used the Internet
and jet travel. They also used the *hawala*[4] money transfer system and a
network of mosques around the world. In other words, they operated in
two worlds. They operated in the modern world—the world of individu-
alism, electronic media, centralized bureaucratic control, the world of

state papers, memos, cell phones, and the Internet. They also operated in the traditional world—the world of family and tribe, and decentralized, socially based authority, the world of *hawala*, and *jituanqiye* (family-based Chinese business conglomerates; *Chaebol* in Korea and *keiretsu* in Japan are examples of similar organizations), religious brotherhoods, and family compounds, a world that dominates whole countries but also, through diaspora and emigration, exists in pockets throughout the world. The terrorists operate in two worlds; we operate in only one. We can intercept electronic messages and track money through the international banking system better than we can track money in the *hawala* system or understand well what goes on in religious brotherhoods. In short, they have more strategic depth than we do.

The advantage the Jihadists acquire from operating in two worlds, from using traditional networks when they need to facilitate their operations, is most evident when it comes to the issue of their security. Our information and intelligence collection capabilities are optimized for the modern world only. Human intelligence as a bureaucratic enterprise developed in Europe along with the European state system. Technical intelligence developed later but also in the world of the state system and centralized bureaucracies. Both human and technical intelligence are adapted to that world. They assume that office and authority go together. If we find out what the prime minister and foreign minister are saying to each other, then we have a good idea what the foreign policy will be. If we want a driver's license, we go to the appropriate office and follow the procedures necessary to get one. In many places around the world, the receding tide of European imperialism has left behind the appearance of nation-states but not the reality. In these places, traditional forms of social organization and, therefore, political authority prevail. In these places, if we really want to know what is going on, we need to hear what tribal elders or religious leaders are saying. Or, we need to know what the local tyrant or strong man is saying, and there is no reason to suppose that he is saying it to the prime minister or foreign minister just because that person happens to have a title and hold an office. He is more likely to be talking candidly to those he trusts, who are likely to be members of his extended family or clan. In these places, if we want a license, we are most likely to get it expeditiously if we know the right person.

As we discovered in Iraq, a country with army divisions in the field, a hierarchical command system and a president with a cabinet or war council may look something like a European nation-state, but this does not mean that it functions like one. Family, clan, and religion have an authority in such places they do not have in Europe or in countries that may fairly be described as European. What was critical in Iraq was not, or not alone, intelligence on the Iraqi military's battle order but information on and influence within Iraq's tribal order. The same is true in Afghanistan and in the tribal areas of Pakistan, which have provided such excellent hiding places for members of al-Qaeda and its senior leadership.

The socially based security advantage that terrorists enjoy and our corresponding socially based intelligence disadvantage is perhaps the most glaring consequence of our inability to operate in the traditional social world, but there are others. Two related ones are, perhaps, most important. First, because they are organizations at risk, terrorist groups tend to recruit from among those they trust, which typically means from among their preexisting social relationships—family, kin, friends, mosque attendees.[5] The strength of traditional social networks and the trust they inspire is an important advantage in the recruiting process. We now have only a limited ability to understand and affect such processes. Second, we think strategic communication and the war of ideas is important for winning the war on terrorism, but for the most part, as far as our adversaries are concerned, that part of the struggle takes place at the level of the individual Imam or tribal elder. We now have only a limited ability to understand or influence that level of traditional communication.[6] In security, recruiting, and communicating, traditional social networks provide our enemies with significant advantages.

These traditional networks manifest themselves in a variety of ways. For example, Robert Kaplan reports that ancient spice trade routes connecting the Middle East and Southeast Asia have facilitated the movement of al-Qaeda's money and ideas. In Afghanistan, family connections between a member of the Northern Alliance and a member of the Taliban overcame their political differences and allowed the Northern Alliance to develop intelligence on Americans held by the Taliban. The 9-11 attackers came to a militant version of Islam on their own, but their entry into the operational world of al-Qaeda came about through a network of militant Muslims that conducted them to Afghanistan and ultimately to bin Laden.[7] To borrow a Defense Department neologism, traditional social and communication networks form the "battlespace" of much of the unconventional conflict in the world.

RESTRUCTURING TO BETTER UNDERSTAND AND
INFLUENCE TRADITIONAL NETWORKS

Not all political violence or even all terrorism gets decisive support from the traditional social world, of course. But the terrorism that threatens us most now and in the foreseeable future does. The international Jihadist movement uses the traditional social world. As we have noted, traditional social and communication networks operate in many places around the world and will continue to do so. We face them now in Iraq, the Middle East, Central Asia, South and Southeast Asia, Northern and Sub-Saharan Africa, and in some places in Latin America. It is important to note, however, that these networks also operate in immigrant communities in the otherwise modern countries of Europe and North America. Indeed, because the networks in those countries can combine what is to us the elusiveness of traditional networks with the latest in modern technology, traditional networks in modern countries may pose the greatest threat. Police agencies are the best organizations to respond to these networks in modern states. But the U.S. government needs a capability to respond to these networks outside the modern setting for two reasons. First, these networks provide advantages to our enemies wherever they operate. Second, if approached properly, it may be easier for U.S. personnel to penetrate and influence traditional social and communication networks in their traditional setting outside the modern world. In the modern world, pockets of the traditional world are small and often not accessible to Americans. In those countries where the traditional world is more prevalent, American personnel are more likely to have access to it, once they step outside the small imitation modern world. From this traditional world we may therefore have better access into traditional networks in the modern world. Africans in Francophone Africa are more likely to know what is going on in African communities in France than the vast majority of people that American officials meet in France.

To get access to traditional networks, however, will require that the United States deploy people who can operate in the austere and possibly violent circumstances that often characterize the nonmodern world. While the austere character of the nonmodern, less economically developed world may be evident, its violent character deserves a word. In the modern world of the nation-state, the state and its designated agencies either control the use of force within the state or seek to eliminate or punish those who do not accept this control. In the traditional world, the control of force is less centralized. In some places, it may be localized and under the control of warlords or strongmen. Almost everywhere in this world, violence is more prevalent than in the modern world and may be endemic. In such a situation, training in personal protection may be necessary and knowledge of guns and experience in their use part of what earn someone respect.

Only two organizations in the U.S. government presume that their personnel will operate in violent and austere circumstances, and have expertise in preparing them to do so and supporting them once they are there: the Defense Department and the CIA. (This is why the State Department should not be the U.S. government organization that focuses on traditional networks.) The CIA should not have responsibility for penetrating and influencing traditional social and communication networks for at least two reasons. First, the Agency's key contribution to national security is its ability and expertise in clandestine operations. This is an expensive skill to maintain and use and a dangerous one. Exposure of a clandestine relationship with the United States endangers both those who conduct them and those who participate in them and creates political costs for the United States. Because of the costs and risks associated with clandestine operations, the U.S. government should use them only when no other way to accomplish a significant objective is available. Understanding and influencing traditional social and communication networks does not need to be done clandestinely and, indeed, is probably best done overtly. None of the key information associated with such networks is "secret." On the contrary it is in the open but now largely invisible to us. It becomes visible over time to an observer educated to understand it as the relationships of trust that he builds slowly reveal the structure and character of traditional networks. As relationships of trust lead to understanding of these networks, they also provide the basis for influencing them. Since "secrets" and clandestine relationships are not necessary, there is no reason to have the CIA involved in the task of understanding traditional networks.

A second reason not to have the CIA involved in understanding traditional networks is that the Agency's history, training, structure, and incentives all focus its Case Officers—its clandestine collectors of intelligence—on modern information systems and bureaucratic structures in nation-states or their post-European imperialism imitations. (The State

Department's history, training, structure, and incentives also focus its Foreign Service Officers [FSOs] on the state-centric world and is another reason that the work of understanding and influencing traditional networks should not be done by FSOs.) The Agency's case officers want to know what key decisionmakers have decided. As collectors, they take this same approach to terrorist organizations. They want to know the plans and intentions of terrorist or insurgent leaders. In addition, as operators, they want to disrupt terrorist organizations. All of this should continue, as should the Agency's work against state organizations. But this work is different from the slower, more time-consuming work of coming to understand traditional social and communication networks. It would be false to say that Case Officers who operate in the midst of traditional networks ignore them. On the contrary, they often come to understand them very well. Still, penetrating and influencing them is not the Agency's priority, and it is not structured nor are its personnel trained to do so. Nor should they be. The CIA's core task is necessary and needs to be done better. Doing it better will take all the Agency's time and resources.

Setting aside the Agency and the Department of State leaves the Defense Department as the organization to understand and influence the traditional social world. Hardly anything, of course, could appear less the work of the Defense Department. But in fact personnel in the Department already do this sort of work. The Army has Foreign Area Officers (FAOs) who become experts in a region and do on occasion become experts as well in some aspects of the traditional social world when this exists in their region. Similarly, Defense Attachés also sometimes gain such knowledge. Finally, when Special Forces (SF) engage in the indirect approach, when they work by, with, and through indigenous forces or personnel, they are often working within traditional social and communication networks. So, too, often are Civil Affairs (CA) and Psychological Operations forces (PSYOP). As we saw in chapter 1, some PSYOP teams in Iraq gathered and disseminated information working through and with traditional social networks, although this is not a doctrinal task for PSYOP.

Of these forces, SOF are best suited to focus on the traditional social world. Defense Attachés have a traditional role that they need to fulfill, reporting on military developments as part of American diplomatic missions. Their focus is the military and the official world of the capital city. New or additional duties, especially any outside the official world, will suffer neglect. FAOs are better able to work in the traditional social world than Attachés and should continue to do so, if they already are, but they too have already existing responsibilities. In addition, as an institution, the FAO bureaucracy would not be able to focus on the traditional social world. Its officers cover all regions of the world, not just those where the traditional world predominates. Of the forces that work in the traditional social world, only the SF, CA, and PSYOP bureaucracies have this experience because their forces are quite often in these environments. For none of these forces, however, is understanding and influencing traditional social and communication networks their sole mission. In order to get the training they need or because they are limited in number and are needed in many places, these forces do not stay in one place for long periods of time, which limits their ability to build relationships of trust. Therefore these SOF units, although the best suited to this new task among current military forces, cannot be dedicated to it. Instead, they should be supplemented by a new cadre of people focused on traditional networks.

What would these experts in traditional social and communication networks do with their knowledge? They would help prepare SF for their training missions and other deployments, alerting them about key figures in traditional networks and about issues that SF should be aware of as they carry out their missions. They would assist embassy Public Affairs Officers and PSYOP personnel in getting their messages out by carrying that message to key figures in traditional communication networks. They would serve as linguistic and social interpreters. They would serve as eyes and ears in places that U.S. and even local officials seldom visit and, for that reason, are places where things of interest to the United States happen. They would be able to assist State Department and other personnel in identifying individuals of interest to the United States. They would report what they learned about traditional social and communication networks. Information they gathered from the Lebanese community in West Africa, for example, might be of interest to U.S. personnel in the Middle East, France, and the tri-border region of Latin America, as well as to analysts and policymakers in Washington. Their information would also be of use to a range of Federal law enforcement and intelligence agencies. They should be key advisers if U.S. forces are needed to deploy to their country or region. In addition to using their knowledge to assist military forces and U.S. government agencies, this new cadre, focused on the traditional social world, would wield influence on its own. This influence would come from the relationships of trust the cadre develop and from the assistance that they would provide from already existing overt U.S. government programs. Ultimately, this cadre should have its own source of funds to provide, in coordination with all the other U.S. government agencies that operate overseas, overt assistance to key leaders and organizations in the traditional social world. Such assistance might in some cases be nothing more than a gift to a village of food. The point in such gifts is not their munificence but the relationship within which they occur.

Accepting that a capability to understand and influence the traditional world and to collect its information would be useful and perhaps even necessary, we can sketch how it might work. We imagine military personnel, not necessarily only from SOF, transferring to this line of work in their late twenties or early thirties, after completing a tour or deployment or two overseas in an area or in a job that has brought them into contact with the traditional social world. After a period of training, which will vary depending on background and initial assignment, they will go to their first tour in a U.S. embassy, taking a job that will allow them to travel and meet a variety of local people. The jobs they hold might include working with security assistance or some other activity in the Defense Attaché's office, the Agency for International Development or even in the political or economic section of the embassy. Whichever embassy job they held, their primary work would be to understand traditional social and communication networks. To allow time to meet and build trust and knowledge, a tour should last four or five years, an unusually long time by the standards of the CIA, the State Department or the Defense Department. How and with whom trust and knowledge were built would depend on the interplay of local circumstances and the skills and background of each individual. A second tour would follow in a neighboring or nearby country, and then a third perhaps in the country of the first tour, with time mixed in for training and education. Long periods spent in a subregion (e.g., western sub-Saharan Africa) and in one or two countries in that subregion are necessary to build relationships, knowledge, and influence.

This brief outline raises a host of questions about the personnel management and organization of these specialists in traditional social networks.[8] For example, these specialists do not need a highly differentiated rank structure. Those who enter this work will not have command of progressively larger numbers of personnel. Their rank structure should not be 0–1 through 0–6 (e.g., in the Army, lieutenant through Colonel) therefore, but correspond more to something like apprentice, journeyman, and master. However these and other such issues are decided—and how they are decided will be critical to the success of these specialists—the key point is that their personnel system will be different from anything now found in the Defense Department. This might suggest that their organization not be part of the Department. But as we have argued, the Department is the best location in the U.S. government for their organization. If the organization must be part of the Defense Department, then it needs to be a separate organization within the Department to have any chance of surviving in the Department bureaucracy. Since the organization will be small, certainly by Defense Department standards, it must be part of some other organization in Defense. Given its function, this new organization should be grouped with, so that it can complement, the other Defense components that focus on the indirect approach.

Once we see the utility of grouping the defense components that specialize in the indirect approach, further consideration suggests that they be not only grouped but also established as a separate organization within DoD. There are two reasons for this. First, in listening to SOF talk about what they do and in reviewing the history of SOF, we came again and again across the fact that the conventional military has neglected SOF generally as well as indirect missions particularly. This results from the nature of these missions. They are indirect because they seek to achieve objectives by working with a population or the forces and personnel of a friendly government. Consequently, the military, valuing most highly direct engagement with an enemy, has treated the indirect approach and those who carry it out as lesser priorities, as our previous discussions of selection and training and roles and missions also indicated. Given this history, it would not be unreasonable to conclude that just as the direct-action elements of SOF did not flourish until separated from the conventional military in their own command, the indirect approach of SOF will not flourish unless all of its components are separated from SOF's direct-action components.

The second reason DoD forces engaged in the indirect approach should be grouped together arises from the fact that success in the indirect approach requires working well not only with local forces and people but also with a variety of U.S. government agencies. As we saw in chapter 3, from the beginning of its involvement with indirect action, the U.S. government has recognized that it could not conduct this mission through the Defense Department alone. Even its earliest post–World War II plans to use Special Forces to wage unconventional warfare in Europe required that SF work with the CIA. As the counterinsurgency era developed, the importance of SF and other SOF working with various government agencies became a matter of policy. Winning "hearts and minds" required the work of the State Department, the Agency for International Development, the CIA, and others.[9] Stabilization operations similarly require working with other government agencies and, increasingly over the past fifteen years or so, with nongovernmental organizations (NGOs). In counterinsurgency, peacekeeping and stabilization operations, perhaps the most critical issue to get right is the mix of force and persuasion or the transition, often gradual and halting, from one to the other, from conflict of varying intensity to what those most immediately affected recognize as more normal, day-to-day life. Since conflict precedes and creates the need for the restoration of normality, it is the Defense Department, by necessity or design the lead agency in the conflict, that must make the difficult transition from bringing force to bear directly on an opponent, and therefore from being a dominant to an equal and ultimately subordinate position of authority vis-à-vis other U.S. government agencies or a reconstituted foreign government and military and police forces, as DoD's more indirect capabilities come to the fore. For this reason, the ability of the Defense Department to work with other agencies is critical for success.

While interagency cooperation is critical for success, it is not something that the military does easily. No agency does it easily, but, with the possible exception of the CIA or the FBI, whose roles are minor compared to DoD's, none finds it as difficult as the military. All other agencies have more in common with each other than they do with DoD. They are civilian and think and operate in a peacetime environment. The Defense Department is military and operates in, or at least thinks foremost about, war. The military thus places the greatest emphasis on and most strongly rewards engaging and closing with the enemy, not with other agencies. In fact, to the extent that working with other agencies distracts Defense from its primary mission, other agencies become the enemy. But since these enemies cannot be engaged and destroyed, they are best ignored. This is, indeed, the military's attitude toward both indirect-action missions generally and the other government agencies associated with such missions.

The military has some justification for neglecting the indirect approach. Such an approach typically takes more time than a direct conventional approach and may not work at all or may produce ambiguous results. Of course, the direct approach does not always work and may produce ambiguous results, but in that case we have only ourselves to blame; and we have the authority and leverage to correct what went wrong. In the wake of 9-11, the use by the CIA during the 1990s of proxies, an example of working by, through, and with indigenous forces to find and kill or capture Osama bin Laden came under attack. Did the proxies really try to find him or did they just take the money they were paid to do so and make up stories to cover their inaction?[10] This is a perennial problem with the indirect approach. How do we know that those we work by, through, and with will do what we want them to do and in the way we want them to do it? If the proxies produce results, did they do it with a level of violence or with human rights abuses that will produce more and even bigger problems later on? These are good and serious objections to the indirect approach.

The fact remains, however, that in the past there have been and in the future there will be instances in which the U.S. government will judge that what is at stake does not warrant the direct military approach or that such an approach is not possible. Although, in retrospect, it would have been worth inserting U.S. forces into Afghanistan to destroy the Taliban and bin Laden's organizational base sooner than we did, this was clear only in retrospect and will not be true for every threat the U.S. faces in the future. An indirect approach to deal with a small threat before it becomes a big threat might be the best course of action. In addition, in many places, having the U.S. forces take the lead will actually make matters worse by undermining the legitimacy of the government we hope to help. In chapter 1 we saw that SF functioned in the Philippines only as advisers, and in close coordination with the State Department, in deference to the Philippine government's political sensitivities. In such cases, an indirect approach will be necessary. It will also be necessary in cases such as the Balkans and Iraq, where it is important to have the locals take responsibility for governance after conventional fighting subsides. Finally, it is important to remember that, given the character of bin Laden's organization and the 9-11 plot, once it was set in motion, even an invasion of Afghanistan by U.S. forces might not have prevented the attack. Some threats that cannot be dealt with by the direct use of military force might be handled by an indirect approach given sufficient lead time and persistence. Some portion of the military should be as adept at the indirect approach as it is with the direct approach. This suggests that there should be a military organization that has as its primary responsibility working by, through, and with indigenous people, and with the other government agencies and NGOs that are necessary in this work.

Pressing the analogy with the development of the Special Operations Command (SOCOM), we suggest establishing a separate Joint Command—perhaps called the Unconventional Warfare Command—that would include SF, CA, PSYOP, and a new cadre, those described above, whose mission is to gather information on and influence traditional social and communication networks. The new command would draw on all services for personnel and would in other respects function much as SOCOM functions now, on the principle that it would pay for training and equipment specifically related to unconventional warfare but would rely on the services for all other support. The command thus would have a Major Force Program in the Defense Budget and have acquisition authority. For example, it would take responsibility for modifying aircraft for PSYOP use. Access to transportation resources for members of the new command might become such an issue that it would need control over some aircraft, although it may be able to rely on Air Force or Army assets for transport. It would also need authority to devise new personnel management procedures, since, as noted, the current Defense Department procedures should not apply to the new cadre focused on traditional social networks. Personnel reforms would have to extend into the Army and other services, however, since the new cadre would have a career progression different from other service personnel. Over time, it might be that the personnel system of the new cadre would better fit at least some CA and PSYOP personnel as well.

The commander of the new command should be a four-star officer. The new command will run into a host of bureaucratic problems and will need an officer at that level, plus considerable assistance from high-ranking civilians in the Defense Department, to establish and maintain itself and make sure that its personnel are not disadvantaged in the promotion process. The primary problem for the new command will be the general disregard for the indirect approach. The command will also have to sort out relations between its components and the intelligence community. For example, SF already collect information—and could learn to collect and report it better—that should interest the intelligence community. The new cadre we have discussed should increase the amount of such intelligence or information available to the U.S. government. The commander of the Unconventional Warfare Command will have to work to force this information into the well-worn paths of the intelligence analysis process. Even if relations with other agencies remain problematic for a time, the new command will give the indirect approach better standing within the Defense Department and improve its ability to support the direct approach of SOF and conventional forces and to carry on such independent indirect missions as foreign internal defense. Altogether, the various activities of the command will give the Defense Department and the U.S. government the global scouts that SF sometimes claim to be.

While a new command might be the best possible solution, it faces major objections, both substantive and bureaucratic. Among the substantive objections, several stand out. First, some might object that in a bureaucracy as big and cumbersome as the U.S. government's is reputed to be, the last thing we need is another new organization. Is it not possible to network existing organizations into something more dynamic, instead of creating another hierarchical organization whose very structure is likely to impede the collaboration it is supposed to foster? As will soon become apparent, we take seriously the need for integration across organizations and make some suggestions about how DoD and the U.S. government can do that better. But such integration does not do away with the need for organizations that foster and protect certain skills and abilities. Indeed, without such organizations, there would be little of worth to collaborate or network with. Of course, we should not create organizations unnecessarily; but we have argued there is a need for an organization in DoD devoted to indirect measures. By all means, do away with organizations that are no longer necessary; but necessary skills require organizations able and willing to fight bureaucratically for their preservation and enhancement. Finally, we should remember that networks are not inherently superior to hierarchies. Each form of organization has advantages and disadvantages.[11] Maximizing the former and minimizing the latter in light of our objectives and challenges is key.

Some might also object that having SF, CA, and PSYOP in an organization that focuses on the indirect approach will make them less able to support conventional forces. On the contrary, an organization properly structured and funded for and devoted to the indirect approach should provide forces better at the indirect approach and therefore better able to use that approach to support conventional forces. SF teams, for example, currently prepare for an array of core tasks and missions. There are not enough time and resources to do this. If they focus on the indirect approach, they will get better at it. They will be able to focus selection and training on these tasks, for example. They will learn more about this mission and doctrine will begin to change and improve, as will what we might call the tactics, techniques, and procedures of engaging with the traditional social world.

A more serious substantive objection is that focusing on the indirect approach will indeed change the selection criteria for SF and therefore soon change the character of these forces. SF currently succeed, those making this objection will argue, because they have a hard edge to their "soft," indirect power. If they become a kind of armed peace corps, they will lose this edge and the respect of the foreign military forces with whom they work. This objection is related to another that concerns relations internal to U.S. SOF. The direct and indirect SOF roles arguably benefit from proximity to one another. Direct-action missions would often be better conducted if they took account of the information and influence that the indirect approach can generate, while the indirect approach may require sophisticated firepower and tactical skills at some points.

We concede that there are serious objections to the proposal to place SOF's direct and indirect approaches in separate organizations. We do not find them compelling, however. First, historically, the indirect approach has included the use of force and there is no reason to suppose that this will change. In fact, in a separate command, SF might find it easier to get into a fight because it will no longer be part of a command that automatically defers to special mission units for all direct-action operations. In so far as there is now a reluctance to use force, this results from political concerns of senior decisionmakers and applies equally to SF and special-mission units.[12] Second, while it is true that the direct and indirect approaches complement each other, it does not follow that they must be part of the same command. Not all complementary capabilities need to be housed in the same organization. Despite the benefits achieved from having the four military services operate effectively together, we need to maintain separate services because this is the best way to preserve critical but different fighting skills. Indeed, effective joint action by the services requires services with vibrant and different approaches. Similarly, given the historical neglect of the indirect approach, it needs a separate organizational existence to flourish and contribute most effectively to national defense.

The bureaucratic objections to this new organization will be legion. For example, SOCOM will likely object to losing significant numbers of its personnel and fear that its budget would be cut to support the new command. The State Department, failing to see the utility of a new cadre devoted to understanding and influencing traditional social and communication networks, will object to the new cadre taking over State Department duties and support ambassadors in their efforts to rein in the new cadre so they do not interfere with the conduct of state-to-state relations. Fearing competition, the CIA will claim first that the new cadre is not necessary, then assert that its case officers already do what the cadre is supposed to do, and finally work behind the scenes through its authority over foreign intelligence collection to limit the activities of the new cadre. Setting up the new agency would require overcoming prejudices and established ways of doing things to such a degree that it would take civilian and probably congressional intervention in the Defense Department and the wider national security apparatus to bring it about. Making it work over the long-term would require constant attention and support from cabinet-level officials.

A critic might note the difficulty and expense of the measures we are proposing and wonder if they are really necessary. After all, the Defense Department has lately been very interested in the cultural aspects of warfare. It has decided to increase language training, and some of the services are requiring cultural awareness training for units before they deploy to Iraq. The military is also devoting more time in its schools and training exercises on working with other agencies and NGOs. Isn't this enough? It may help. When it comes to terrorism and insurgency, however, we need to acknowledge that the underlying phenomenon is not cultural but social. Unless we get better at understanding and influencing the traditional social world, we will not deal effectively with the major problem currently before us. More generally, unless we get better at mastering and using to our advantage the indirect approach to our enemies, we will be less effective in defending our way of life than we should be.

RESTRUCTURING TO IMPROVE COMMAND AND CONTROL
AGAINST SMALL, LETHAL GROUPS

Establishing a separate command focused on the indirect approach is critical for improving this capability. It will also have an unintended benefit. Those elements of SOF not in this new organization—the special mission units, the SEALs, the Rangers, the 160th Special Operations Aviation Regiment, and Air Force Combat Controllers and Pararescue personnel—will form an organization of their own. This new organization—perhaps called the Special Operations Strike Command[13]—would retain SOCOM's current service-like responsibilities and authorities but would focus on direct-action missions. This organizational change would allow the Strike Command to focus on the second of the two problems with which we began this chapter: small, very lethal groups.

Dealing with these groups and their efforts to acquire very lethal weapons will raise a host of political, technological, legal, strategic, operational, and tactical issues. A raid to capture or kill individuals in a teeming city or to stop a ship on the high seas will entail great political and operational risks, which decisionmakers will have to weigh against various potential benefits. In these respects, operating against small, very lethal groups will be similar to the effort to capture Mohammed Farah Aideed in Mogadishu recounted in chapter 4. A new Special Operations Strike Command will not, in and of itself, give the United States a better ability to conduct such operations. By focusing on the direct-action mission, the new command is likely to develop excellent tactics, techniques and procedures, but as the case of SOF in Somalia shows, tactical or technical expertise is not by itself the key to an excellent outcome for the United States. The operation in Somalia was plagued and eventually undone by a series of failures: a failure to clarify and then communicate policy to the field, the American public, and other relevant audiences; a failure to weigh the costs of the operation against its possible benefits; a failure to supervise forces in the field; a failure to coordinate operations with policy on an iterative basis; a failure by tactical commanders to inform political decisionmakers of changing operational realities and risks; a failure by tactical commanders to be aware of or heed the complex domestic and international political environment in which the operation was taking place. We may categorize these failures as failures in command and control. Ultimately, our direct-action capability will improve only if command and control of SOF improves.

In its most general sense, the sense we are using the term here, "command and control" is what allows military operations to achieve a political purpose. Elected officials establish goals the achieving of which, they believe, will ensure the nation's security. Civilian and military officials in charge of the military in turn sort out a military strategy, a plan for using military means to achieve these policy goals. Based on this strategy, the military develops operational plans that explain in detail how the military will carry out the specific missions and tasks of the military strategy. In principle, then, one should be able to trace the justification for each military operation, and the training and equipping that make it possible, to a policy goal. It is this policy rationale for each operation that provides the basis for evaluating whether that operation serves policy and whether, therefore, policy directs operations. Furthermore, in a democracy, since the policymakers are elected, command and control ensures not only that civilians control the military but also that the military ultimately carries out the will of the people.

Command and control should mean more, however, than the arrangements by which elected civilian officials exercise authority over the military. Command and control arrangements should ensure, to the extent they can, that policy decisions and military operations are coordinated. The most important thing that should be coordinated is the potential risk and gain of an operation. Effective command and control should include determining if the political and operational risk of a military operation is commensurate with the importance of the policy objective it is intended to serve. If it is, then the possible gain from the operation may equal or exceed its risk, and it would make sense to undertake the operation. The case of Somalia is an exemplary instance of failure to coordinate policy and military operations or to manage risk by keeping the potential costs of a military operation in proportion to the hoped-for gain. Whether or not we accept the importance of the Clinton administration's policy, the fact is that no senior civilian decisionmaker understood the high level of risk involved in Task Force Ranger's direct action missions to capture Aideed and his lieutenants. Therefore, they were not in a position to judge whether the possible gain was worth the risk. Indeed, after the October 3 battle, both President Clinton and Secretary of State Christopher admitted that they had not been paying sufficient attention to these operations. In this case, in the most fundamental sense, then, policy and operations were not coordinated and command and control failed.

A possible objection to speaking of political risk management in connection with command and control is that it might appear to be cynical. The risk to be managed, one might argue, is only the risk to the political standing of the administration in power. When it comes to issues of national security, such calculation of personal interest, of political viability, one might argue, should be unacceptable. Discussion of political considerations, however, does not imply that the president or his aides have only a cynical interest, one tied only to their political survival, in the outcome of a military operation. To succeed, any policy requires public support. Therefore, even a president who had no regard for his own political future, who selflessly thought only about the good of the country, should have a strong interest in the support of public opinion for what he wants to do. The public good demands, then, that the president consider the political risks of military operations, since a failed operation might discredit a policy critical to long-term national well-being. This is particularly true of the direct-action missions that SOF undertake, because the risks are so high. Weighing the risks of such missions and having in place an effective system of command and control to manage them will remain important.

Unfortunately, the system in place at the time of the SOF operation in Somalia is the same system that is in place now. It is a system that is not conducive to developing comprehensive and balanced policy objectives, formulating comprehensive strategies to achieve those objectives, and encouraging the flow of information between policymakers and operators—all requirements for success, as the example of Somalia shows. To address this issue, we should distinguish between its "horizontal" aspect—developing across the Defense Department and the U.S. government comprehensive objectives and strategies that integrate all elements of American power—and its "vertical" aspect—implementing these strategies with operations that further our objectives.

Horizontal Integration

Consider first the issue of developing comprehensive, integrated objectives and strategies. Currently both the Defense Department and the national security bureaucracy are organized around dominant organizations dedicated to expertise in a single functional area. The State Department excels at diplomacy, the Defense Department at applying military force, the CIA at spying and so on. Within each organization, powerful under secretaries or their equivalents control largely independent fiefdoms dedicated to policy development, military assessments, financial or legal issues, acquisition, and other areas of functional expertise. Yet many current security problems, including countering terrorism and the proliferation of CBRN weapons, are so complex that addressing them requires the integrated expertise of many U.S. and even international or nongovernmental agencies. Often, there is no time to integrate solutions by handing problems from one functional body of expertise to another until finally, fully coordinated, they appear on the desk of the secretary of defense or the president. Worse, internally consistent and vigorous recommendations often never reach the secretary or the president, because they are watered down by the leaders of the functional organizations who are powerful enough to delay and neuter any recommendations they do not like. These leaders are consumed by the functional problems their organizations were created to fix, and any recommendations that run counter to their organization's perceived interests seem like inherently bad ideas. They have little personal or professional incentive to look at problems and corresponding solutions beyond the scope of their own organizations.

Periodically the president or secretary of defense sits down with principal subordinates and manages to craft an integrated solution to a major problem. This sometimes works in a crisis, when all attention is focused on one problem, but as a routine matter these busy leaders generally do not have time to hammer out integrated solutions to complex problems. Moreover, they are constrained by the political liabilities of routinely overriding powerful personalities and institutional interests. If the president or secretary want integrated solutions to complex problems, and want them quickly, they need supporting organizations to produce and take responsibility for such products. They need to empower and hold accountable teams and team leaders to draw upon but cut across functional areas of expertise to produce sound, integrated solutions that they can then quickly adapt to changing circumstances.

This is precisely what many large, successful businesses have done over the last decade or so, and for essentially the same reasons. The explosion of global information has enabled competitors to quickly obtain capital and enter the market more easily than previously was the case. Historic industry leaders like IBM and General Motors suddenly found their competitive environment was much more dynamic. To compete, they had to create teams that would quickly integrate experts from engineering, design, marketing, financing, etc. and produce high-quality products quickly with an ever present attention to market fluctuations. They could no longer afford to let independent bastions of expertise wring marginal efficiencies out of a slow coordination process that rarely deviated much from the status quo.

How would these "horizontal integration" teams work? Consider first how they would work within the Defense Department to counter the threat of terrorists with CBRN weapons. The secretary would authorize an individual with the relevant experience and leadership skills to organize a team to integrate the counterproliferation expertise now divided among various organizations within the department. The purpose of the team would be to develop strategies and plans to deal with proliferation and to oversee the implementation of these plans and associated budgetary and acquisition issues. The team would not be a task force. It would be a permanent structure, or as permanent as the problem it was designated to deal with. Comprehending the problem and solution in an end-to-end fashion, the team would use its authority to intervene selectively to ensure progress, mostly at the strategic level where the efforts of functional organizations tend to compete and work at cross-purposes, but down to whatever level of detail was required to ensure successful outcomes.

To succeed, the teams will require four things. First, the Department's leadership must provide a clear, written mandate that identifies what the team is to accomplish and why. The leadership must also explain the criteria by which the team's performance will be evaluated and how feedback will be provided so that it can modify its performance. Second, the group and its own leadership must be allowed to decide how to accomplish its objectives. The group must decide what expertise is needed, and it must be able to get that expertise. The group leader must be able to "hire" and "fire" group members. The presumption is the group's output is acted upon absent compelling reasons to the contrary. Third, the team must have office space, information technology resources, other administrative support, and members committed for specific periods of time and levels of effort. Finally, the group must receive rewards based on individual and group performance. Performance evaluations should be based on individual and group results. The group leader must be able to reward and sanction members by having some authority over their performance evaluations.

Making the transition to new "horizontal" organizations will be difficult. In particular, achieving unity of effort requires, at one level, violating the principle of unity of command. The experts who populate the teams that produce integrated solutions essentially report to two leaders. On the one hand, they remain part of the organization whose expertise they represent, and to which they will return after their service on the integration team. On the other hand, they can be rewarded or released by the team leader if they are not loyal and dedicated to producing the best overall solution to the problem the team has been charged to solve. This "dual authority" problem—reporting to two leaders—is the single point of failure for such horizontal teams. If the secretary of defense, for example, does not impress upon his immediate subordinates the importance of collaboration and information sharing, they may instruct the experts they send to the teams to protect organizational interests at all costs. In such cases, the teams may deadlock and produce "least common denominator" products that satisfy all the individual members of the team but are substantially inconsistent and ineffective.

However, if the Defense Department can make the transition to such empowered, collaborative teams, it will help deal with some of the most intractable problems that the Department and the American people face. The effect would be even greater if such teams took hold across the government to deal with key national security issues. Again, these would not be the customary interagency deliberative bodies, or even the interagency executive committees that the Clinton administration used to manage some of its more difficult problems, but small permanent organizations with authority, derived from the president, over both their agendas and their own resources, devoted to developing policies and strategies and reporting directly to the Principals Committee (i.e. national security cabinet-level authorities). Again, comprehending the problem and solution in an end-to-end fashion, these teams would use their authority to intervene selectively at the strategic level where different agencies are found to be working at cross-purposes, but could delve into the activities of specific agencies to obtain information when success required doing so. In the case of counterterrorism, we have a precedent for such an organization, at least with regard to a group having authority from cabinet-level officials and reporting to them directly in order to overcome barriers to effective problem-solving.[14]

Vertical Integration

As we have noted, these integration teams must have the authority to dig into the details of policy implementation. They must constantly monitor implementation once the policy is set, adjusting course as they receive feedback on progress or the lack of it. This means that the teams, whether operating in the Defense Department or across the government's national security apparatus, must look into the details of military operations as well. This is the "vertical" aspect of command and control. It assumes a degree and quality of communication between policymakers and operators that is rare for a variety of reasons.

First, in the American tradition we separate the military from politics to preserve the freedom of politics.[15] This has come to mean separating policymaking from military operations. In the typical American understanding, the politicians lay out the objectives and then, when military force becomes necessary, leave the military professionals alone to figure out the best way to get things done. This approach may make sense in large-scale conventional warfare[16] but, as we saw in the case of Somalia, is problematic for independent special operations. Nevertheless, it is a deeply ingrained prejudice and an obstacle to effective command and control of strategic direct-action missions. As we saw in chapter 4, President Clinton appealed to this traditional understanding of how policymakers and operators should communicate when explaining his lack of oversight of operations in Somalia. Given this traditional understanding, politicians have good reason to take a "hands off" approach to military operations. Overruling, changing, or "interfering" in military operations carries political risks for any politician who attempts it. Lyndon Johnson continues to pay the price posthumously for "interfering" in the bombing of North Vietnam. As noted in chapter 4, Secretary of Defense Aspin was harshly criticized after the October 3 battle in Mogadishu because he had previously refused to send all the military equipment to Mogadishu that various commanders had requested at various times. The most recent example of the costs of civilian "interference" in military affairs comes from the experience of Secretary of Defense Donald Rumsfeld. Less deferential to the military than his immediate predecessors, Rumsfeld reportedly antagonized the senior military leadership and eventually managed to antagonize key figures in the Congress as well. So troubled were his relations with the military and Congress that, immediately prior to September 11, rumors circulated that Rumsfeld would be the first member of the cabinet replaced.[17] Some of Rumsfeld's problems may have resulted from his style but at least some of them resulted from an effort to probe into the details of military planning and operations rather than merely give general guidance and allow the military to do the rest.

Other obstacles to effective communication between policymakers and operators, and thus to command and control, arise from the character of those involved in this task. Politicians as a group bring to the role of risk assessment an unsurpassed sensitivity to the state of public opinion and thus to political risk—at least, they hope they do. Their ability to assess operational risk is less reassuring, however. Politicians tend to lack understanding of special operations and often of military matters altogether. JCS chairman Hugh Shelton reportedly "blanched" at a suggestion that President Clinton made about how SOF might attack bin Ladin.[18] The chairman was a former commander of the Special Operations Command (the only time this has happened) and presumably had a thorough knowledge of what SOF could do. The chairman was probably shocked that the Commander-in-Chief would have proposed the U.S. military undertake an operation more suitable for the make-believe of a Hollywood action movie than the unforgiving terrain of Afghanistan. This episode is telling since, as far as we know, no dialogue developed between the military and policymakers to weigh the level of the President's concern over bin Laden against the risks and possible benefits of various operational options in Afghanistan. The military simply concluded that the politicians were unreasonable, while the politicians concluded that the military was unhelpful.

Ignorance is not the only problem with civilian attempts to direct and control the use of SOF. Civilian prejudices may also be a problem. Although, as noted in chapter 5, it is easy to overstate this point, political leaders may sometimes look too favorably on SOF and become victims of wishful thinking.[19] Politicians want the military to achieve policy objectives at a politically acceptable cost in lives and dollars. Frustrated with what appears to be the inability of conventional commanders to give them this, some politicians may be inclined to turn to SOF as a silver bullet. These forces can go abroad in small numbers, are relatively cheap, are more expendable than other military personnel (they are double or triple volunteers) and may be able to keep a low profile. Politicians will thus have a tendency to discount the risks inherent in special operations in hopes of achieving their policy objectives on the political cheap. Something like this seems to have been behind the suggestion that Clinton made to Shelton. The "cheapness" of SOF appears to lower the political risk of using them. Yet, an inability to understand the operational risks involved in their use leads politicians to underestimate the chance of operational failure and hence to underestimate the political risk they run by using special forces. In other words, when civilians direct the use of SOF, civilian preferences and prejudices paradoxically may create precisely the political risks that politicians think they are avoiding.

Military leaders bring their own baggage to the task of commanding and controlling SOF. Senior commanders understand regular military operations. In addition, they have reached the rank they hold because they have demonstrated sensitivity to the larger political world in which the armed forces must survive. This should make these officers effective interlocutors between the worlds of policy and operations. However, most officers at the senior ranks who deal with political leaders have no experience with special operations and have only a limited understanding of the requirements and risks of these missions. The SOF officer with experience in the Pentagon on 9-11 presented in chapter 1 commented that the senior officers he dealt with did not know a lot about SOF. This follows from two facts. First, as we have noted elsewhere in this account, the military has traditionally not valued SOF as much as it has conventional forces. Promotions to senior positions come more easily, therefore, to officers from conventional military backgrounds. This has changed somewhat recently (witness the elevation of Shelton to the JCS chairmanship) but is still largely the case. Second, special operations differ from conventional operations, emphasizing certain principles of war that differ from those conventional commanders rely on and understand.[20] Senior commanders therefore are not necessarily well-informed about the requirements of special operations. In addition, as we have noted on several occasions, they often have prejudices against SOF.[21] The combination of ignorance of and prejudice against SOF that marks conventional commanders means that those with whom civilians are most in contact and who hold positions in the military bureaucracy between politicians and special operators are limited in their ability to provide the risk assessment and control that should accompany any consideration of using these forces.

Should politicians bypass the conventional military leaders and work directly with the commanders of special forces? The units that plan and conduct direct-action missions know their operational realities better than anyone else. The commanders of these units have the best feel for their ability to succeed. But their judgment about operational risk should be suspect. The direct-action units live to fight. They will take every opportunity to do so.[22] They may tend, therefore, when speaking to decisionmakers, to underestimate operational risk even unconsciously, for fear that talk of risk will deprive them of an opportunity to fight. Wishful thinking on the part of civilians and the drive to fight characteristic of special units is, potentially, a dangerous combination.

For a variety of reasons, then, the prospects for effective "vertical" communication between policymakers and operators are not as good as they should be for consistently effective direct-action missions. Could communication be made better? It is not difficult to state what effective communication should produce. If operations are to achieve the objectives that policymakers establish, and, in doing so, the risk of a military operation is to be commensurate with the importance of the policy objective it is intended to serve, then the goals and restraints of policy must inform operational planning and execution, just as the possibilities and problems of operations must inform policymaking. How might this situation be brought about? Somehow, policymakers and operators must learn something about how each other sees things, so the politicians can trust the operators and the operators can understand the political constraints under which they must operate.

A possible way to help bring this situation about would be for policymakers and operators to participate in realistic simulations of the approval, conduct, and possible consequences of direct-action missions. The integration teams in the Defense Department and across the national security apparatus should be involved in these simulations, but they should include as well the secretaries of state and defense, the national security advisor and, above all, the president. These senior leaders will be the ones making decisions on the most important operations. Such exercises will give the civilian decisionmakers an opportunity to ask questions, to probe the planning and thinking of SOF. Such interaction will also educate military leaders about the civilians for whom they work and the political realities that must govern military operations. To be effective, these exercises need to be done with persons other than the most senior commanders in the military as the principal interlocutors. These senior officers should be present, but in the background, involved as advisers. This is particularly true of the JCS chairman, who is by law the principal military adviser to the president. The principal military interlocutors should be the officers directly responsible for conducting direct-action missions. And these exercises need to be done not once, at the beginning of an administration, as a pro forma effort to make the civilians and the military feel good about each other, but repeatedly, in a realistic way. They also need to be done with the actual decisionmakers and not with lower-ranking substitutes, as is too often done now. These substitutes will not be the ones making the decisions when they are made for real. These exercises should not take the place of the briefings that presidents and senior advisers receive about particularly risky operations as part of the process of getting approval for them. These should continue. The exercises proposed here will educate all involved so that these operational briefings might give rise to more informed decisionmaking.[23]

A number of objections to such exercises will arise. Critics will probably object that they risk civilian interference in military operations and violate the traditional American understanding of how the military and civilians should work together. As we have suggested, this is not so much an objection as a description of an obstacle to something that needs to be done. Furthermore, the fact that the president and his advisers are involved in thinking through all aspects of a military operation does not mean that they should or will have live video and audio feeds from the helmets of troops during the operation and give orders to turn left or right. In some cases, an operation may allow for communication between operators and the highest levels of the U.S. government even as the operation unfolds, for example at certain staging points, but this communication will not become necessary at every stage simply because of the exercises proposed here. On the contrary, approval of operations and delegation of authority might be more forthcoming, more appropriately given, and more strictly adhered to, if there is more understanding and hence more trust between military and civilian decisionmakers.

Civilian and military officials might object to the kind of exercises we have outlined for various reasons. Given the prominent role that the president should take in these exercises, the secretary of defense might

object, for example, believing that the exercises undermine his authority. The exercises may imply to him and, more important, will imply to
others, at least initially, that the president somehow lacks faith in his
abilities. The secretary is also likely to object that the exercises give other
members of the National Security Council some say in how "his" forces
are used and confuses the chain of command that runs from the president through him to commanders in the field. Senior military commanders will also object for a similar reason. They will not like being upstaged,
as they are likely to see it, by the more junior officers who command
direct-action units, units to which they may not be well disposed to begin
with. These concerns and resentments will create opportunities for the
president's critics to take political advantage.

These various concerns and resentments will be difficult to deal with.
In fact, there is no way they can be simply overcome. No new structure
or training program will take care of them. They are deeply embedded
in the way that the U.S. government and its personnel from the lowest
to the highest ranking do business. Perhaps they can be eased by arguing that the exercises proposed here are a necessary complement to the
more technological revolution in military affairs currently changing the
way that the U.S. military fights. This revolution is increasing the speed
at which the U.S. military operates. What has not increased correspond-
ingly is the quality and speed of the decisionmaking that authorizes military operations. One of the time-consuming requirements for this decisionmaking is the need to build the political context in which decisions
are made. Part of this political work or coalition building needs to be
done within the Executive branch.[24] The exercises proposed here could
help in a sense prefabricate the necessary coalitions by building among
key policymakers a shared understanding of what risks are worth taking.
Leadership will be important as always, and although training is not a
cure-all, it will help too. For good reason, the military insists that it must
train as it plans to fight. When it comes to direct action missions, this
training must include the president and his principal advisers.

AN AGENDA TO RESTRUCTURE SOF

Right now and for the foreseeable future, we need to get the most that
we can from SOF as practitioners of both their direct and indirect

approaches. In so far as this concerns training, tactics, techniques, and procedures, the forces will take care of this themselves, if they are resourced to do so. Giving them the maximum freedom to operate and produce results consistent with comprehensive American interests and careful vetting of risks and possible benefits requires restructuring not only SOF but decisionmaking in the Defense Department and the National Security Council. To that end we have recommended the following changes:

- Establish a separate command—perhaps called the Unconventional Warfare Command—to take charge of SOF's indirect action capabilities
- Supplement those capabilities with a new one dedicated to understanding and influencing traditional social and communication networks.
- Establish another separate command—perhaps called the Special Operations Strike Command—to take charge of SOF direct-action capabilities.
- Create integrated teams to manage these forces properly. These teams should be given the authority and resources to tackle the four or five most important and intractable security problems that the Defense Department faces. Similar teams should operate across the U.S. government's national security departments and agencies.
- Institute a frequent series of exercises, under the direction of the National Security Council, involving the highest level decisionmakers and the commanders of the special-mission units. The exercises would be designed to improve command and control of SOF's direct action capabilities.

These changes amount to a restructuring not just of SOF but of some elements of the national security apparatus. This results not from a desire to make this apparatus more SOF-friendly but from a recognition that the new prominence of SOF and the need to restructure these forces, as well as the need to update the national security apparatus, all result from the changing security environment we face now and are likely to continue to face for some time.

CONCLUSION

WE WROTE THIS BOOK to explain SOF's core attributes and limitations, how to employ them well, and how to better prepare them for future challenges. Describing what SOF are like, and how difficult it is to raise, train, and equip the highly competent SOF the United States has, was necessary in order to clearly identify the critical characteristics that distinguish SOF from conventional and even other elite forces. SOF can modify or improve on these characteristics to some extent in order to better meet future security challenges, but it cannot abandon them in the main without ceasing to be SOF.

The reader may test the extent to which the book succeeded in explaining key SOF attributes and issues by rereading the first chapter. What at first reading was simply an introduction to the diverse forces and what they do can now be read with greater appreciation for nuance and controversy. For example, the reader should now understand our disapproval of the increasingly popular prescription for how U.S. forces should change that we cited in the introduction; the notion that the Army should become like the Marine Corps, the Marines like SOF, and SOF like the CIA. If this book has succeeded in explaining the core attributes of SOF, the reader will understand that the Marines cannot become like SOF because they lack the selection, training, equipment, and experiential base to conduct special operations. As chapter 2 illustrated, preparing for special operations is a full-time activity that requires a training base with years of military experience. The Marines would have to abandon what they are very good at—expeditionary warfare—in order to become special operations forces. In effect, the Marines concluded as much when they decided to assign Marine forces full-time to SOCOM. Similarly, SOF would have to abandon or significantly weaken some of their special skills to invest in and practice intelligence tradecraft if they wanted to be like the CIA. Rather than asking forces to mimic the characteristics of other forces, something they are not likely to do well, it makes more sense to adjust and improve each type of force to the changing security environment and then make them work well together when that is necessary, which it increasingly is.

With respect to how SOF should be employed, it should be obvious that SOF are tremendously useful forces. Chapter 3 demonstrated that they have been repeatedly raised up in response to the demands of the security environment, until finally Congress required that standing SOF be maintained so they would be available and prepared when contingencies arise that demand their abilities. However, as chapter 4 (on Somalia) illustrated, it is possible to employ SOF to poor effect. To use SOF well, their enabling and limiting characteristics must be understood, and the most appropriate SOF units must be used to tackle the most pressing security problems in the context of a sensible strategy. Only in this way can SOF provide maximum strategic value to the nation.

What makes SOF special is now generally agreed upon at the Special Operations Command (SOCOM), and reflected in its policy and doctrine. However, as we discussed in chapter 5, the Command's leadership does not equally support all SOFs' unique capabilities. SOCOM favors SOFs' direct action missions over their indirect action missions. Also, while SOCOM's leaders acknowledge that a unifying attribute of SOF missions is the difficult and politically sensitive environments SOF operate in, the leaders pay more attention to the operational than the political challenges. Hence SOF missions sometimes take place without appropriate oversight from political authorities, as happened in Somalia and as is reflected in SOCOM's refusal to allow psychological operations forces to commingle with policy authorities in the Washington area. SOCOM's leadership also seems to agree with the conventional force bias against independent SOF operations for independent strategic effect, as illustrated by SOCOM's lethargic response to the secretary of defense's decision to assign SOCOM the lead in the war on terrorism.[1] SOCOM's slow response was reported just after the terrorist attacks of September 11, 2001. Even after being officially assigned the mission in 2004, concerns that SOCOM is still not providing strategic direction for the war persist.

A penchant for employing SOF in support of conventional forces, and for emphasizing SOF direct action at the expense of SOFs' indirect capabilities, arguably was less of a problem in the 1990s, when U.S. defense strategy emphasized preparedness for two major theater wars. Smaller contingency operations occurred frequently during the 1990s, but with the exception of Somalia, SOF were used primarily as supporting forces. Other instances of small, independent missions for SOF, such as assisting in the hunt for drug lords in South America were not of strategic import. Now, however, with the United States engaged in a long war against Islamic extremists using terrorist and insurgent tactics around the globe, emphasizing SOF direct action at the expense of SOFs' indirect capabilities is a major liability.

As we argued in chapters 5 and 6, Islamic extremism and other irregular threats are the proper strategic focus for SOF and the area where SOF can provide the greatest strategic value. SOF are less a model for information-age transformation of conventional forces than they are a model for how to fight irregular warriors with discrimination, at low cost, and through emphasis on indirect methods. Information-age forces will crowd out some SOF direct action missions, but SOF are the preferred forces for countering terrorism and insurgency, and their effectiveness in these areas would reduce pressure to sidetrack transformation of conventional forces for information-age warfare.

SOF can best focus their strategic attention on irregular threats as part of a broader, coherent national strategy for the war on terrorism. To date there remains insufficient consensus in Washington on what it will take to defeat the Islamic extremists. As we argue in chapter 7, the terrorists enjoy greater strategic depth than the United States by virtue of the ability to operate within traditional social networks. The United States Government must understand these networks in order to be effective at dissuading traditional leaders and populations from supporting terrorists. Understanding and having the ability to influence traditional networks also will better enable us to attack the terrorist organizations. Currently, however, the United States lacks the ability to comprehend and influence traditional social networks supporting the terrorists. It is imperative that we develop this capability, and it makes sense to organize it in the Department of Defense along with SOFs' best indirect mission capabilities.

Splitting SOCOM into two commands and putting additional resources into SOFs' indirect capabilities would require profound organizational and cultural changes. There is an understandable reluctance to try solving complex problems with large organizational reforms, so many of which fail and all of which are costly. Yet some problems can be solved only by reorganization, and we have frequently raised up new commands and collapsed old ones together in the past as strategic circumstances seemed to dictate. In fact, currently there is high-level support for a new "Africa Command" to give due attention to that part of the world. So the issue is not costs or some artificial limit on the number of commands the Pentagon can have. The only real question is whether a new command dedicated to forces that excel in indirect missions would be helpful. It would be.

The Pentagon now believes that it must fight terrorists on a global basis with indirect military methods,[2] and SOCOM also now emphasizes the indirect approach as a major part of its strategy in the war on terror.[3] Yet twenty years after the creation of SOCOM and five years after the terror attacks of September 11, 2001, there is ample evidence that SOF indirect action capabilities will not be properly resourced or employed under existing command arrangements. The decision to let the larger portion of SOCOM's force structure for civil affairs and psychological operations forces (in the reserves) return to the Army, where they are to be integrated with conventional forces, is just the most recent indication of the Pentagon and SOCOM's tendency to treat forces whose primary strategic value is indirect missions as less important members of the SOF community.[4] This decision contrasts sharply with the attention SOCOM leaders are giving to raising the rank of SOF leaders who specialize in direct action missions.[5] Other examples of SOCOM priorities in favor of direct action in recent years were reviewed in chapters 5 and 6. Only a separate command will ensure resources and priority missions for SOF indirect action, and open the possibility of their being augmented by improved abilities to understand and influence traditional social networks. This is not likely to happen, however.

Most senior military leaders will see such change as unnecessary. They will rightly point out that SOFs' direct and indirect capabilities are mutually reinforcing, and they will ignore the point that SOFs' direct and indirect capabilities could and must still collaborate, even if housed in two separate commands. No one will deny that we need independent SOF indirect action operations, but the real issue, which is what it takes to get and support them well, is not likely to be addressed.

The primary reason for this is the persistent discomfort of conventional military commanders with independent SOF operations and particularly indirect missions, a recurrent theme in this book. It is true that this discomfort declined as SOCOM made efforts to focus on direct action and support to conventional-force operations. However, the conventional military's discomfort with independent indirect action missions persists as we discussed in chapter 5, and cannot be overcome without political intervention.

Some civilian observers also are not supporters of independent strategic special operations, arguing that their ability to deliver results is overblown and that they tend to be micromanaged.[6] In some cases, the concern about high risks for little effect is justified. As we argued in chapter 5, independent unconventional warfare missions generally are not worthwhile when directed against well-prepared authoritarian regimes. However, in most cases it does make sense for SOF to take the lead on combating terror and insurgency. The charge that civilian leaders tend to inappropriately micromanage SOF operations is not true, although conventional military leaders have done so on numerous occasions. It is more true to say that political leaders launch SOF and hope for the best, sometimes then holding SOF accountable for the difficult judgment calls about acceptable risks. This is not right.

When independent SOF missions make sense, they require close oversight by and support from political leaders, as demonstrated in chapter 4 and as observed by the United States Senate in its superb report on Task Force Ranger in Somalia. SOF must perform within the bounds of U.S. strategy, culture, and ethics, which requires difficult judgment at times. SOF independent operations for strategic effect carry risks, but the risks have to be considered relative to the threat and U.S. objectives. Both the threat and the objectives may change quickly. Insulating SOF from political authorities or filtering SOF command and control through a hierarchy of conventional-force commanders does not make sense when SOF are given the strategic lead for operations. Recognizing this, Congress allowed for the possibility of SOCOM's command and control of strategic special operations. Such operations should not be undertaken without direct oversight from political authorities who are familiar with SOF and the operation in question.

Restructuring SOF for greater strategic effect will not accomplish all that it should, absent reform of the larger national security bureaucracy. The policy chaos demonstrated in chapter 4 unfortunately is symptomatic of Washington decision-making. Rigidly stovepiped bureaucracies, which are unable to collaborate quickly on defense or national security matters as critical issues develop, are the norm. SOF has no authoritative source for strategic oversight of its strategic missions on a recurring basis. The secretary of defense and president are too busy to fulfill this function. Collaborative and empowered interagency teams, and integrated strategy and mission teams within the Defense Department, are necessary to provide effective oversight of SOF strategic missions. In short, creating a command to ensure that SOFs' indirect capabilities are resourced and applied for strategic effect, and allowing SOFs' direct action missions to be directly overseen by senior political authorities, would be more likely if we had a strategically functioning national security bureaucracy rather than the independent cabinet-level fiefdoms that currently prevail and constantly thwart attempts to integrate all instruments of national power toward common purposes.

The recommendations in this book require major organizational and cultural changes, both in SOF and in the broader national security community. SOCOM must get used to taking the lead in the field and working closely with authorities in Washington. The national security bureaucracy in Washington must adopt a more collaborative decision-making system to produce and choose among integrated strategic options, monitor progress in their implementation, and adjust and adjudicate risk rapidly in response to developments. Some of the recommendations made here run counter to conventional wisdom, and others, such as reforms in Washington decision-making, have been made by many others. We believe these changes are as necessary as they are difficult. If they are not made, progress against terrorism and insurgency will languish, and typically heroic tactical efforts by SOF may be used to poor effect or even end in strategic setbacks.

It is a staple of organizational reform wisdom to note that the best time to make reforms is when an organization is enjoying success. Resources are available and operational demands are manageable. It is also politically the most difficult time to reform, as all those who are accustomed to the current way of doing business will see less need to change. The alternative is to wait until a crisis makes it apparent that the current state of affairs is inadequate to needs. Then reform will be demanded, but there will be little time to think through the options. This book was written to help those so inclined think through the options, and the sooner the better.

NOTES

INTRODUCTION

1. "Remarks by the President at the Citadel," The Citadel, Charleston, South Carolina, December 11, 2001, http://www.whitehouse.gov/news/releases/2001/12/20011211–6.html, accessed December 17, 2003.

2. *Department of Defense Dictionary of Military and Associated Terms*, Joint Publication 1–02, April 12, 2001 (As Amended Through May 9, 2005), p. 493, http://www.dtic.mil/doctrine/jel/new_pubs/jp1_02.pdf, accessed August 14, 2005.

3. Anna Simons, *The Company They Keep* (New York: The Free Press, 1997) discusses this issue.

4. In addition to the Special Operation Commands, which are part of the regional commands, there is a separate Special Operations Command in Korea, SOCKOR.

5. The definitions of SOF missions are based on *United States Special Operations Forces Posture Statement 2003–2004* (n.d., n.p.), pp. 36–37.

1. SPECIAL OPERATIONS FORCES AND THE WAR ON TERRORISM

1. The Counterterrorism Security Group (CSG) consists of representatives from the U.S. government agencies principally involved in countering terrorism (e.g., Defense, State, FBI, CIA). Richard Clarke, the chief counterterrorism official on the National Security Council, chaired the meetings of the CSG until he retired from the government after September 11.

2. The seven phases are: psychological preparation; initial contact; infiltration; organization; buildup; employment; and demobilization. See FM 3–05.201, *Special Forces Unconventional Warfare Operations*.

3. The position was recently elevated to a one-star (general/flag officer) position.

4. "The tank" refers to the meeting room where the Joint Chiefs of Staff meet to receive briefings and make decisions.

5. The Northern Alliance was a largely Tajik organization opposed to the Taliban's control of Afghanistan. It was widely considered the only effective military force in Afghanistan resisting the Taliban. In the fall of 2001, it was operating in the north central area of Afghanistan.

6. Mazar-e-Sharif is a town in northern Afghanistan where prisoners with hidden weapons attacked guards and killed an American, Johnny Michael Spann.

7. Abdul Rashid Dostum's National Islamic Movement, a part of the Northern Alliance, controlled several north central provinces of Afghanistan in the fall of 2001.

8. Massoud was the leader of the Northern Alliance. The U.S. government had contact with Massoud during the 1990s and considered him the best leader with whom to work against the Taliban. For details of the U.S. government's efforts to work with Massoud, see Steve Coll, *Ghost Wars: The Secret History of the CIA, Afghanistan, and bin Laden, from the Soviet Invasion to September 10, 2001* (New York: Penguin, 2004).

9. Before deploying, SF teams isolate themselves to plan and prepare for the upcoming mission.

10. Warrant officers are commissioned officers who specialize in technical fields.

11. The DoD Dictionary of Military Terms defines "special mission unit" as a "generic term to represent a group of operations and support personnel from designated organizations that is task-organized to perform highly classified activities." http://www.dtic.mil/doctrine/jel/doddict/data/s/04972.html, accessed August 9, 2006.

12. A Joint Operations Center is a facility containing personnel from different services that controls and manages operations.

13. AC-130 aircraft with side-mounted guns, including a 40-mm Bofors cannon, a 105-mm Howitzer cannon, and a 25-mm gun.

14. U.S. military forces assisting the civilian and military agencies of another government in defending that government and its people from subversion, lawlessness, and insurgency.

15. The C-130 is a propeller transport aircraft. Air Force Special Operations Forces fly modified versions of this aircraft, for example, the MC-130 Combat Talon.

16. At that slow a speed, airplanes tend to stall and fall from the sky. They therefore are said to hang in the sky on their propellers.

17. A Joint Special Operations Task Force is a military organization composed of special operations units from more than one service, for example,

Army Special Forces and Navy SEALs. It may also have some conventional units assigned.

18. The military conceives of conventional operations unfolding in four phases. Phase four, or transition, is the process of restoring civilian control through reorganizing government and restoring basic services. Assisting with this transition is a principal task of Civil Affairs units.

19. The Abu Sayaf Group (ASG) split from the Moro National Liberation Front (MNLF) as the MNLF conducted peace negotiations with the Philippine government in the 1990s. The ASG aims to create a Muslim state but has often seemed to be little more than a criminal gang.

2. SELECTION AND TRAINING

1. United States Government Accountability office, "Special Operations Forces: Several Human Capital Challenges Must Be Addressed to Meet Expanded Role," GAO–06–812, July 2006, pp. 29–35.

2. SOCOM, 2005 Annual Report, at: http://www.socom.mil/Docs/2005_Annual_Report.pdf, p. 18. Accessed October 27, 2005.

3. Sheila Nataraj Kirby, Margaret C. Harrell, and Jennifer Sloan, "Why Don't Minorities Join Special Operations Forces?" *Armed Forces and Society* 26 (Summer 2000):533.

4. Kirby et. al., "Why Don't Minorities Join Special Operations Forces?" p. 539.

5. Ronald Smothers, "A Hate-Crime Tale's Surprising Turn," *The New York Times*, September 23, 1996, p. A10; John Kifner, " ...And a Racial Shooting," *The New York Times*, December 17, 1995, p. A4; Philip Shenon, "Militias Aim to Lure Elite Army Troops, U.S. Generals Fear," *The New York Times*, March 22, 1996, p. A1.

6. Kirby et. al., "Why Don't Minorities Join Special Operations Forces?" p. 530.

7. On swimming, see ibid., p. 532, and note 8, p. 544.

8. Ibid., p. 543.

9. http://www.training.sfahq.com/quali_special_forces_available_f.htm, accessed April 29, 2005.

10. Tom Vanden Brook, "U.S. Elite Forces Face Shortfall," *USA Today*, July 3, 2006, p. 1; Richard Lardner, "Road to Elite Service Is Grueling Challenge," *Tampa Tribune*, May 31, 2005; Seth Hettena, "Navy Unit Goes Public to Recruit," *Philadelphia Inquirer*, October 11, 2005, p. A12; Ann Scott Tyson, "Pulling No Punches in Push for Navy SEALs; Pentagon Looking to Increase Ranks Without Easing the Tough Training," *Washington Post*, June 20, 2006, p. A3; Janice

Burton, "18Xs Make Mark, Initial Entry SF Soldiers Earn Praise of Senior SF NCOs," *Special Warfare* 19 (July–August, 2006): 28.

11. Fred L. Schultz, "Mar SOC: Just Call Them Marines," *Proceedings* 132 (January, 2006): 48–51.

12. Officers, Foreign Military Training Unit, "The Foreign Military Training Unit: Kingmakers, Not Kings," *Marine Corps Gazette* 90 (August 2006): 41.

13. Paul McHugh, "Building Elite Forces for Military of Future," *San Francisco Chronicle*, May 14, 2006, p. 1.

14. Major General Dennis J. Hejlik, Major Cliff W. Gilmore, and Sergeant Major Matthew P. Ingram, "Special Operations Marines and the Road Ahead," *Marine Corps Gazette* 90 (August, 2006): 40.

15. Dan Morgan, "Secret Army Account Linked to Contra Aid; North, Secord Possibly Involved, Official Says," The Washington Post, April 22, 1987, p. A1.

16. See Anna Simons, *The Company They Keep: Life Inside the U.S. Army Special Forces* (New York: The Free Press, 1997), pp. 116–123, for differences on integrity among SF teams.

17. Government Accounting Office, "Army Ranger Training: Safety Improvements Need to be Institutionalized," GAO/NSIAD-97-29, January 1997, p. 2.

18. Dick Couch, *The Finishing School: Earning the Navy SEAL Trident* (New York: Crown, 2004), p. 18.

19. Douglas C. Waller, *The Commandos: The Inside Story of America's Secret Soldiers* (New York: Dell, 1994), pp. 192–193.

20. Tony Perry, "New Navy SEALs Undeterred by Recent Loss of 11," *Los Angeles Times*, October 3, 2005, p. B3.

21. McHugh, "Building Elite Forces for Military of Future."

22. Perry, "New Navy SEALs Undeterred by Recent Loss of 11."

23. Couch, *The Finishing School*, p. 52.

24. Major Will Cotty, Captain Brendon Bluestein, and Jat Thompson, "The Whole-Man Concept: Assessing the SF Soldier of the Future," *Special Warfare* 17 (April, 2005): 19–21.

25. Waller, *The Commandos*, p. 72.

26. Major Jonathan A. Blake, "SFQC Phase II: Building a Warrior," *Special Warfare* 18 (July 2005): 2–7.

27. McHugh, "Building Elite Forces for Military of Future."

28. H. Arkes and C. Blumer, "The Psychology of Sunk Cost," *Organizational Behavior and Human Decision Processes*, 35 (1985): 124–140.

29. Hejlik, Gilmore, and Ingram, "Special Operations Marines and the Road Ahead," p. 40; Officers, Foreign Military Training Unit, "The Foreign Military Training Unit: Kingmakers, Not Kings," 42–43.

30. Chris Lamb, Review of *Psychological Operations Lessons Learned*, Occasional Paper, National Defense University Press, September, 2005, p. 107.

31. Barlow Soper, Gary E. Milford, Gary T. Rosenthal, "Belief When Evidence Does Not Support Theory," *Psychology and Marketing* 12 (August, 1995): 415–422 summarize the research on Maslow's theories.

3. HISTORY

1. http://www.army.mil/cmh-pg/documents/RevWar/revra.htm, accessed February 4, 2005. Rangers and the kind of warfare they conducted are a principal concern of John Grenier, *The First Way of War: American War Making on the Frontier, 1607–1814* (Cambridge: Cambridge University Press, 2005).

2. http://www.army.mil/cmh-pg/documents/RevWar/revra.htm, accessed February 4, 2005.

3. Grenier, *The First Way of War*, pp. 87, 91, 113, 131, 161, 196.

4. Robert M. Utley, "The Contribution of the Frontier to the American Military Tradition," in James P. Tate, ed., *The American Military on the Frontier, The Proceedings of the 7th Military History Symposium, United States Air Force Academy, 30 September–1 October 1976* (Washington, DC: Office of Air Force History and United States Air Force Academy, 1978), p. 7.

5. Clayton D. Laurie, "'The Chanting of Crusaders': Captain Heber Blankenhorn and AEF Combat Propaganda in Word War I," *The Journal of Military History* 59 (July 1995): 475, 479, 481; Stanley Sandler, "*Cease Resistance: It's Good for You!": A History of U.S. Army Combat Psychological Operations* (n.p.: United States Army Special Operations Command, Directorate of History and Museums, 1999), p. 21.

6. Colonel Michael E. Haas, USAF, Retired, *Apollo's Warriors: United States Air Force Special Operations During the Cold War* (Maxwell Air Force Base, Alabama: Air University Press, 1997), p. 8.

7. William T. Y'Blood, "Any Place, Any Time, Anywhere: The 1st Air Commando Group in World War II," *Air Power History* 48 (Summer, 2001): 11.

8. Col. Irwin L. Hunt, Officer in Charge of Civil Affairs, Third Army and American Forces in Germany, Report, *American Military Government of Occupied Germany, 1918–1920*, March 4, 1920, quoted in Harry L. Coles and Albert K. Weinberg, *Civil Affairs: Soldiers Become Governors* (Washington, D.C.: Center of Military History, United States Army, 1964; reprinted 2004), pp. 6–7.

9. Coles and Weinberg, *Civil Affairs*, pp. 24, 19, 20, 28, 22.

10. In addition to Coles and Weinberg, *Civil Affairs*, this discussion of Civil Affairs draws on Earl F. Ziemke, "Civil Affairs Reaches Thirty," *Military Affairs* 36 (December, 1972): 130–133.

11. Grenier, *The First Way of War*, p. 141.

12. "CS and CSS Soldiers May Attend Ranger School," *Army Logistician* 37 (July/August, 2005): 45.

13. Letter, General of the Army Dwight D. Eisenhower, Headquarters, US Forces, European Theater, Office of the Commanding General, quoted in Alfred H. Paddock, *U.S. Army Special Warfare, Its Origins* (Lawrence: University Press of Kansas, 2002; revised edition), p. 20.

14. Senate Select Committee to Study Governmental Operations with respect to Intelligence Activities, *Foreign and Military Intelligence*, 94th Congress, Second Session, 1976 S. Rept. 94–755, Book IV, p. 26; Andrei Zhdanov, "Report on the International Situation to the Cominform," September 22, 1947, http://www.cnn.com/SPECIALS/cold.war/episodes/04/documents/cominform.html, accessed July 30, 2003.

15. Foreign Relations of the United States (hereafter FRUS), http://www.state.gov/www/about_state/history/frus.html, documents 243, 244, 245.

16. E. Lilly, "Short History of the Psychological Strategy Board," December 21, 1951, National Security Council Staff Papers, NSC Secretariat Series, Box 6, Dwight Eisenhower Library, p. 36–37; Paddock, *U.S. Army Special Warfare*, p. 56; FRUS, "Memorandum for the Secretary of the State-Army-Navy-Air Force Coordinating Committee to the Under Secretary of State," document 242.

17. FRUS, Document 283, 291; Paddock, *U.S. Army Special Warfare*, pp. 43–45, 48.

18. Paddock, *U.S. Army Special Warfare*, pp. 57–60, 64; General Albert C. Wedemeyer, *Wedemeyer Reports!* (New York: Henry Holt, 1958), pp. 91, 95.

19. FRUS, documents 253, "Psychological Operations," December 9, 1947; FRUS document 256, "Coordination of Foreign Information Measures (NSC 4) Psychological Operations (NSC 4-A)," December 17, 1947; and "Report to National Security Council on Coordination of Foreign Information Matters," December 15, 1947; FRUS 269, March 29, 1948; Senate Report, 1976, p. 28; Forrest C. Pogue, *George C. Marshall: Statesman* (New York, Viking Press, 1987), pp. 152, 192–196.

20. Lilly, "Short History of the Psychological Strategy Board," pp. 62–64, 75–76, 78–79.

21. Paddock, *U.S. Army Special Warfare*, pp. 61, 63, 91–94; Lilly, "Short History of the Psychological Strategy Board," p. 86.

22. Paddock, *U.S. Army Special Warfare*, pp. 97, 94 (cf. p. 147), 100–101, 118, 102–103, 107.

23. Paddock, 131; Thomas K. Adams, *US Special Operations Forces in Action: The Challenge of Unconventional Warfare* (London: Frank Cass, 1998), pp. 57–58

24. NSAM 124, http://www.cs.umb.edu/jfklibrary/images/nsam124a.jpg, accessed September 19, 2002.

25. Shelby L. Stanton, *Green Berets at War, U.S. Army Special Forces in Southeast Asia, 1956–1975* (Novato, California: Presidio Press, 1985), pp. 38–39; Let-

ter, DA Office of the Chief of Staff, Subj: Special Warfare Field Visit to Vietnam and Okinawa, 13–30 Jan 63, dated 30 Jan 63, p. 3, quoted in "Outline History of the 5th SF Group (Airborne), Participation in the CIDG Program, 1961–1970," p. 11, http://www.ehistory.com/vietnam/pdf/sfcidg.pdf, accessed October 1, 2002. See also, Adams, p. 85; Andrew Krepinevich, *The Army and Vietnam* (Baltimore: Johns Hopkins University Press, 1986), pp. 70–71; Colonel Francis J. Kelly, *Vietnam Studies, U.S. Army Special Forces, 1961–1971* (Washington, D.C., Department of the Army, 1973), pp. 4, 19–44.

26. William B. Rosson, General, USA, (retired), "Four Periods of American Involvement in Vietnam: Development and Implementation of Policy, Strategy and Programs, Described and Analyzed on the Basis of Service Experience at Progressively Senior levels" (Ph.D. diss., Oxford University, 1979), pp. 149–151.

27. Kelly, *Vietnam Studies*, p. 49.

28. Ibid., pp. 34; 46–48; Krepinevich, *The Army and Vietnam*, pp. 73–75.

29. Richard H. Shultz Jr., *The Secret War Against Hanoi : The Untold Story of Spies, Saboteurs, and Covert Warriors in North Vietnam* (New York: Perennial, 2000) is the most complete account of covert special operations in Vietnam.

30. Joe Wagner, "Army Special Forces: Step Child or Child Prodigy?" *Armed Forces Management* 12 (May 1966): 55.

31. David W. Hogan, *Raiders or Elite Infantry? The Changing Role of the U.S. Army Rangers from Dieppe to Grenada* (Westport, Connecticut: Greenwood Press, 1992), p. 160.

32. Rosson, "Four Periods of American Involvement in Vietnam," p. 124.

33. Hogan, *Raiders or Elite Infantry?* p. 160.

34. J. W. Partin, "Interview with General E. C. Meyer," Arlington, Virginia, July 14, 1988, p. 2 (typescript in possession of the author).

35. *Rescue Mission Report* (Washington, D.C.: Joint Chiefs of Staff, 1980), p. 60.

36. The Introduction provides definitions of these missions. In response to the changing operational environment, SOF's missions have changed. Humanitarian assistance, helping foreign governments deal with humanitarian problems, and theater search and rescue operations to recover personnel, are no longer considered SOF missions, while counterproliferation and information operations now are.

37. Susan Marquis, *Unconventional Warfare: Rebuilding U.S. Special Operations Forces* (Washington, D.C.: Brookings Institute Press, 1997), pp. 144–146. Marquis' account is the most complete.

38. Statement of the Honorable Richard L. Armitage, Assistant Secretary of Defense for International Security Affairs in "To Combat Terrorism and Other Forms of Unconventional Warfare," A Hearing Before the Subcommittee on

Sea Power and Force Projection of the Committee on Armed Services, United States Senate, 99th Congress, Second Session, on S. 2453, To Enhance the Capabilities of the United States to Combat Terrorism and Other Forms of Unconventional Warfare, August 5, 1986, p 18; Interview with David S. C. Chu, October 30, 2000, Assistant Secretary for Program Analysis and Evaluation, 1988 to 1992; Henry L. T. Koren, Jr., "Congress Wades into Special Operations," *Parameters* (December 1988): 71.

39. Armitage, "To Combat Terrorism and Other Forms of Unconventional Warfare," pp. 39–40.

40. Report to the Chairman, Subcommittee on Military Readiness, Committee on National Security, House of Representatives, "Special Operations, Opportunities to Preclude Overuse and Misuse," Government Accounting Office, GAO/NSIAD-97-85, May 1997.

41. Linda Robinson, *Masters of Chaos: The Secret History of the Special Forces* (New York: PublicAffairs, 2004), pp. 130–134.

42. Quoted in United States Special Operations Command, History, 15th Anniversary (n.p., 2002), p. 6.

43. Quoted in Adams, *US Special Operations Forces in Action*, pp. 10–11.

44. On this issue, see Steve Coll, *Ghost Wars: The Secret History of the CIA, Afghanistan, and bin Laden, from the Soviet Invasion to September 10, 2001* (New York: Penguin 2004), pp. 497–502, 570.

45. Matthew Rosenberg, "Effort in Afghanistan Gets More Conventional," *Philadelphia Enquirer*, September 15, 2002, p. A14; James Brooke, "Pentagon Tells Troops in Afghanistan: Shape Up and Dress Right," *New York Times*, September 12, 2002, p. B21.

46. "Afghan About Face," *Washington Post*, October 1, 2002, p.A1.

47. Ahmed Rashid, *Taliban: Militant Islam, Oil, and Fundamentalism in Central Asia* (New Haven: Yale University Press, 2000), p. 100.

48. Major Jonathan A. Blake, "SFQC Phase II: Building a Warrior," *Special Warfare* 18 (July 2005): 2–7.

4. SOMALIA

1. Robert B. Oakley, "An Envoy's Perspective," *Joint Forces Quarterly* no. 2 (Autumn 1993): 46.

2. It even has been asserted that U.S. officials, mainly in the Pentagon, wrote UN resolutions on Somalia, promoting nation building. Walter Clarke and Jeffrey Herbst, "Somalia and the Future of Humanitarian Intervention," *Foreign Affairs*, 75 (March/April 1996): 73. The drafting, however, took place privately at the U.S. mission to the United Nations (Ambassador Albright) and the NSC, where Ambassador Albright and Tony Lake were champions of assertive

multilateralism. Secretary of Defense Les Aspin admitted later, however, that the Pentagon had approved the resolutions.

3. "Great care was taken to develop an approved, well-defined mission with attainable, measurable objectives prior to the operation commencing. Disarmament was excluded from the mission because it was neither realistically achievable nor a prerequisite for the core mission of providing a secure environment for relief operations. Selective 'disarming as necessary' became an implied task which led to the cantonment of heavy weapons and gave UNITAF the ability to conduct weapons sweeps." Joseph P. Hoar, "A CINC's Perspective," *Joint Forces Quarterly* no. 2 (Autumn 1993): 58.

4. Robert B. Oakley, "An Envoy's Perspective," *Joint Forces Quarterly* no. 2 (Autumn 1993): 48.

5. A briefing provided by LTG Robert Johnson in the Pentagon in 1993 underscored his appreciation of SOF and their value in Somalia. A conversation between Ambassador Oakley and the author in the summer of 2005 confirmed he had the same opinion. Ambassador Robert Oakley read this chapter and made numerous helpful recommendations.

6. Ambassador Albright made the statement on March 26, 1993. She is quoted to this effect in John R. Bolton, "Wrong Turn in Somalia," *Foreign Affairs* 73 (January/February 1994): 62.

7. "Chapter VII" refers to the seventh chapter of the UN charter, which authorizes the use of force in response to "threats to the peace, breaches of the peace, and acts of aggression."

8. Keith B. Richburg, "Aideed Exploited U.N.'s Failure to Prepare," *Washington Post*, December 5, 1993.

9. Most of the details here concerning the conflict between Aideed and the UN on June 5 comes from Tom Farer's "Report of an Inquiry, Conducted Pursuant to Security Council Resolution 837, Into the 5 June 1993 Attack on UN Forces in Somalia."

10. Richburg, "Aideed Exploited," *Washington Post*, December 5, 1993.

11. Barton Gellman, "The Words Behind a Deadly Decision; Secret Cables Reveal Maneuvering Over Request for Armor in Somalia," *Washington Post*, October 31, 1993.

12. "Hope Behind the Horror," *Economist*, June 19, 1993: 41.

13. Brigadier General Wesley Taylor, the Deputy Assistant Secretary of Defense for Policy and Missions in the Office of the Assistant Secretary of Defense (Special Operations and Low-Intensity Conflict), advised against the mission in a memorandum to the Under Secretary of Defense (Policy) on July 27, 1993, and in an earlier position paper of June 15, 1993.

14. "Rejecting 'facile solutions like get Aideed and all will be well,' Hoar concluded, 'If the only solution for Mogadishu is a large-scale infusion of troops

and if the only country available to make this commitment is the U.S., then its time to reassess." Barton Gellman, "The Words Behind a Deadly Decision," *Washington Post*, October 31, 1993.

15. State Department sources said the cable was not ignored, but that "the new policy…was not worked out fully until after the October 3 firefight." Keith B. Richburg, "U.S. Envoy to Somalia Urged Policy Shift Before 18 GIs Died," *Washington Post*, November 11, 1993.

16. Following quotations are from Gellman, "The Words Behind A Deadly Decision."

17. Mark Bowden, *Blackhawk Down: A Story of Modern War* (New York: Atlantic Monthly Press, 1999).

18. Elaine Sciolino, "Puzzle in Somalia: The U.S. Goal," *New York Times*, October 5, 1993.

19. Ann Devroy, "Collapse of U.S. Collective Action May Force Second Look at Bosnia," *Washington Post*, October 8, 1993.

20. Michael R. Gordon with John H. Cushman, "Mission in Somalia; After Supporting Hunt for Aideed, U.S. is Blaming U.N. for Losses," *New York Times*, October 18, 1993.

21. "President Responds to Recent Violence Against U.S. Forces," *Washington Times*, October 7, 1993.

22. President William Clinton, "Message to the Congress Transmitting a Report on Somalia October 13th, 1993," the American Presidency Project website: http://www.presidency.ucsb.edu/ws/index.php?pid = 47197, accessed September 6, 2006.

23. Secretary of State Cyrus Vance resigned in protest over the decision to attempt the Iranian Hostage rescue, a low point for President Carter. Prior to that, Secretary of Defense James Schlesinger was fired over the handling of the *Mayaguez* crisis, which ironically was seen as a high point in the Ford administration. Secretary of Defense Robert McNamara resigned over Vietnam. On Schlesinger's demise, see Christopher Jon Lamb, *Belief Systems and Decision Making in the Mayaguez Crisis* (Gainesville, Florida: The University of Florida Press, 1989): 209–212.

24. See discussion on "the Somalia Syndrome" in Richard H. Shultz, "Showstoppers: Nine Reasons Why We Never Sent Our Special Operations Forces After al-Qaeda Before 9/11," *The Weekly Standard*, January 26, 2001, p. 28.

25. Eric V. Larson and Bogdan Savych, American Public Support for U.S. Military Operations from Mogadishu to Baghdad (Santa Monica, CA: RAND, 2005) provides a good discussion of this point.

26. Report from Senators John Warner and Carl Levin, "Review of the Circumstances Surrounding the Ranger Raid on October 3–4, 1993 in Mogadishu, Somalia," September 29, 1995, p. 50. Hereafter, cited as Senate Report.

27. On SOCOM's position, see General Powell's testimony, Senate Report, p. 26. For the position of the Office of the Assistant Secretary of Defense (Special Operations and Low-Intensity Conflict), see note 13.

28. Senate Report, p. 50.

29. Senate Report, pp. 49–50.

30. Senate Report, p. 39.

31. Senate Report, p. 49.

32. Senate Report, for Aspin comments, p. 41; for Hoar comments, pp. 39–40.

33. Shultz, "Showstoppers," p. 28.

5. SOF ROLES AND MISSIONS

1. The secretary of defense also assigns primary and collateral functions to amplify statutory roles and missions identified by Congress. John Collins, "Roles and Functions of U.S. Combat Forces: Past, Present, and Prospects," Washington, January 1993 (CRS Report for Congress no. 93–72 S); John M. Collins, Library of Congress, Congressional Research Service, "Military Roles and Missions: A Framework for Review," Washington, May 1, 1995 (CRS Report for Congress no. 95–517 S); and Chairman, Joint Chiefs of Staff Report on Roles, Missions and Functions of the Armed Forces of the United States, February 1993.

2. Samuel Huntington, "National Policy and Transoceanic Navy," U.S. Naval Institute *Proceedings* (May 1954): 483; quoted in "Strategic Employment of Special Operations Forces and Requirements for Success, Phase II," National Institute for Public Policy, December 1992; Contract Number MDA 903-91-C-0030, a study conducted for the Office of the Assistant Secretary of Defense (Special Operations/Low-Intensity Conflict), p. 1.

3. Colin S. Gray, "Handfuls of Heroes on Desperate Ventures: When Do Special Operations Succeed?" *Parameters* 29 (Spring 1999): 2–24.

4. United States Special Operations Command, *Special Operations Forces Posture Statement*, 2003–2004, p. 33.

5. James F. Dunnigan, *The Perfect Soldier* (New York, Citadel Press Books, 2003).

6. Christopher Lamb, "Perspectives on Emerging SOF Roles and Missions," *Special Warfare* (July 1995), and Centre for Conflict Studies Univeristy of New Brunswick, "Special Operations: Military Lessons from Six Selected Case Studies," Contract FO 1600-80-DO299 with JFK School, Fort Bragg, Fall 1982: 261; 264.

7. J. Paul de B. Taillon, The Evolution of Special Forces in Counterterrorism: The British and American Experiences (Westport, CT: Praeger, 2001).

8. Department of Defense, Annual Report to President and Congress, 1998, Chapter Four, Special Operations Forces. Available at http://www.defenselink.mil/execsec/adr98/chap4.html, accessed February 10, 2005.

9. Linda Robinson, *Masters of Chaos* (New York: Perseus Books Group, 2004), 365, attributed to Major General Geoffrey Lambert.

10. Thomas K. Adams, *U.S. Special Forces in Action: The Challenge of Unconventional Warfare* (London and Portland, OR: Frank Cass, 1998).

11. Edward Luttwak, *Strategy: The Logic of War and Peace* (Cambridge: Harvard University Press, 2001): 113–116; 153. Guerrillas and terrorists also employ a relational maneuver response to superior military strength, and also are critically reliant on accurate assessments of enemy weaknesses for success. However, the weakness they are trying to exploit—at least initially—is the self-restraint of regular forces constrained from destroying them with indiscriminate firepower for fear of causing excessive civilian casualties.

12. For a good theoretical treatment of how commando missions exploit enemy weakness, see William H. McRaven's *Spec Ops: Case Studies in Special Operations Warfare: Theory and Practice* (Novato, CA: Presidio, 1995). McRaven distinguishes between catching the enemy unprepared (not likely), and catching him off guard (quite possible). He notes surprise is a necessary but not a sufficient condition for success and chides special operations tacticians who focus unduly on surprise.

13. Colin Gray, "Strategic Employment of Special Operations Forces and Requirements for Success, Phase II," National Institute for Public Policy, December 1992; Contract Number MDA 903-91-C-0030, a study conducted for the Office of the Assistant Secretary of Defense (Special Operations/Low-Intensity Conflict).

14. James Lukas, *Kommando: German Special Forces of World War II* (New York: St. Martin's Press, 1985).

15. John M. Collins, *Special Operations Forces: An Assessment*, (Washington, D.C.: National Defense University Press, 1994). Collins quotes Section 1453, Department of Defense Authorization Act, 1986 (P.L. 99–145; 99 Stat. 760), July 29, 1985.

16. Susan Marquis' book, *Unconventional Warfare: Rebuilding U.S. Special Operations Forces* (Washington, D.C.: Brookings Institution Press, 1997) an otherwise authoritative account of the creation of SOCOM, says little about Congressional intent in this regard; see p. 146. However, an unpublished paper by James K. Bruton, which benefits from interviews with major participants, is more helpful. It includes the results of interviews with Noel Koch, who underscored that Congress really just wanted better commandos, and had no intention of precisely defining SOF's strategic role. James K. Bruton, "U.S. Special Operations Command: Does the Current Organization Fulfill the Original Intent," Unpublished Paper for Strategic Studies Research Seminar, John Hopkins University, November 30, 1994, p. 28.

17. Richard H. Shultz, "Showstoppers: Nine Reasons Why We Never Sent Our Special Operations Forces After al-Qaeda Before 9/11," *The Weekly Standard* 9 (January 26, 2004): 32.

18. John Keegan, *Intelligence in War: Knowledge of the Enemy from Napoleon to al-Qaeda* (New York: Knopf, 2003), p. 343.

19. Michael E. Hass, *In the Devil's Shadow: U.N. Special Operations during the Korean War* (Annapolis, MD: Naval Institute Press, 2000), p. 204.

20. Lucien S. Vandenbroucke, *Perilous Options: Special Operations as an Instrument of U.S. Foreign Policy.* (New York: Oxford University Press, 1993): 181. Also Eliot A. Cohen's *Commandos and Politicians: Elite Military Units in Modern Democracies* (Cambridge: Harvard University Press, 1978).

21. For example, Senator Sam Nunn, "Domestic Missions for the Armed Forces," Strategic Studies Institute, U.S. Army War College, February 1993.

22. GlobalSecurity.org website. According to the website, the Clinton administration's Presidential Decision Directive 25 exempted the Joint Special Operations Command from the Posse Comitatus Act of 1878, Title 18 USC Section 1385, PL86–70, Sec. 17[d], which makes it illegal for military and law enforcement to exercise jointly. The site claims that SOCOM units and the FBI's Hostage Rescue Team routinely train together now.

23. As a rule, the Posse Comitatus Act of 1878 limits military involvement in civil affairs. However, over time, Congress made exceptions to the act, including the use of military personnel to suppress insurrection (Title 10 USC Sections 331–334), to assist in the case of crimes involving nuclear materials (Title 18 USC Section 931), and in "Emergency Situations" involving chemical or biological weapons (Title 10 USC Section 382). Stephen Young, "The Posse Comitatus Act: A Resource Guide," http://www.llrx.com/features/posse.htm, accessed March 2, 2005.

24. Eric Schmitt, "Commandos Get Duty on U.S. Soil," *New York Times*, January 23, 2005.

25. According to one insider with knowledge of the issue, by 1994 DoD had formally rejected offers to take responsibility for all paramilitary operations at least three times over the previous four decades. James K. Bruton, personal interview with Robert A. Mountel, January 6, 1994, cited in Bruton, "U.S. Special Operations Command: Does the Current Organization Fulfill the Original Intent," p. 14, fn. 34, based on a January 6, 1994, personal interview with Robert A. Mountel (Colonel, USA, Ret). Col. Mountel has Special Forces experience dating from the 1950s, and after retirement he worked until 1994 on special operations as a civilian for the Army. Specific examples are offered in Kathryn Stone's *All Necessary Means: Employing CIA Operatives in a Warfighting Role Alongside Special Operations Forces*, U.S. Army War College Strategy Research Project, July 4, 2003, p. 13.

26. Section 1208 of PL 108–375, the Ronald W. Reagan National Defense Authorization Act for Fiscal Year 2005. The new funding authority for SOF was limited to $25 million per year through 2007 to collectively fund both USSOCOM and CIA paramilitary activities. This authority expires at the end of 2007.

27. Kathryn Stone, *All Necessary Means*; Jennifer D. Kibbe, "The Rise of the Shadow Warriors," *Foreign Affairs* 83 (March/April 2004); Philip L. Mahla, and Christopher N. Riga, "An Operational Concept for the Transformation of SOF into a Fifth Service," Monterey, CA: Naval Postgraduate School, June 2003; CRS Report on SOF Issues

28. Kathryn Stone, *All Necessary Means*, 20.

29. John MacGaffin, "Clandestine Human Intelligence: Spies, Counterspies, and Covert Action," in *Transforming U.S. Intelligence*, eds. Jennifer E. Sims and Burton Gerber (Washington, DC: Georgetown University Press, 2005), pp. 89–90. See also Rowan Scarborough, "Green Berets Take On Spy Duties: Pentagon seeks intelligence options," *Washington Times*, February 19, 2004, p. 1.

30. Senior Defense Official, U.S. Department of Defense, Office of the Assistant Secretary of Defense (Public Affairs) News Transcript, January 24, 2005. Accessed on April 2, 2007 at: http://www.defenselink.mil/transcripts/transcript.aspx?transcriptid=1667.

31. "McCain Expects Hearings on Defense Intelligence Unit: Pentagon Disputes Some of Post Report," *Washington Post*, January 24, 2005, pg. 2.

32. For example, Robert Kelly, "US Army Special Forces Unconventional Warfare Doctrine: Engine of Change or Relic of the Past," Research Paper, Naval War College, January 7, 2000.

33. See Mindaugas Rekasius, "Unconventional Deterrence Strategy," (Monterey: Naval Postgraduate School, 2005).

34. Current SOF doctrine notes: "Operational and strategic staffs and commanders must guard against limiting unconventional warfare to a specific set of circumstances or activities.... The most prevalent mistake is the belief that unconventional warfare is limited to guerrilla warfare or insurgency." Joint Publication 3-05, *Doctrine for Joint Special Operations*, December 17, 2003, II–7, 8.

35. Christopher J. Lamb, "Review of Psychological Operations Lessons Learned from Recent Operational Experience," Occasional Paper, National Defense University Press, September 2005.

36. Adams, *U.S. Special Forces in Action*; particularly chapter 11 and quotations from USSOCOM Commander, Wayne Downing, pp. 10–11. See also General Wayne A. Downing, "Joint Special Operations in Peace and War," *Joint Forces Quarterly* 8 (Summer 1995): 24.

37. Sean Taylor, "The Battle of Mari Ghar," *Defense News*, June 26, 2006: 42.

38. Adams' *U.S. Special Forces in Action* is the best source for these arguments, but much the same sentiment is often expressed in the pages of *Special Warfare*,

the JFK Special Warfare Center and School magazine. See Colonel Gary M. Jones, and Major Christopher Tone, "Unconventional Warfare: Core Purpose of Special Forces," *Special Warfare* 12 (Summer 1999): 4–15; Colonel Michael R. Kershner, "Unconventional Warfare: The Most Misunderstood Form of Military Operations," *Special Warfare* 14 (Winter 2001): 2–7; Captain Robert Lee Wilson, "Unconventional Warfare: SF's Past, Present and Future," *Special Warfare*, 14 (Winter 2001): 24–27; MAJ Mike Skinner, "The Renaissance of Unconventional Warfare as an SF Mission," *Special Warfare*, 15 (Winter 2002): 16–22. See also de B. Taillon, *The Evolution of Special Forces in Counter-Terrorism* for an historic overview of the tension between the Special Forces and the "Ranger" approach to special operations.

39. The full text of the memo is available at http://www.usatoday.com/news/washington/executive/rumsfeld-memo.htm, accessed October 8, 2004.

40. Linda Robinson, "Men on a Mission: U.S. Special Forces are retooling for the war on terror," *U.S. News and World Report*, September 11, 2006.

41. David Tucker and Christopher Lamb, "Restructuring Special Operations Forces for Emerging Threats," Strategic Forum No. 219, Institute for National Strategic Studies, National Defense University, January 2006.

6. SOF AND THE FUTURE OF WARFARE

1. Christopher J. Lamb and James Pryzstup, "Beigun no Toransufohmehshon to Higashi Ajia no Anzenhoshou (Transformation of the U.S. Military and East Asian Security)," *Kokusai Mondai*, 539 (February 2005): 2743.

2. Andrew Krepinevich, "Cavalry to Computer: The Pattern of Military Revolutions," *The National Interest* 37 (Fall 1994): 1.

3. Ibid., p. 8.

4. Eliot Cohen, "A Revolution in Warfare," *Foreign Affairs* 75 (March/April 1996): 51.

5. David Tucker and Christopher Lamb, "Peacetime Engagements," in Sam Sarkesian, ed., *America's Armed Forces: A Handbook of Current and Future Capabilities* (Westport, CT: Greenwood Publishing, 1996), p.298.

6. Quotes are from George W. Bush's speech at the Citadel, September 23, 1999.

7. Vice Adm. (retired) Arthur Cebrowski, "New Rules for a New Era," *Transformation Trends*, October 21, 2002; http://www.oft.osd.mil/library/library_files/trends_163_transformation_trends_21_october_issue.pdf., accessed October 26, 2005.

8. Ibid.

9. Department of Defense, *Transformation Planning Guidance*, p. 3. http://www.oft.osd.mil/library/library_files/document_129_Transformation_Planning_Guidance_April_2003_1.pdf., accessed October 27, 2005.

10. Colin Gray, "Strategic Employment of Special Operations Forces and Requirements for Success, Phase II," National Institute for Public Policy, December 1992; Contract Number MDA 903–91-C-0030, a study conducted for the Office of the Assistant Secretary (Special Operations/Low-Intensity Conflict).

11. Cebrowski, "New Rules for a New Era."

12. Eliot Cohen, "What's in a Name: World War IV," Wall Street Journal, November 20, 2001.

13. "JFCOM Examines How to Make Conventional Troops More "SOF-Like," Inside the Pentagon, September 4, 2003; and "Rumsfeld's Pick for Army Chief Seen as Step Toward Big Changes," Inside the Army, June 16, 2003.

14. Gordon Lubold, "Small U.S. Marine Units Poised for Power," Defense News, May 24, 2004, p. 18.

15. Bradley Graham, "Larger Special Operations Role Being Urged on Marines," Washington Post, May 8, 2005; and U.S. Department of Defense News Release, "Secretary of Defense Approves Marine Special Operations Command," No. 1127-05, November 1, 2005.

16. Stephen Biddle, "Special Forces and the Future of Warfare: Will SOF Predominate in 2020?" Strategic Studies Institute, U.S. Army War College, May 24, 2004.

17. SOCOM, 2005 Annual Report; http://www.socom.mil/Docs/2005_Annual_Report.pdf, p. 18, accessed October 27, 2005.

18. Adrian Erckenbrack, "Transformation: Roles and Missions for ARSOF," Special Warfare 15 (December 2002): 2–8.

19. William H. McRaven, Spec Ops: Case Studies in Special Operations Warfare Theory and Practice, (Novato, CA: Presidio Press, 1995), pp. 13ff, 381–82, 389.

20. "Should Army Special Forces Take Leading Role in Postwar Iraq?" Inside the Army, August 25, 2003.

21. Thomas W. O'Connell, Assistant Secretary of Defense for Special Operations and Low-Intensity Conflict, "Ensuring SOF's Training, Equipment and Leadership," Special Operations Technology 2 (May 2004): 34–36.

22. "Rumsfeld's Pick for Army Chief Seen as Step Toward Big Changes," Inside the Army, June 16, 2003.

23. David Litt, "Special Ops Forces Are 'Tool of Choice,' " National Defense, February 2003: 20. David Litt is a U.S. ambassador who served as a political adviser to the Commander, SOCOM.

24. Megan Scully and Gina Cavallaro, "Special Forces Brain Drain," Defense News, May 3, 2004; and Richard Lardner, "Senior Soldiers In Special Ops Being Lured Off," Tampa Tribune, March 21, 2005.

25. "Special Operations Clamors for Better ISR," Aviation Week and Space Technology, February 23, 2004.

26. SOCOM, 2005 Annual Report; http://www.socom.mil/Docs/2005_An-nual_Report.pdf, p. 27, accessed October 27, 2005.

27. Gregory L. Vistica, "Military Split on How to Use Special Forces in Terror War," *Washington Post*, January 5, 2004.

28. Robert Oakley and T. X. Hammes, "Securing Afghanistan: Entering a Make-or-Break Phase?" *Strategic Forum*, Institute for National Strategic Studies, no. 205, March 2004; and *U.S. News and World Report*, "The Hunt for Bin Laden," May 10, 2004.

29. James A Gavrilis, "The Mayor of Ar Rutbah," *Foreign Policy* 151 (November/December 2005): 28–36.

30. Linda Robinson, *Masters of Chaos*, (New York: Perseus Books Group, 2004), pp. 245ff.

31. Michael Hirsh and John Barry; "The Salvador Option," *Newsweek*, Web Exclusive; http://www.msnbc.msn.com/id/6802629/site/newsweek/, accessed April 18, 2005.

32. Richard H. Shultz, "Showstoppers: Nine Reasons Why We Never Sent Our Special Operations Forces After al-Qaeda Before 9/11," *The Weekly Standard* 9 (January 26, 2004): 32.

33. Steve Coll, *Ghost Wars: The Secret History of the CIA, Afghanistan, and Bin Laden, from the Soviet Invasion to September 10, 2001* (New York: Penguin, 2004), pp. 422, 497–529.

34. By late 2003 there was open, public debate on this subject. See "Should Army Special Forces Take Leading Role in Postwar Iraq?" *Inside the Army*, August 25, 2003.

35. Army Field Manual, FM 31-20 and Adrian Erckenbrack, "Transformation: Roles and Missions for ARSOF." Erckenbrack cites SOF imperatives as the need to "understand the environment, engage the threat discriminately, apply capabilities indirectly, develop multiple options, and anticipate and control psychological effects."

36. Sidney E. Dean, "US Army Special Forces at Threshold of Transition," *Pentagon Brief*, May 15, 2003, p. 2. "General Brown's ideal 21st Century special operator combines 'a warrior ethos with language proficiency, cultural awareness, political sensitivity, and the ability to maximize information-age technology.'"

37. Robert D. Kaplan, "War on Terrorism: Indian Country," *Wall Street Journal*, September 21, 2004.

38. Ann Scott Tyson and Dana Priest, "Pentagon Seeking Leeway Overseas: Operations Could Bypass Envoys," *Washington Post*, February 24, 2005. SOCOM's commander has denied this report. See Linda Robinson, "Men on a Mission: U.S. Special Forces Are Retooling for the War on Terror." *U.S. News and World Report*, September 11, 2006.

39. Christopher Lamb, *Review of Psychological Operations Lessons Learned from Recent Operational Experience* (Washington, D.C.: National Defense University Press, 2005). The three firms SOCOM later contracted with for functional expertise in persuasive communications were all located in Washington, D.C. David Pugliese, "Special Ops Hires Firms to Improve US Image," *Federal Times*, September 5, 2005.

40. Jennifer D. Kibbe, "The Rise of the Shadow Warriors," *Foreign Affairs* 83 (March/April 2004): 102–115.

41. Matthew G. Karres and Michael Richardson, "Innovation from Below: The Role of Subordinate Feedback in Irregular Warfare Operations," Master's Thesis, Naval Postgraduate School, Monterey, CA, June 2001.

42. Erckenbrack, "Transformation: Roles and Missions for ARSOF," 2.

43. SOF leadership emphasizes transforming SOF capabilities to conduct small surgical operations with minimal risk to the employed force. Thomas W. O'Connell, *Special Operations Technology*, 33.

44. Christopher Lamb, *Review of Psychological Operations*.

45. Robinson, "Men on a Mission."

46. These observations are based on author discussions with members of the SOF community and reactions from the community to studies conducted by the authors.

47. Others have also concluded SOF require organizational changes to improve performance. Philip L. Mahla and Christopher N. Riga, "An Operational Concept for the Transformation of SOF into a Fifth Service," Master's Thesis, Monterey, CA: Naval Postgraduate School, June 2003; also Robinson, *Masters of Chaos*, p. 361.

48. Foreword, *Transformation Planning Guidance*.

49. A recent Pentagon language initiative reportedly will require all junior officers to complete a foreign language course, and eventually will demand that all general officer and flag officer candidates be bilingual. See "QDR Will Put 'Major Emphasis' on Shoring Up Foreign Language Capabilities, DOD Official Says," Inside Defense.com Defense Alert, October 27, 2005; http://insidedefense.com/secure/defense_docnum.asp?f = defense_2002.ask&docnum = 10272005_oct27b, accessed November 4, 2005

50. Even SOF find they must further improve their capabilities in these areas in order to be effective. See Janice L Burton, "Language Transformation Plan to Build Culturally Savvy Soldiers," *Special Warfare*, 18 (September 2005): 14.

51. On top of a $30 billion program reduction in 2004, another cut of more than $30 billion was planned for 2005. See "Pentagon to Slash $32 Billion from Service Budgets; More Cuts May Follow," InsideDefense.com Defense Alert, November 2, 2005; http://insidedefense.com/secure/defense_docnum.asp?f = defense_2002.ask&docnum = 1122005_nov2b, accessed November 4, 2005.

7. RESTRUCTURING SPECIAL OPERATIONS FORCES

1. This chapter draws upon arguments previously made in David Tucker and Christopher Lamb, "Restructuring Special Operations Forces for Emerging Threats," *Strategic Forum* no. 219, Institute for National Strategic Studies, National Defense University, January 2006.

2. Zawahiri's letter was posted at http://www.dni.gov/release_letter_101105.html. Stephen Ulph argues that the letter may be a fake; http://www.jamestown.org/news_details.php?news_id = 145, accessed October 18, 2005.

3. An assumption criticized at length in David Tucker, "The Unconventional Threat to Homeland Security," in Paul Stockton, ed., *Homeland Security* (New York: Oxford University Press, 2007).

4. "*Hawala* is an alternative or parallel remittance system. It exists and operates outside of, or parallel to 'traditional' banking or financial channels. It was developed in India, before the introduction of western banking practices, and is currently a major remittance system used around the world. It is but one of several such systems; another well known example is the 'chop', 'chit' or 'flying money' system indigenous to China, and also, used around the world... . The components of *hawala* that distinguish it from other remittance systems are trust and the extensive use of connections such as family relationships or regional affiliations. Unlike traditional banking or even the 'chop' system, *hawala* makes minimal (often no) use of any sort of negotiable instrument. Transfers of money take place based on communications between members of a network of *hawaladars*, or *hawala* dealers." http://www.interpol.int/Public/FinancialCrime/MoneyLaundering/hawala/default.asp#2, accessed May 31, 2005.

5. On this point, consider Doug McAdam, "Recruitment to High Risk Activism: The Case of Freedom Summer," *The American Journal of Sociology* 92 (July, 1986): 64–90. See also Marc Sageman, *Understanding Terrorist Networks* (Philadelphia: University of Pennsylvania Press, 2004).

6. C. A. Bayly, *Empire and Information: Intelligence Gathering and Social Communication in India, 1780–1870* (Cambridge University Press, 1996) presents a useful case study of some of the issues in this paragraph.

7. Robert Kaplan, *Imperial Grunts: The American Military on the Ground* (New York: Random House, 2005), p. 36; Gary C. Schroen, *First In: An Insider's Account of How the CIA Spearheaded the War on Terror in Afghanistan* (New York: Ballantine Books, 2005), pp. 190–191.

8. Further details on a possible personnel system are available in Anna Simons and David Tucker "Improving Human Intelligence in the War on Terrorism: The Need for an Ethnographic Capability," Office of Net Assessment, Office of the Secretary of Defense, December 2004.

9. National Security Action Memorandum 182, "United States Overseas Internal Defense Policy," September, 1962.

10. Steve Coll, *Ghost Wars: The Secret History of the CIA, Afghanistan, and bin Laden, from the Soviet Invasion to September 10, 2001* (New York: Penguin, 2004), p. 379 describes such an episode.

11. On this point, see Francis Fukuyama and Abram Shulsky, *The "Virtual Corporation" and Army Organization* (RAND: Santa Monica, 1997).

12. On the preference for special mission units over SF for direct action, see Gregory Vistica, "Military Split on How to Use Special Forces In Terror War," *The Washington Post*, January 5, 2004. For constraints on use of force by SF and special-mission units, compare Mark Bowden, *Killing Pablo: The Hunt for the World's Greatest Outlaw* (New York: Penguin, 2001), p. 148, who is reporting on special-mission units, and Kaplan, *Imperial Grunts*, pp. 63–64, who is reporting on SF.

13. This name and the mission of the command would return SOCOM to something like the original vision of General Edward Myers, a key early supporter of an improved direct-action capability. See J. W. Partin, "Interview with General E. C. Meyer," Arlington, Virginia, July 14, 1988 (typescript in author's possession).

14. David Tucker, *Skirmishes at the Edge of Empire: The United States and International Terrorism* (Westport, CT: Praeger, 1997), pp. 109–131.

15. A version of the following arguments appeared in David Tucker, "Counterterrorism and the Perils of Preemption: Problems of Command and Control," in Betty Glad and Chris Dolan, eds., *Striking First: The Preventive War Doctrine and the Reshaping of U.S. Foreign Policy* (New York: Palgrave MacMillan, 2004).

16. Eliot A. Cohen, *Supreme Command: Soldiers, Statesmen and Leadership in Wartime* (New York: Free Press, 2002) believes it does not.

17. Richard Lowry, "Bombing at the Pentagon," *National Review* 53 (September 3, 2001): 36–37.

18. Daniel Benjamin and Steven Simon, *The Age of Sacred Terror* (New York: Random House, 2002), p. 318.

19. A point suggested by Eliot Cohen, *Commandos and Politicians, Elite Military Units in Modern Democracies* (Cambridge: Center for International Affairs, 1978), pp. 77, 101.

20. On the difference between regular and special operations, in addition to McRaven cited above, compare Joint Publication 3-0, *Doctrine for Joint Operations*, p. II-1 with Joint Publication 3-05, *Doctrine for Joint Special Operations*, pp. I-4, 5, especially what the latter says about mass and surprise.

21. Bowden, *Killing Pablo*, pp. 148, 216 reports some examples of senior officer attitudes toward SOF.

22. Sean Naylor, *Not a Good Day to Die: The Untold Story of Operation Anaconda* (New York: The Berkley Publishing Group, 2004) provides examples.

23. For recommendations on an institutional vehicle for such simulations, see Christopher Lamb and Irving Lachow, "Reforming Pentagon Strategic Decision Making," *Strategic Forum* No. 221, Institute for National Strategic Studies, National Defense University, July 2006.

24. For a more detailed discussion of this issue, see David Tucker, "The RMA and the Interagency: Knowledge and Speed vs. Sloth and Ignorance?" *Parameters* 30 (Autumn 2000): 66–76.

CONCLUSION

1. Bradley Graham, "Shortfalls of Special Operations Command Are Cited," *Washington Post*, November 17, 2005, p. A02.

2. The 2006 Quadrennial Defense Review argues that "This war [on terror] requires the U.S. military to adopt unconventional and indirect approaches." Secretary of Defense Donald Rumsfeld, "2006 Quadrennial Defense Review," Department of Defense, p. 1. Greg Jaffe, "Rumsfeld Aims To Elevate Role of Special Forces," *Wall Street Journal*, February 18, 2006, p. 1.

3. USSOCOM, Special Operations Forces Posture Statement, 2006, pp. 5–6.

4. Joshua Kucera, "Civil Affairs, Psyops Shift Away From SOCOM," *Jane's Defence Weekly* March 22, 2006.

5. Richard Lardner, "Special Ops Command Gets Extra Clout," *Tampa Tribune*, February 13, 2006.

6. Lucien S. Vandenbroucke, *Perilous Options: Special Operations as an Instrument of U.S. Foreign Policy* (New York: Oxford University Press, 1993).

BIBLIOGRAPHY

Adams, Thomas K. *US Special Operations Forces in Action: The Challenge of Unconventional Warfare.* London: Frank Cass, 1998.

Arkes, H., and C. Blumer. "The Psychology of Sunk Cost." *Organizational Behavior and Human Decision Processes,* 35 (1985): 415–422.

Armitage, Richard L., Assistant Secretary of Defense, International Security Affairs. "To Combat Terrorism and Other Forms of Unconventional Warfare." A Hearing before the Subcommittee on Sea Power and Force Projection of the Committee on Armed Services, United States Senate, 99th Congress, Second Session, on S. 2453. "To Enhance the Capabilities of the United States to Combat Terrorism and Other Forms of Unconventional Warfare." August 5, 1986.

Army Field Manual, FM 31–20.

Bayly, C. A. *Empire and Information: Intelligence Gathering and Social Communication in India, 1780–1870.* Cambridge University Press, 1996.

Benjamin, Daniel, and Steven Simon, *The Age of Sacred Terror.* New York: Random House, 2002.

Biddle, Stephen. "Special Forces and the Future of Warfare: Will SOF Predominate in 2020?" Strategic Studies Institute, U.S. Army War College, May 24, 2004.

Blake, Jonathan A., Major. "SFQC Phase II: Building a Warrior." *Special Warfare.* 18 (July, 2005): 2–8.

Bolton, John R. "Wrong Turn in Somalia." *Foreign Affairs* 73 (January/February, 1994): 56–67.

Bowden, Mark. *Killing Pablo: The Hunt for the World's Greatest Outlaw.* New York: Penguin Books, 2001.

————. *Blackhawk Down, A Story of Modern War. New York: Atlantic Monthly Press,* 1999.

Brooke, James. "Pentagon Tells Troops in Afghanistan: Shape Up and Dress Right." *New York Times,* September 12, 2002.

Bruton, James K. "U.S. Special Operations Command: Does the Current Organization Fulfill the Original Intent." Unpublished Paper for Strategic Studies Research Seminar, John Hopkins University. November 30, 1994.

Burton, Janice. "18Xs make Mark, Initial Entry SF Soldiers Earn Praise of Senior SF NCOs." *Special Warfare* 19 (July–August, 2006): 28.

——. "Language Transformation Plan to Build Culturally Savvy Soldiers." *Special Warfare* 18 (September 2005): 14–18.

Bush, George, "Remarks by the President at the Citadel." The Citadel, Charleston, South Carolina. December 11, 2001. http://www.whitehouse.gov/news/releases/2001/12/20011211–6.html, accessed December 17, 2003.

Cebrowski, Arthur, Vice Adm. (retired). "New Rules for a New Era." *Transformation Trends.* October 21, 2002; http://www.oft.osd.mil/library/library_files/trends_163_transformation_trends_21_october_issue.pdf.

Centre for Conflict Studies, University of New Brunswick. "Special Operations: Military Lessons from Six Selected Case Studies." Contract FO 1600-80-DO299. JFK School, Fort Bragg, Fall 1982.

Chairman, Joint Chiefs of Staff. Report on Roles, Missions and Functions of the Armed Forces of the United States. February, 1993.

Chu, David S. C. Assistant Secretary for Program Analysis and Evaluation, 1988 to 1992. Interview. October 30, 2000.

Clinton, William. "Message to the Congress Transmitting a Report on Somalia, October 13th, 1993." http://www.presidency.ucsb.edu/ws/index.php?pid = 47197, accessed September 6, 2006.

Clarke, Walter, and Jeffrey Herbst. "Somalia and the Future of Humanitarian Intervention." *Foreign Affairs* 75 (March/April 1996): 70–85.

Cohen, Eliot A. *Supreme Command: Soldiers, Statesmen and Leadership in Wartime.* New York: The Free Press, 2002.

——. "What's in a Name: World War IV." *Wall Street Journal,* November 20, 2001.

——. "A Revolution in Warfare." *Foreign Affairs* 75 (March/April 1996): 37–55.

——. *Commandos and Politicians: Elite Military Units in Modern Democracies.* Cambridge: Harvard University Press, 1978.

Coles, Harry L., and Albert K. Weinberg, *Civil Affairs: Soldiers Become Governors.* Washington, D.C.: Center of Military History, United States Army, 1964; reprinted 2004.

Coll, Steve. *Ghost Wars: The Secret History of the CIA, Afghanistan, and bin Laden, from the Soviet Invasion to September 10, 2001.* New York: Penguin, 2004.

Collins, John M. "Roles and Functions of U.S. Combat Forces: Past, Present, and Prospects." Washington, January 1993 (CRS Report for Congress no. 93–72 S).

———. Library of Congress, Congressional Research Service, "Military Roles and Missions: A Framework for Review." Washington, May 1, 1995 (CRS Report for Congress no. 95-517S).

———. *Special Operations Forces: An Assessment*. Washington, D.C.: National Defense University Press, 1994.

Cotty, Major Will, Captain Brendon Bluestein, and Jat Thompson. "The Whole-Man Concept: Assessing the SF Soldier of the Future." *Special Warfare* 17 (April, 2005): 18–22.

Couch, Dick. *The Finishing School: Earning the Navy SEAL Trident*. New York: Crown, 2004.

"CS and CSS Soldiers May Attend Ranger School." *Army Logistician*. 37 (July/August, 2005): 45.

Dean, Sidney E. "US Army Special Forces at Threshold of Transition." *Pentagon Brief*, May 15, 2003.

Department of Defense. *Dictionary of Military and Associated Terms*. Joint Publication 1–02. April 12, 2001 (As Amended Through May 9, 2005). http://www.dtic.mil/doctrine/jel/new_pubs/jp1_02.pdf, accessed August 14, 2005.

———. Annual Report to President and Congress. 1998. http://www.defenselink.mil/execsec/adr98/chap4.html

———. *Transformation Planning Guidance*. http://www.oft.osd.mil/library/library_files/document_129_Transformation_Planning_Guidance_April_2003_1.pdf

Devroy, Ann. "Collapse of U.S. Collective Action May Force Second Look at Bosnia." *Washington Post*, October 8, 1993.

Doctrine for Joint Special Operations. Joint Publication 305, December 17, 2003.

Downing, General Wayne A. "Joint Special Operations in Peace and War." *Joint Forces Quarterly* 8 (Summer 1995).

Dunnigan, James F. *The Perfect Soldier*. New York: Citadel Press, 2003.

"Hope Behind the Horror," *Economist* June 19, 1993.

Erckenbrack, Adrian. "Transformation: Roles and Missions for ARSOF." *Special Warfare* 15 (December 2002): 2–8.

Farer, Tom. "Report of an Inquiry, Conducted Pursuant to Security Council Resolution 837, Into the 5 June 1993 Attack on UN Forces in Somalia."

Fukuyama, Francis, and Abram Shulsky. *The "Virtual Corporation" and Army Organization*. Santa Monica: RAND, 1997.

Government Accountability office. "Special Operations Forces: Several Human Capital Challenges Must Be Addressed to Meet Expanded Role." GAO-06-812, July 2006.

Government Accounting Office. Report to the Chairman, Subcommittee on Military Readiness, Committee on National Security, House of Representatives. "Special Operations, Opportunities to Preclude Misuse." GAO/NSI-AD-97-85, May 1997.

———. "Army Ranger Training: Safety Improvements Need to be Institutionalized." GAO/NSIAD-97-29, January 1997.

Field Manual 3-05.201, Special Forces Unconventional Warfare Operations.

Foreign Relations of the United States. http://www.state.gov/www/about_state/history/frus.html

Gavrilis, James A. "The Mayor of Ar Rutbah." *Foreign Policy* 151 (November/December 2005): 28–36.

Gellman, Barton. "The Words Behind a Deadly Decision; Secret Cables Reveal Maneuvering Over Request for Armor in Somalia." *Washington Post*, October 31, 1993.

Gordon, Michael R. with John H. Cushman. "Mission in Somalia; After Supporting Hunt for Aided, U.S. is Blaming U.N. for Losses." *New York Times*, October 18, 1993.

Graham, Bradley. "Shortfalls Of Special Operations Command Are Cited." *Washington Post*, November 17, 2005.

———. "Larger Special Operations Role Being Urged on Marines." *Washington Post*, May 8, 2005.

Gray, Colin S. "Handfuls of Heroes on Desperate Ventures: When Do Special Operations Succeed?" *Parameters* 29 (Spring 1999): 2–24.

———. "Strategic Employment of Special Operations Forces and Requirements for Success, Phase II." National Institute for Public Policy, December 1992. Contract Number MDA 903-91-C-0030.

Grenier, John. *The First Way of War: American War Making on the Frontier, 1607–1814.* Cambridge: Cambridge University Press, 2005.

Haas, Colonel Michael E., USAF, Retired. *Apollo's Warriors: United States Air Force Special Operations During the Cold War.* Maxwell Air Force Base, Alabama: Air University Press, 1997.

———. *In the Devil's Shadow: U.N. Special Operations During the Korean War.* Annapolis, MD: Naval Institute Press, 2000.

Hejlik, Major General Dennis J., Major Cliff W. Gilmore, and Sergeant Major Matthew P. Ingram. "Special Operations Marines and the Road Ahead." *Marine Corps Gazette* 90 (August, 2006): 39–41.

Hettena, Seth. "Navy Unit Goes Public to Recruit." *Philadelphia Inquirer* October 11, 2005.

Hirsh, Michael, and John Barry. "The Salvador Option." *Newsweek.* Web Exclusive http://www.msnbc.msn.com/id/6802629/site/newsweek/, accessed April 18, 2005.

Hoar, Joseph P. "A CINC's Perspective." *Joint Forces Quarterly*, 2 (Autumn 1993).

Hogan, David W. *Raiders or Elite Infantry? The Changing Role of the U.S. Army Rangers from Dieppe to Grenada*. Westport, CT. Greenwood Press, 1992.

Jaffe, Greg. "Rumsfeld Aims To Elevate Role Of Special Forces." *Wall Street Journal*, February 18, 2006.

"JFCOM Examines How to Make Conventional Troops More SOF-Like." *Inside the Pentagon*, September 4, 2003.

Johnson, Lieutenant General Robert. "Briefing," Washington, D.C., 1993.

Joint Publication 3-0, *Doctrine for Joint Operations*.

Joint Publication 3-05, Doctrine for Joint Special Operations.

Jones, Gary M., and Major Christopher Tone. "Unconventional Warfare: Core Purpose of Special Forces." *Special Warfare* 12 (Summer 1999): 4–15.

Kaplan, Robert D. *Imperial Grunts: The American Military on the Ground*. New York: Random House, 2005.

———. "War on Terrorism: Indian Country." *Wall Street Journal*, September 21, 2004.

Karres, Matthew G., and Michael Richardson. "Innovation from Below: The Role of Subordinate Feedback in Irregular Warfare Operations." Master's Thesis, Naval Postgraduate School, Monterey, CA, June 2001.

Keegan, John. *Intelligence in War: Knowledge of the Enemy from Napoleon to al-Qaeda*. New York: Knopf, 2003.

Kelly, Colonel Francis J. *Vietnam Studies, U.S. Army Special Forces, 1961–1971*. Washington, D.C.: Department of the Army, 1973.

Kelly, Robert. "US Army Special Forces Unconventional Warfare Doctrine: Engine of Change or Relic of the Past." Research Paper, Naval War College, January 7, 2000.

Kershner, Michael R. "Unconventional Warfare: The Most Misunderstood Form of Military Operations." *Special Warfare* 14 (Winter 2001): 2–7.

Koren, Henry L. T. Jr. "Congress Wades Into Special Operations." *Parameters* 18 (December 1988): 62–74.

Kibbe, Jennifer D. "The Rise of the Shadow Warriors." *Foreign Affairs* 83 (March/April, 2004): 102–115.

Kirby, Sheila Nataraj, Margaret C. Harrell, and Jennifer Sloan. "Why Don't Minorities Join Special Operations Forces?" *Armed Forces and Society* 26 (Summer 2000): 523–546.

Krepinevich, Andrew. *The Army and Vietnam*. Baltimore: The Johns Hopkins University Press, 1986.

———. "Cavalry to Computer: The Pattern of Military Revolutions." *The National Interest* 37 (Fall 1994): 30–42.

Kucera, Joshua. "Civil Affairs, Psyops Shift Away From SOCOM." *Jane's Defence Weekly*, March 22, 2006.

Lamb, Christopher, and Irving Lachow. "Reforming Pentagon Strategic Deci-sion Making." *Strategic Forum* No. 221, Institute for National Strategic Stud-ies, National Defense University, July 2006.

Lamb, Christopher J., and James Pryzstup, "Beigun no Toransufohmehshon to Higashi Ajia no Anzenhoshou" (Transformation of the U.S. Military and East Asian Security). *Kokusai Mondai* 539 (February 2005): 27–43.

Lamb, Christopher J. "Review of Psychological Operations Lessons Learned from Recent Operational Experience." Occasional Paper, National Defense University Press, September 2005.

———. *Belief Systems and Decision Making in the Mayaguez Crisis.* Gainesville, Florida: The University of Florida Press, 1989.

Lardner, Richard. "Special Ops Command Gets Extra Clout." *Tampa Tribune,* February 13, 2006.

———. "Senior Soldiers in Special Ops Being Lured Off." *Tampa Tribune,* March 21, 2005.

———. "Road to Elite Service Is Grueling Challenge." *Tampa Tribune,* May 31, 2005.

Larson, Eric V., and Bogdan Savych. *American Public Support for U.S. Military Operations from Mogadishu to Baghdad.* Santa Monica, CA: RAND, 2005.

Laurie, Clayton D. "'The Chanting of Crusaders:' Captain Heber Blankenhorn and AEF Combat Propaganda in Word War I." *The Journal of Military His-tory* 59 (July, 1995): 1–58.

Lilly, E. "Short History of the Psychological Strategy Board," December 21, 1951, National Security Council Staff Papers, NSC Secretariat Series, Box 6, Dwight Eisenhower Library.

Litt, David. "Special Ops Forces Are 'Tool of Choice.'" *National Defense,* Febru-ary 2003.

Lowry, Richard. "Bombing at the Pentagon." *National Review* 53 (September 3, 2001): 36–38.

Lubold, Gordon. "Small U.S. Marine Units Poised for Power." *Defense News,* May 24, 2004.

Lukas, James. *Kommando: German Special Forces of World War II.* New York, St. Martin's Press, 1985.

Luttwak, Edward. *Strategy: The Logic of War and Peace.* Cambridge: Harvard University Press, 2001.

Marquis, Susan. *Unconventional Warfare: Rebuilding U.S. Special Operations Forces.* Washington, D.C.: Brookings Institute Press, 1997.

Mahla, Major Philip L., and Major Christopher N. Riga. "An Operational Con-cept for the Transformation of SOF into a Fifth Service." Monterey, CA: Naval Postgraduate School, June 2003.

McAdam, Doug. "Recruitment to High Risk Activism: The Case of Freedom Summer." *The American Journal of Sociology* 92 (July 1986): 64–90.

"McCain Expects Hearings On Defense Intelligence Unit: Pentagon Disputes Some of Post Report." *Washington Post*, January 24, 2005.

McHugh, Paul. "Building Elite Forces for Military of Future." *San Francisco Chronicle*, May 14, 2006.

McRaven, William H. *Spec Ops: Case Studies in Special Operations Warfare: Theory and Practice*. Novato, CA: Presidio, 1995.

Morgan, Dan. "Secret Army Account Linked to Contra Aid; North, Secord Possibly Involved, Official Says." *The Washington Post*, April 22, 1987.

National Security Action Memorandum 182, "United States Overseas Internal Defense Policy." September, 1962.

Naylor, Sean. *Not a Good Day to Die: The Untold Story of Operation Anaconda*. New York: The Berkley Publishing Group, 2004.

Nunn, Sam. "Domestic Missions for the Armed Forces," Strategic Studies Institute, U.S. Army War College, February 1993.

Oakley, Robert B. "An Envoy's Perspective," *Joint Forces Quarterly* 2 (Autumn 1993): 44–55.

Oakley, Robert, and T. X. Hammes. "Securing Afghanistan: Entering a Make-or-Break Phase?" *Strategic Forum*. Institute for National Strategic Studies, no. 205, March 2004.

O'Connell, Thomas W., Assistant Secretary of Defense for Special Operations and Low-Intensity Conflict. "Ensuring SOF's Training, Equipment and Leadership." *Special Operations Technology* 2 (May 2004): 34–36.

Officers, Foreign Military Training Unit. "The Foreign Military Training Unit: Kingmakers, Not Kings." *Marine Corps Gazette*, 90 (August, 2006): 41–43.

Paddock, Alfred H. *U.S. Army Special Warfare: Its Origins*. Lawrence, Kansas: University Press of Kansas, 2002; revised edition.

Partin, J. W. "Interview with General E. C. Meyer." Arlington, Virginia, July 14, 1988.

"Pentagon to Slash $32 Billion from Service Budgets; More Cuts May Follow," InsideDefense.com Defense Alert, Nov. 2, 2005 http://insidedefense.com/secure/defense_docnum.asp?f = defense_2002.ask&docnum = 1122005_nov2b, accessed Nov. 4, 2005.

Perry, Tony. "New Navy SEALs Undeterred by Recent Loss of 11." *Los Angeles Times*. October 3, 2005.

Pogue, Forrest C. *George C. Marshall: Statesman*. New York, Viking Press, 1987.

"President Responds to Recent Violence Against U.S. Forces." *Washington Times*. October 7, 1993.

Pugliese, David. "Special Ops Hires Firms to Improve US Image." *Federal Times* September 5, 2005.

"QDR Will Put 'Major Emphasis' on Shoring Up Foreign Language Capabilities, DOD Official Says." Inside Defense.com Defense Alert, October 27, 2005; http://insidedefense.com/secure/defense_docnum.asp?f = defense_2002.ask&docnum = 10272005_oct27b.

Rashid, Ahmed. *Taliban: Militant Islam, Oil and Fundamentalism in Central Asia.* New Haven: Yale University Press, 2000.

Richburg, Keith B. "Aideed Exploited U.N.'s Failure to Prepare." *Washington Post*, December 5, 1993.

———. "U.S. Envoy to Somalia Urged Policy Shift Before 18 GIs Died." *Washington Post*, November 11, 1993.

Rekasius, Mindaugas. "Unconventional Deterrence Strategy." Master's Thesis. Monterey: Naval Postgraduate School, 2005.

Rescue Mission Report (Washington, D.C.: Joint Chiefs of Staff, 1980.

Robinson, Linda. "Men on a Mission: U.S. Special Forces Are Retooling for the War on Terror." *U.S. News and World Report*, September 11, 2006.

———. *Masters of Chaos: The Secret History of the Special Forces.* New York: Public Affairs, 2004.

Rosenberg, Matthew. "Effort in Afghanistan Gets More Conventional." *Philadelphia Enquirer*, September 15, 2002.

Rosson, General William B., USA, (retired). "Four Periods of American Involvement in Vietnam: Development and Implementation of Policy, Strategy and Programs, Described and Analyzed on the Basis of Service Experience at Progressively Senior Levels." Ph.D. dissertation, Oxford University, 1979.

Rumsfeld, Donald, Secretary of Defense. Memorandum. http://www.usatoday.com/news/washington/executive/rumsfeld-memo.htm, accessed October 8, 2004.

"Rumsfeld's Pick for Army Chief Seen as Step Toward Big Changes." *Inside the Army.* June 16, 2003.

Sageman, Marc. *Understanding Terrorist Networks.* Philadelphia: University of Pennsylvania Press, 2004.

Sandler, Stanley. *"Cease Resistance: It's Good for You!": A History of U.S. Army Combat Psychological Operations.* N.p.: United States Army Special Operations Command, Directorate of History and Museums, 1999.

Scarborough, Rowan. "Green Berets Take on Spy Duties: Pentagon Seeks Intelligence Options." *Washington Times*, February 19, 2004.

Scully, Megan, and Gina Cavallaro. "Special Forces Brain Drain." *Defense News*, May 3, 2004.

Schultz, Fred L. "MarSOC: Just Call Them Marines." *Proceedings.* 132 (January, 2006): 48–51.

Schmitt, Eric. "Commandos Get Duty on U.S. Soil." *New York Times*, January 23, 2005.

Schroen, Gary C. *First In: An Insider's Account of How the CIA Spearheaded the War on Terror in Afghanistan*. New York: Ballantine Books, 2005.

Sciolino, Elaine. "Puzzle in Somalia: The U.S. Goal." *New York Times*, October 5, 1993.

Senate Select Committee to Study Governmental Operations with Respect to Intelligence Activities, Foreign and Military Intelligence, 94th Congress, Second Session, 1976 S. Report 94–755, Book IV.

Shultz, Richard H. Jr. "Showstoppers: Nine Reasons Why We Never Sent Our Special Operations Forces After al Qaeda Before 9/11." *The Weekly Standard*, 9 (January 26, 2004).

———. *The Secret War Against Hanoi: The Untold Story of Spies, Saboteurs, and Covert Warriors in North Vietnam*. New York: Perennial, 2000.

"Should Army Special Forces Take Leading Role in Postwar Iraq?" *Inside the Army*. August 25, 2003.

Simons, Anna. *The Company They Keep*. New York: The Free Press. 1997.

Simons, Anna, and David Tucker. "Improving Human Intelligence in the War on Terrorism: The Need for an Ethnographic Capability." Office of Net Assessment, Office of the Secretary of Defense, December 2004.

Skinner, Mike. "The Renaissance of Unconventional Warfare as an SF Mission." *Special Warfare* 15 (Winter 2002): 16–22.

Soper, Barlow, Gary E. Milford, Gary T. Rosenthal. "Belief When Evidence Does Not Support Theory." *Psychology & Marketing*. 12 (August, 1995): 415–422.

"Special Operations Clamors for Better ISR." *Aviation Week and Space Technology*. February 23, 2004.

Stanton, Shelby L. *Green Berets at War, U.S. Army Special Forces in Southeast Asia, 1956–1975*. Novato, CA: Presidio Press, 1985.

Stone, Kathryn. "All Necessary Means: Employing CIA Operatives in a Warfighting Role Alongside Special Operations Forces." U.S. Army War College, Strategy Research Project, July 4, 2003.

Taillon, J. Paul de B. *The Evolution of Special Forces in Counterterrorism: The British and American Experiences*. Westport, CT: Praeger, 2001.

Tucker, David. "The Unconventional Threat to Homeland Security." In Paul Stockton, ed., *Homeland Security*. New York: Oxford University Press, 2007.

———. "The RMA and the Interagency: Knowledge and Speed vs. Sloth and Ignorance?" *Parameters* 30 (Autumn 2000), pp. 66–76.

———. *Skirmishes at the Edge of Empire: The United States and International Terrorism*. Westport, CT: Praeger, 1997.

Tucker, David, and Christopher Lamb. "Restructuring Special Operations Forces for Emerging Threats." Strategic Forum No. 219, Institute for National Strategic Studies, National Defense University, January 2006.

———. "Peacetime Engagements." In Sam Sarkesian, ed. *America's Armed Forces: A Handbook of Current and Future Capabilities*. Westport, CT: Greenwood Publishing, 1996.

Tyson, Ann Scott. "Pulling No Punches in Push for Navy SEALs; Pentagon Looking to Increase Ranks Without Easing the Tough Training." *Washington Post*, June 20, 2006.

Tyson, Ann Scott, and Dana Priest. "Pentagon Seeking Leeway Overseas: Operations Could Bypass Envoys." *Washington Post*, February 24, 2005.

United States Department of Defense News Release, "Secretary of Defense Approves Marine Special Operations Command." No. 1127-05, November 1, 2005.

United States Special Operations Command, *Special Operations Forces Posture Statement*, 2006.

———. 2005 Annual Report, http://www.socom.mil/Docs/2005_Annual_Report.pdf. Accessed October 27, 2005.

———. *Special Operations Forces Posture Statement*, 2003–2004.

———. *History, 15th Anniversary*. N.p.. 2002.

U.S. News and World Report. "The Hunt for Bin Laden," May 10, 2004.

Utley, Robert M. "The Contribution of the Frontier to the American Military Tradition." in James P. Tate, ed. *The American Military on the Frontier, The Proceedings of the 7th Military History Symposium, United States Air Force Academy, 30 September–1 October 1976*. Washington, DC: Office of Air Force History and United States Air Force Academy, 1978.

Vanden Brook, Tom. "U.S. Elite Forces Face Shortfall." *USA Today*, July 3, 2006.

Vandenbroucke, Lucien S. *Perilous Options: Special Operations as an Instrument of U.S. Foreign Policy*. New York: Oxford University Press, 1993.

Vistica, Gregory L. "Military Split on How to Use Special Forces in Terror War." *Washington Post*, January 5, 2004.

Wagner, Joe. "Army Special Forces: Step Child or Child Prodigy?" *Armed Forces Management* 12 (May, 1966).

Waller, Douglas C. *The Commandos: The Inside Story of America's Secret Soldiers*. New York: Dell, 1994.

Warner, John, and Carl Levin. "Review of the Circumstances Surrounding the Ranger Raid on October 3–4, 1993 in Mogadishu, Somalia." September 29, 1995.

Wedemeyer, Albert C., General. *Wedemeyer Reports!* New York: Henry Holt, 1958.

Wilson, Robert Lee. "Unconventional Warfare: SF's Past, Present and Future." *Special Warfare* 14 (Winter 2001): 24–27.

Y'Blood, William T. "Any Place, Any Time, Anywhere: The 1st Air Commando Group in World War II." *Air Power History* 48 (Summer, 2001): 5–16.

Young, Stephen. "The Posse Comitatus Act: A Resource Guide." http://www.llrx.com/features/posse.htm

Zhdanov, Andrei. "Report on the International Situation to the Cominform." September 22, 1947. http://www.cnn.com/SPECIALS/cold.war/episodes/04/documents/cominform.html, accessed July 30, 2003

Ziemke, Earl F. "Civil Affairs Reaches Thirty." *Military Affairs* 36 (December, 1972): 130–133.

INDEX

Northern Iraqi Oil Company, 35
North Vietnam, 92, 163, 228
Nunn-Cohen amendment, 97, 98

Oakley, Robert, 109, 112, 128, 133, 137, 249n5
Office of the Assistant Secretary of Defense, Special Operations and Low-Intensity Conflict (OASD(SO-LIC)), xi, 97; disagreement of with Special Operations Command over Somalia, 136, 249n13;
Office of the Chief of Psychological Warfare, 84
Office of the Secretary of Defense, 108
Office of Strategic Services (OSS), 77; denied most sensitive intelligence, 78
Office of the Under Secretary of Defense for Policy, 121
operational security (OPSEC), impeding operational coordination, 33
Operation Eagle Claw. See Desert One
Operation Enduring Freedom (OEF), 25
Operation Enduring Freedom, role of Special Forces in, 36–38
Operation Iraqi Freedom (OIF), 25, 156, 160, 194
Operation Just Cause, 99
Operation Restore Hope, 108
Operations Directorate, Joint Staff, vice director of, 1

Pace, Frank, 84, 85
paramilitary operations, 168–169
pararescue personnel, 11, 222; qualifications of enlisted volunteers for, 47–48; qualifications of officers to volunteer for, 47; reasons of for joining SOF, 44; selection and training of, 54
Patriotic Union of Kurdistan, 33
peace enforcement operations, 15; in Somalia, 114
Pentagon, attack on, September 11, 2001, 1–4; conventional forces represented in, 7; evacuation of ordered, 3;

hypervigilance of after September 11, 2002, 4; resistance of to SOF reform, 97–98
Persian Gulf, 99
Peshmerga, 156
phase four, of conventional military operation, 33; defined, 243n18
Philippines, 36–38, 72, 80, 156, 217
Phoenix program, 94
plane crash, 21–22, 26–28; and rewarding risk taking, 50
Pointe du Hoc, 74
population, attitude of conventional forces to, 163, 176; role of in unconventional warfare, 14, 103, 113, 175; relevance of to SOF, 132, 148, 153, 156;
Powell, Colin, 109, 111, 121, 140; opposition of to deployment of armor to Somalia, 124
Predator, 18
principals committee, 227
propaganda, 72; attitude of Americans toward, 80; attitude of military toward, 80
psychological operations, attitude of conventional military toward, 72–73, 85, 88; attitude of military toward, 83–84; attitude of State Department toward, 83; and Civilian Irregular Defense Groups, 91; civilian and SOCOM leadership limiting role of, 173–176, 194, 198, 238; conflict of with information operations, 32; definition of by Central Intelligence Agency, 83; description of, xix; and guerrilla warfare, 87; inherently ambiguous, 66; in Italy, 83; inadequacy of in Somalia, 113, 115; in Korean War, 85; lack of planning for in Iraq, 29; measuring the effectiveness of, 31; 66; military operation as an example of, 24–25; office of disbanded by War Department, 73; organizational issues related to, 81–82; part of information operations, 172; in peacetime, 80; renewed interest in

evidence of, 180, 181; and the future of SOF, 183–204; and jointness, 187; and SOF-like forces, 187–188
translators. *See* interpreters
Truman, Harry 77; disbanding of Office of Strategic Services by, 79; and Truman doctrine, 80
Turkey, 33, 36, 80, 105, 156

unconventional conflict, 98, 99
unconventional warfare, in Afghanistan, 102–103, 161–162; in colonial America, 69; comparison of with direct action, 102; constraints on U.S. conduct of, 162; decline of interest in after cold war, 100, 173; description of, xviii; different from counterinsurgency, 93; distancing SOF from, 101; doctrinal phases of, 6; and expectations of SOF, 5; failure to employ in Iraq, 194–195; foreshadowing of by George Crook, 71; and indigenous forces, 70, 74, 88, 92, 99, 102, 143, 149, 176; interagency character of, 215–217; and lethal technologies, 206–207; personal traits required for success in, 60–61; plan for in Afghanistan, 6, 15, 17; plans for well received, 6; role of population in, 14, 92; role of traditional networks in, 207–209; and small very lethal groups, 206–207, 222; SOCCENT planning for, 6, 7, 17; Special Forces and, 173, 193; as SOF mission, 143, 173; and transformation of warfare, 181, 202–203; transition of to counterinsurgency, 15; two critical problems of, 205. *See also* asymmetric threats; guerrilla warfare; indirect missions; irregular warfare
Unconventional Warfare Command, 218–221, 237–238
underwater demolition teams (UDTs), 73–74, 78; development of into SEALs, 89; kept in service after World War II, 79; in Korean War, 85, 86
United Nations, 52; in Somalia, 107; differences of with State and Defense

Departments over operations in Somalia, 109–111
United Nations Operations in Somalia I and II (UNOSOM I and II), 112, 114; desire of to establish credibility of UN peacekeeping operations, 119; Italian participation in, 121; political strategy of, 115
United Nations Security Council Resolution 794, 108
United Nations Security Council Resolution 837, 118
United States, strategic confusion of in Somalia, 116
United States Agency for International Development (USAID), 91
United States Military Assistance Command, Vietnam (MACV), 91
United States Military Assistance Command, Vietnam—Studies and Observation Group (MACV—SOG), 92
United Task Force (UNITAF), 109, 114
unmanned aerial vehicle (UAV), 18
Utley, Robert, 71
Uzbekistan, 15; deployment of Air Force SOF to, 20
Uzbek Army, Special Forces training of, 15–16

Vietcong, 91, 92
Vietnam War, activities of SOF in, 90–91; influence on military leaders of, 5

Waco. *See* Branch Davidian compound
war on terrorism, xiv; costs of and impact on transformation, 203–204; direct action in, 193–194; and effect of on SOF, 44, 165, 171, 202–203; and effect of on training, 39; importance of indirect missions in, 175–176; SOCOM lead in, 194, 236; SOF willingness to share missions in, 191–195; Special Forces operations in, 38; and transformation, 202–203
War Department, 73; receives clandestine operations capability from Office of Strategic Services, 79–80; and